PRISON

PRISON

Five hundred years of life behind bars

Edward Marston

The National Archives

First published in 2009 by

The National Archives
Kew, Richmond
Surrey, TW9 4DU, UK

www.nationalarchives.gov.uk

The National Archives brings together the Public Record
Office, Historical Manuscripts Commission, Office of Public
Sector Information and Her Majesty's Stationery Office.

A catalogue card for this book is available
from the British Library.

ISBN 978 1 905615 33 9

Jacket illustrations: *front* prisoner from Pentonville's
photograph albums, 1875-6 (PCOM 2/98); *back* the Fleet prison
courtyard, from Ackerman, *The Microcosm of London*, 1808-10,
illustrated by Pugin and Rowlandson (TopFoto.co.uk).
Design by Goldust Design
Printed in Malta by Gutenberg Press

CONTENTS

Preface   7

Introduction: Life Behind Bars   9
1   The Great Gaols of London   24
2   The State of Eighteenth-century Prisons   51
3   Rat-infested Prison Hulks   76
4   A Most Victorian Zeal   101
5   No Place for a Woman   130
6   Suffragettes and the New Century   157
7   Prisoners of Two World Wars   179
8   The Last Executions   202
    Conclusion   226

A Note on Sources   232
Further Reading   234
Index   235
Acknowledgements   240

PREFACE

Prison has always played a part in my life. As a boy, I cycled past Cardiff prison on my way to school, wondering when my next-door neighbour would be released and how long it would be before his next conviction. Then, while acting in a student production at Oxford, I visited the prison in the hope of persuading the governor to let us perform the play there. Built on the site of a medieval castle, the prison incorporated many of its features, and you could almost feel the accumulated weight of past prisoners' oppression and despair.

After graduation I led an evening class at Winson Green Prison in Birmingham, teaching drama to ten or twelve inmates in a locked room. The limited space meant that we were largely confined to recording plays on a tape recorder provided by the prison Commission. The prisoners especially enjoyed Eugene O'Neill's *The Iceman Cometh* and Samuel Beckett's *Waiting for Godot*, two dramas about people killing time, as well as Sam and Bella Spewack's comedy *My Three Angels*, set in a penal colony in French Guiana around 1900.

Sessions were lively and there was always a warm response to the plays. The mood changed abruptly on 19 November 1962, when I arrived on the eve of an execution. There was a tense atmosphere in the prison and mingled fear and resentment among the inmates. My students worked hard on Tennessee Williams' *Cat on a Hot Tin Roof* for a couple of hours, and I thought I'd taken their minds off the hangman. As I left, however, one of them asked me if I'd like to bet on whether the condemned man screamed as he was taken to the gallows. I declined the invitation.

All that I knew of the case at the time was what I'd read in the *Birmingham Mail* and heard from the prison staff. It was only while researching this book that I was able to look at the relevant file in the

National Archives (PCOM 9/2209) and discover the full details. Oswald Grey was a 20-year-old Jamaican immigrant who shot dead Thomas Bates, a shopkeeper, before stealing money from the till. When arrested, Grey still had ten rounds of ammunition on him. The jury needed only a quarter of an hour to find him guilty.

In a touching letter to his father, Grey showed genuine remorse and was clearly bewildered by what was happening to him. He was assessed by a consultant psychiatrist as having the mental age of a ten-year-old. During his time in prison, he was quiet but cheerful, playing board games with the officers. He was hanged on 20 November by Harry Allen, assisted by Samuel Plant. Cause of death was given as 'fracture dislocation between the 2nd and 3rd vertebrae'. The length of the drop was seven feet nine inches. After the execution, it was an inch and a quarter longer. Other macabre details may be found in the file; what is not recorded is the profound effect that the event had on the entire prison population, inmates and officers alike.

The emphasis in this book is at all times on the stories of individual prisoners and prison reformers. Through their experiences, I have tried to build up a picture of what it was like to be incarcerated during a period of some five hundred years or more. Throughout that time, the nature and purpose of imprisonment changed radically and evolved into the system we now have today. There has been no room to discuss the many significant improvements that have taken place in recent decades, or indeed to discuss certain aspects of prison history, such as borstals, alien internees and prisoners of war, which merit their own studies. All that I have tried to do is to find a narrative path through the mass of available material and let a large number of faces peer out over the high stone walls.

Edward Marston

INTRODUCTION

Life Behind Bars

He that is taken and put into prison or chains is not
conquered, though overcome, for he is still the enemy.

Thomas Hobbes, 1651

This book begins with a taste of the kind of extraordinary prison stories explored within its pages. Consider Ranulf Flambard, the scheming bishop of Durham, once-favourite of two Norman kings, who in 1100 shinned down a rope to escape from the Tower of London after plying his keepers with wine (see p. 26). Consider Eleanor Cobham, Duchess of Gloucester, who in 1441 was accused of treason and sorcery; her activities were thought to have included burning a wax effigy of King Henry VI. She was sentenced to the penance of walking through the streets of London in her shift for three days, carrying a lit taper and attended by officials including the lord mayor. She then spent 14 years imprisoned in Peel Castle on the Isle of Man.

Consider Mary Wade, who was only 11 years of age in 1789 when she was condemned to death for stealing a few bits of clothing; after three months in Newgate, her sentence was commuted to transportation, and she became the youngest female convict to be sent to Australia (see p. 73). Consider James Edward Spiers, an armed robber sentenced to fifteen lashes in Wandsworth Prison in 1930. When justices of the peace gathered to watch his punishment, Spiers flung himself from his cell tier three storeys above, landing broken and bloody at their feet.

Last of all, consider Ivor Novello, the songwriter and actor whose debonair image was at odds with his offence of misusing petrol coupons during the Second World War. Although his prison experience would have been civilized compared with that of inmates in previous centuries, his spirit was nonetheless broken within weeks of his detention in Wandsworth alongside fellow inmates like 'Mad' Frankie Fraser (see p. 228).

The fates of these prisoners reveal something of the range of experience that has been endured in British prisons. They also say something about the changing nature and severity of incarceration over the centuries, and about the effects that being locked up can have on the mind and behaviour of offenders. Through their cases – and through those of many other malefactors – this book traces the development of prisons from being places where people were simply held pending trial to institutions that served as punishments in themselves. Medieval prisons were used for temporary detention: it was not until many centuries later that penal institutions became part of an integrated national system under a Prison Commission with clear objectives.

Although there are many interesting aspects of prisons, the emphasis here will remain on the people involved: staff, officials, reformers and architects, as well as the prisoners themselves. Penal history has a bewildering abundance of statistics, but it is only individual stories that can give them life and colour.

Nine centuries of prisons
This history begins over nine hundred years ago with the Norman Conquest and the building of the great Tower of London. Its main focus is on the five hundred years from the Tudor period – when the Tower became an emblem of the monarch's arbitrary and bloody power – to the abolition of capital (and corporal) punishment in the 1960s, which set the scene for today's prison regime.

This Introduction begins with a look at how prisons and punishment evolved in the medieval years following the Norman Conquest, a time when prisoners had to pay for their fetters, food and accommodation, and barbaric punishments and trial by ordeal were often inflicted.

Chapter One focuses in on the Tower of London as well as the early years of the great London prisons: the Clink, the Marshalsea, Newgate, the Fleet and the Compters. From the start, the Tower was a royal prison, and its occupants did not always enjoy legal process: freedom was dependent on the whim of a king or queen. Torture was often a feature of imprisonment, most famously employed by the Tudors, and the fate of the Protestant martyr Anne Askew, the only woman on record to have been racked in the Tower, proved that no one was exempt (see p. 32). Equally perilous were the other London prisons, where life was cheap and unregulated conditions meant that abuses like overcrowding, starvation, disease and violence were rife.

Chapter Two explores the appalling conditions still prevalent in eighteenth-century prisons, as well as customs such as transportation, torture and the ghoulish public spectacle of Tyburn executions. It introduces the great reformers such as John Howard, whose seminal work *The State of Prisons in England and Wales* was the first objective, detailed study of the system. Howard noted that a large proportion of those behind bars had been imprisoned for debt, which became a hopeless cycle as prisoners incurred additional debts 'inside' and had little hope of discharging them. Whole families lived within prison walls, just like the family inhabiting the Marshalsea in Dickens' *Little Dorrit*. When the Fleet Prison was finally closed, one debtor had been there for forty years.

Prison hulks, the authorities' solution to overcrowding, are covered in Chapter Three: many military as well as civilian prisoners, including those awaiting transportation, were from the 1770s kept in rotting warships moored on the Thames, the Medway and elsewhere. Thanks to the meticulous work of Henry Mayhew and John Binny, we have a grim record of life on board. The scandal continued until 1859 and included horrors such as the story of thirty prisoners of war thrown into the sea at Portsmouth in 1811 – because the hospital hulk would not receive them unwashed. Few of the exhausted, emaciated men survived the incident.

During the same period, there was considerable reform as prisons at last became part of a centralized system. Victorian prisons, explored in Chapter Four, combined solitary confinement with a punitive rule of silence. It is not surprising that inmates were sometimes driven to insanity or suicide. Flogging was used on the unruly, and daily sessions on the treadmill or the crank, or picking oakum, added to the pain of incarceration. Prisoners such as Oscar Wilde have left vivid memoirs of serving a sentence in the reign of Queen Victoria.

Women prisoners also suffered harsh conditions, with the additional pain of separation from their children. Chapter Five explores female prisons in the Victorian era, focusing on the work of the great reformer Elizabeth Fry, who in her white gown brought stillness and purpose to the chaotic prison world and challenged society's attitudes to its convicted. The chapter ends with the story of Florence Maybrick, a Victorian lady convicted of murder who suffered so greatly in prison that she feigned tuberculosis by impaling herself to draw blood for her spittoon – in the hope of having her case reconsidered.

Chapters Six and Seven cover two new groups of prisoners created in the twentieth century: the suffragettes and the conscientious objectors. Both were on the whole unaccustomed to privation, and were treated with severity by the authorities in the mistaken belief that this would alter consciences. The suffragettes were force-fed with rubber tubing; the conscientious objectors were bullied and punished; but both groups were resilient and found ways of surviving prison life – for example in Maidstone prison, 'conchie' Clifford Allen beat the silent system to play chess with a man five cells away, by whispering moves at slops time. Many prisoners emerged from confinement with their health broken – but lived to tell their incredible stories in books, articles and sound recordings which shed light on the regime experienced by all prisoners.

The story concludes with Chapter Eight's look at the tradition of execution and famous hangmen such as Calcraft, Berry and Pierrepoint. It focuses on John Lee, the man who three times escaped death on the gallows and subsequently described in graphic detail the experience of the condemned man – 'the clang of the bell … a wrench as of a bolt drawn …'. The chapter documents the changing public attitudes to capital punishment – from relish in the Tyburn executions to public outrage at the hangings of Evans, Bentley and Ruth Ellis – that brought the gradual move towards abolition.

Early punishments

When William the Conqueror took power in 1066, he inherited the long and elaborate law code laid down by King Cnut (1017–35) which, ironically, recommended 'gentle punishment' for transgressors: mutilation, castration and whipping were common penalties for certain offences.

The use of the stocks and the pillory was popular. Both forms of imprisonment exposed their victims to public derision and attack. Those with their legs in the stocks could at least use their arms to ward off missiles. No such protection was offered to those caught in the *healsfanger* or neck-trap, a precursor of the pillory. The head was a tempting target for sticks, stones, rotten fruit, dead cats and animal dung. More than one offender who thought he had been spared the death sentence learned that it had simply been given a different name.

Women, too, had to withstand the stocks and the pillory, the favoured penalty for bawds, whores and scolds. The sharp-tongued shrew was set in *cathedra stercoris* (on her shitting-chair, an early form of commode or close-stool) and paraded around her town or village to endure public mockery and be pelted with missiles. Ordeal by fire was another penalty: the victim was made to carry a red-hot bar of iron, pick a stone from a cauldron of boiling water or walk over seven red-hot ploughshares while blindfold and barefoot. Innocence could only be established if the victim showed no sign of injury afterwards. Those whose hands or feet were inevitably burned were punished with branding, nose-slitting or the loss of their hands, penalties carried out before a ghoulish and unsympathetic audience.

Capital punishment was used for the most serious crimes. Sodomy was punishable by 'burning on a pyre' and, in the case of bestiality, both man and beast were to be burned or buried alive 'so as to remove all trace whatever of this heinous crime … their flesh, if any remained, to be fed to the dogs'.

Prisons of the Conquest

The arrival of William the Conqueror in 1066 ushered in a new reign of terror. While he recognized the codes of law of his predecessors, he also took pains to build a strong central government that could impose its will on the nation. Castles and cathedrals were the twin pillars of Norman might. Although he forced London to accept his rule, the Conqueror never trusted its citizens, and immediately set in motion the building of the Tower of London, a massive and menacing stronghold that gave him complete protection and could act as a secure prison.

The familiar motte and bailey castles sprung up all over the country, built first of wood and then of stone, their fortifications being steadily improved over the years. Sites were carefully selected so that use could be made of natural defences such as rocks, hills or lakes. Local peasants were pressed into service to provide the labour. All of these castles had dungeons where malefactors could be kept before trial or where hostages could be held.

Often portrayed as a ruthless and bloodthirsty tyrant, the Conqueror favoured mutilation and a system of fines rather than wholesale slaughter of law-breakers. His appointment in 1070 of Lanfranc as archbishop of Canterbury was a turning point in the history of imprisonment. Lanfranc committed himself to the task of rooting out corruption in the Church and getting rid of clerical laxity. In support of this commitment, his Monastic Constitutions of 1076 provided for bishops to have their own prisons. Some used their respective palaces as places of custody, while others drew on accommodation offered by various sheriffs. Bishops who had lay estates often claimed rights of prison within them, thus exerting power over a wider sphere of the populace.

Clerks were controlled by a different system of law to that imposed on laymen. Before trial, they could be confined in lay or bishops' prisons. Many claimed benefit of clergy, because ecclesiastical law was less stringent and punishments tended to be more lenient. Curiously, felons could plead their clergy after conviction as well as before it, in the hope of a lighter sentence. The Crown did not approve of this apparent escape-hatch, and it made sure that benefit of clergy was not permissible for crimes such as high treason. Women, of course, had no access to benefit of clergy.

If priests or clerks could expect more moderate treatment in ecclesiastical courts, this was not the case for monks. Lanfranc's Constitutions made clear provision for monastic prisons. Hitherto, Benedictine monks and those of other orders could suffer corporal punishment, isolation from their fellows, exclusion from services and, as an ultimate penalty, excommunication. But no allowance was made for an actual place of confinement. Lanfranc corrected that situation, giving abbots rights of discretionary imprisonment over unruly monks that were exploited to the hilt. No court of appeal existed for transgressors.

The Normans were a practical people. As the numbers of offenders steadily rose, it became costly and inconvenient to house them in places of custody while they awaited trial. Bishops and barons alike therefore used bail, frankpledge and property attachment as a means of keeping people out of prison until they appeared before a judge. For treason, arson and other serious offences, no bail was possible – nor could a suspected felon avoid prison if his arrest had been at the direct order of the king or one of the king's judges.

Another characteristic of the Normans was their fondness for hunting, which meant that they guarded their forests with great vigilance and that laws relating to trespass and poaching were rigidly enforced with harsh punishments. Those caught stealing game were imprisoned in forest prisons, lodges or lock-ups specifically built for the purpose. There they stayed until it was time to be tried; those convicted faced blinding, castration or other forms of mutilation.

The Assize of Clarendon

It was not until the reign of Henry II (1154–89), the first Plantagenet king, that public law and administration took on a firmer shape. By the time of the Assize of Clarendon in 1166, Henry and his councillors felt the need to reform the whole system of local jurisdiction. In doing so, they supplied proof that juries of presentment (obtaining information on oath about crimes) and recognition (dealing with disputes as to lay or clerical tenure) were already being used as a part of the legal system. Of particular interest is the seventh clause of the resulting act:

> And in several counties where there are no gaols, let such be made in a borough or some castle of the king at the king's expense and from his wood, if one be near, or from some neighbouring wood at the oversight of the king's servants, to the end that the sheriffs may be able to guard those who shall be arrested by the officials accustomed to do this, or by their servants.
>
> David C. Douglas and George W. Greenaway (eds),
> *English Historical Documents 1042–1189*

Royal prisons were therefore established throughout the kingdom, in castles, gatehouses of towns, monasteries, mills or even manor houses. It meant that whenever a criminal was arrested, there was always somewhere within reach in which to hold him. From this time onwards, all criminal cases had to be tried in the king's courts before justices appointed by the king, instead of being handled by court-leets on private estates.

The injunction to site gaols in one of the king's castles or boroughs was easier for some sheriffs to obey than others. In a county such as Gloucester, there was a county town acting as a nucleus for the whole region. Counties like Berkshire, Wiltshire and Somerset had no such dominant community with an existing castle in the possession of the Crown. Their sheriffs had to be imaginative, but at least they were now spared the cost of prison maintenance. Theoretically, the costs of operating the network of gaols now fell upon the Crown: kings were therefore eager to defray their expenses by making sure that prisoners were not detained in large numbers for long periods.

The most effective way to control costs was by means of regular gaol deliveries, releasing prisoners *en bloc* to face local or (after 1170) royal justices. This not only made room for new offenders, it also established that prisoners were still alive and had not simply been allowed to rot away in chains. In the reign of Henry III (1216–72), gaol deliveries were still a necessary part of the system. Some 40 or so gaols seem to have existed by 1258, and those most frequently delivered in that year were Gloucester (six times), Ilchester, Lincoln, Northampton and York – all relatively remote from London.

Alongside the system of royal prisons were clusters of municipal gaols and lock-ups, some of which were local ventures while others were established under charter. In addition, there was a series of franchise prisons owned by lay barons or leading ecclesiastics. Most of these related to customary rights of certain manors, divisions of counties or liberties within towns granted by Plantagenet kings. As no support came from the royal exchequer, money for the upkeep of these prisons had to come from the owner's purse. His expenses were, however, limited: the owner or keeper was responsible only for keeping the inmates in custody. There was no legal obligation to supply food, water, bedding, fuel, furniture, clothing or anything else to the prisoners. These were chargeable items, and keepers exploited their position mercilessly, making their captors pay for their own imprisonment.

There was a further anomaly. Because a prison was owned as a personal and private right, it could be transferred or sold to anyone. Prisoners could wake up one day to discover that they and their prison were now the property of an entirely new owner. They might even find themselves conveyed under a marriage settlement to a daughter, or inherited by a son. In theory, nothing could stop a franchise prison stocked with debtors from being signed over to someone else in payment of a debt.

Astonishingly, a few profit-making debtors' prisons did actually survive into the nineteenth century, and it was not until 1852 that the Act to Abolish Franchise Prisons was passed, finally sweeping away all the system's abuses. One of the last still operating was the notorious Swansea prison, owned by the Duke of Beaufort and providing him with a steady income. Justice Falconer commented at the time that such prisons ought no longer to exist – yet they had done so unchallenged for hundreds of years, without the close supervision of a controlling authority.

Disease, starvation and beatings

How did the prisoners fare in medieval prisons? Given that feudal society was hierarchical, that depended very much on their station in life. Men of noble rank were held in honourable confinement, while the meanest conditions sufficed for the lower orders. For example, Jordan of Bianney was a knight accused and later convicted of felony. While Jordan was held in Winchester gaol, King John allowed him out twice a day to practise fencing in preparation for a duel. Every time Bianney left his apartment, however, another man occupied it as a hostage. Such an *exeat* would never have been granted to those nearer the bottom of the social scale.

The common experience was a dreadful one. Those unable to buy favours from their keeper were crammed into fetid cells that were cold, damp and bare. There was no segregation of the sexes. Disease – often linked to bad water – was rife and epidemics spread quickly. Medical facilities were non-existent. There was little concern for prisoners' welfare, and their suffering was only alleviated by charitable bequests. Some might be allowed out to beg, while others simply thrust their hands through the barred windows of their cell, hoping for money or food from passers-by. Many died as a result of illness, starvation, savage beatings meted out by a gaoler, injuries suffered at the hands of other prisoners or sheer despair.

In 1295 inmates were kept in York prison for an indefinite time because the visit of the perambulating justices was delayed by the Welsh war. Their numbers gradually swelled, and a 'great multitude' of them perished from lack of food in the overcrowded cells. In response to the scandal, a special commission was hastily assembled to try the remainder of the prisoners, who were close to death. Such a calamity was not an isolated phenomenon.

As he was not paid a salary, the keeper of a prison derived his income solely from the inmates. Out of that income, he had to pay assistants. It is not surprising, therefore, that he kept their number to a minimum or employed members of his family. Gaols had to make a profit to survive, and so every penny was squeezed out of the unlucky inmates.

Irons were a necessary part of the stock-in-trade of prisons: lack of sufficient staff to control the intake meant that prisoners had to be handicapped or immobilized, and the prisoner had to pay for the irons to be affixed and removed. In one of the earliest recorded instances, a charge of sixpence was levied on a prisoner in 1194 when he was fitted with an iron neck-collar. Money could always be used to bribe a keeper into replacing heavy irons with light ones, but this recourse was beyond the reach of the many debtors who cluttered the gaols.

Desperate criminals were also restrained by heavy chains, leg fetters, manacles, neck rings, gyves and other instruments fashioned by black-smiths. Men and women alike felt the chafing presence of iron. Solitary confinement was reserved for those suspected of serious crimes or those most liable to attempt an escape.

Keepers were subject to severe penalties for escapes, yet some still succumbed to the lure of a hefty bribe. Other escapes were effected by force or guile. When Prince John attacked Salisbury castle in 1194, several prisoners took the opportunity to flee through the broken walls. And during the civil war that attended the accession of Henry III in 1216, there were escapes from gaols in Warwick, Kenilworth, Worcester and York. Fourteen years later, there was another multiple escape from Winchester prison.

Not all escapes were successful. Some foundered, and prisoners died or were put to death as a consequence. The brave Welsh rebel Gruffydd ap Llewellyn achieved an unwelcome fame in 1244 by falling to his death while descending a series of knotted sheets at the Tower of London.

'Strong and heavy punishment'

The use of torture on spies, political prisoners and those who defied the established religion was common. Pain could be inflicted by something as simple as a thumbscrew or by a contraption as complicated as a rack. Fire and water could also be used persuasively. We shall see in the next chapter how torturers refined their art in the Tower and made even innocent victims confess to the most hideous crimes.

In some prisons, stocks were set up in the cells themselves so that inmates suffered a double imprisonment. Irons were, of course, a form of torture, as well as a means of control.

One of the worst tortures was that described as *peine forte et dure* (strong and heavy punishment). Introduced by a statute of Edward 1 in 1274, it was usually reserved for those who remained mute when accused. According to the statute, the obstinate prisoner should be shut

> in a windowless airless damp dungeon, naked except for a loin cloth,
> stretched out on the back, and iron weights placed upon the chest,
> increased each day. The first day three morsels of rotten coarse bread,
> second day three draughts of water from the stagnant pool next the
> prison door – no spring or fountain water to be permitted – the third
> day three morsels of bread and then alternate days of the same diet until
> death supervenes.

Victims were spreadeagled with their wrists and ankles held firm by ropes. A board was placed on their chests so that the weights could be balanced on them. It was really a case of execution by slow torture. The old, weak and infirm would be the first to perish, but even the youngest and strongest would eventually succumb as their ribs were cracked open and they were pressed to death. It remained popular until well into the eighteenth century: a print dating from around 1750 shows 'Wm.Spiggot under Pressure in Newgate for not Pleading to His Indictment'.

The combination of strong ropes, mouldy bread, rank water and heavy weights loosened many tongues, but confession was effectively in vain: once the excrutiating punishment had been ordered, it could not be stopped. It is a sobering comment on the entrenched brutality of the penal system that this torture was not legally abolished until 1828.

Medieval women

One of the paradoxes of the medieval period in England is that those who had neither political power nor physical strength were punished with greater severity. Male legislators seemed determined to control, subdue and harass women. A wife who killed her husband was guilty of a crime even worse than murder: she was said to have committed *petit trahison* (petty treason), and was liable to be burned at the stake. The only more heinous crime was high treason, for which the penalty was being hanged, drawn and quartered.

While dreaming up his 'gentle' punishments, King Cnut had decreed that all adulteresses should have their ears and nose cut off. A male offender was simply exiled. Any hint of sexual licence among women was punished by whipping or public humiliation in the stocks. In 1244 Anne of Lodburie (Lothbury) was ducked to death in the well in the churchyard of St Giles, Cripplegate, as a warning to the whores who peopled the area. In 1282 Henry le Waleis, Mayor of London, built the Tun – so called because of its barrel shape – as a lock-up for those caught in breach of the City's curfew. Those most often arrested were prostitutes, pimps and their clients.

Respectable women subjected to rape in the thirteenth century received little help from the law. If a woman were impregnated as a result of the assault, judges would dismiss the case on the strange grounds that the female body needed to secrete a certain seed for conception to take place, and this only occurred if the woman in question was sexually satisfied. The cruel suggestion was that pregnancy was, in effect, enjoyment of rape. A victim not only had to bear the stigma of giving birth to a bastard, she had also to watch the rapist evade punishment instead of suffering castration.

Women were hanged as indiscriminately as men for a wide range of crimes. Hangmen were rarely adept and made their victims suffer long and agonizing deaths. In 1263 Ivette of Bolsham was convicted of a felony and hanged at nine o'clock in the morning. She remained conscious until the pain was too much to bear, then lapsed into a coma. At sunrise on the following morning, to the amazement of everyone, she was still somehow alive. She was revived and the circumstances of her case were reported to King Henry III, who issued a pardon for her.

Another particularly callous punishment for women was the *fossa*, a pit or pond full of water. This made its appearance in England in the early twelfth century and consisted of a rounded chamber in the base of a castle into which prisoners were lowered by rope or ladder. Left in the dark and in the water, women were often allowed to starve to death, their pleas and prayers completely disregarded.

Scolds endured a more public penalty. They were fitted with the branks, an iron bridle that enclosed the head and included a vicious mouthpiece that pressed down on the tongue. In the interests of marital harmony, the scolds were marched around the town so that nagging wives could take note of what might befall them if they continued their shrewish behaviour. No equivalent punishments existed for bad-tempered or mean-spirited men who badgered their womenfolk.

Branks were also routinely used against witches, real or imagined. Laws against witchcraft originate from the time of the Anglo-Saxons: ecclesiastical and secular courts had concurrent jurisdiction and witches got short shrift in both of them. Those who were merely whipped, put in the stocks or imprisoned in a scold's bridle were grateful. Mutilation and death by drowning were other options available to judges of the day. Watching a witch being dipped into a river until she was drowned was a spectacle that always drew large and vociferous crowds.

Cheek by jowl

Medieval prisons were always highly visible in the community and thus had a great immediacy for people. Where a town was built around a castle, the shadow of the prison fell across it every day. Everyone therefore lived cheek by jowl with torture and suffering. The howls of pain that emanated from a castle or a town gaol would have a cautionary effect on all who heard them. Because no long sentences of coercive imprisonment were given, there was regular traffic in and out of the institutions. Nobody was left unaware of the evils and abuses taking place behind prison walls.

Notwithstanding the fear of prison, criminals of every hue carried on plying their trades. Cities like London had their own criminal underworld replete with brothels, gambling dens, rowdy taverns and safe hiding places for any outlaws. The absence of any effective police force meant that countless crimes went unnoticed or unreported. Sheriffs responsible for law and order in their respective counties had only limited resources on which to call. Local constables were rarely the nimblest and most alert members of a community.

One fact was impressed on every mind throughout the Middle Ages: prison was a universal threat, affecting all ranks of society. Kings such as Edward II, Richard II and Henry VI were thrust behind bars, even archbishops were imprisoned and government ministers were also immured in castle dungeons. Nobody was safe, although, as we have seen, conditions were often better for those higher up the social scale. Nonetheless, those arrested for petty crimes shared an experience that befell some of the highest in the land. Those who made and enforced the law sometimes ended up in exactly the same position as those who violated it.

Merrie England

Generations of writers, artists and even certain historians have looked back on the Middle Ages through rose-tinted spectacles. What they saw was an England that was free, unspoiled, cheerfully unsophisticated and based on sound Christian values. A typical description of this Utopia can be found in F. M. Salter's *Medieval Drama in Chester*, written in 1955.

> It is an England with a deep sense of homogeneity of man and beast and
> fowl, of all living things; an England deeply devout, into every moment
> of whose life religion entered as a living force; an England merry in the
> sunshine, in the springtime, in the summer festivals, an England whose
> sanity and wholesomeness ought to be an inspiration to all who come after.

Nothing explodes the myth of Merrie England as completely as a study of crime and punishment in the period. The dominant themes are cruelty, oppression, injustice, class conflict, torture and open revolt.

Peasants who danced in the summer festivals led harsh lives marked by low wages, mean housing, the burdensome impositions of Church and State, the plague and other recurrent disasters. Laws multiplied with each reign and crippling punishments awaited those who broke them.

Castles and prisons erected to keep the people in subjection became symbols of hatred as well as apprehension. During riots or uprisings, one of the first acts was to liberate prisoners and burn down the gaols. During the Peasants' Revolt of 1381 the mob marched to London and they took the prisons of Newgate and the Fleet. They went on to seize the Tower, that defining emblem of power and imprisonment.

In 1450 Jack Cade led another peasant army from Kent. Some 5,000 protestors were joined in London by resident shopkeepers, craftsmen, apprentices and even a knight and two members of parliament. Their numbers were further swelled by soldiers and sailors returned from the French Wars. All of them subscribed to the Complaint of the Poor Commons of Kent, a manifesto that protested against the feeble kingship of Henry VI, unfair taxes, corruption in government at local and national level, and the damaging effects of the loss of France.

Seething with anger, the mob entered the city, tore open the prisons and resorted to looting. The lord treasurer was killed and his head was put on a spike along with those of some royal favourites. The rebels were eventually driven out of the city and suffered many casualties. They were appeased, pardoned and promised that the terms of their manifesto would be met. Cade and his men retired with a sense of triumph.

A week later Cade learned that his pardon had been revoked and that he was now a wanted man. Killed in a skirmish at Heathfield, he was taken to London in a cart, his naked body exposed all day to the citizens. Cade was then beheaded and quartered. While his head was stuck on London Bridge alongside those of other traitors, the four quarters were sent to Blackheath, Gloucester, Norwich and Salisbury for public exhibition. The familiar cycle of open rebellion and violent suppression was repeated once again.

As usual, the prisons affected were rebuilt and swiftly refilled. The next chapter looks in more detail at some of the capital's infamous institutions, from the Tower of London to Newgate, and explores their impact on human lives great and small.

CHAPTER ONE

The Great Gaols of London

In London, and within a mile I ween
There are of jails and prisons full eighteen,
and sixty whipping-posts and cages,
Where sin with shame and sorrow hath due wages.
For though the Tower be a castle royal,
Yet there's a prison in't for men disloyal.

All the Workes of John Taylor, the Water Poet, 1630

The Norman fortress

The Tower of London is today dwarfed by high-rise buildings and engulfed by urban sprawl. However, when it was first built on the north bank of the Thames in 1068, it dominated the skyline and loomed over the whole city (see plate 1). Designed by Gundulph, Bishop of Rochester, and constructed of imported Caen stone, it was like nothing Londoners had ever seen before – tall, stark, alien, imposing, threatening and apparently impregnable. William the Conqueror had brought it into being both to safeguard the city and to protect himself from its citizens. It was a fortress, a palace, a prison, a centre of government and a place of sanctuary. Winchester remained the Norman capital, and one of the three annual crown-wearings occurred there. The other two venues were Gloucester and London, and in the latter city the Tower took on growing importance.

It was not the only castle built along the river by the new king.

While the Tower was in London's north east, Baynard's Castle and Montfichet Castle stood in the west of the city. All three were daunting edifices, but the Tower was supreme. Defended on one side by the broad back of the Thames – which its entrance on the first floor faced, reached by a wooden staircase – its walls were 90 feet high, thick and solid, 15 feet wide at the base and tapering slightly towards the uppermost parts. Above the battlements were four turrets, three of which were square while the one on the north-east corner was circular. The vaulted basement of the Tower contained a well that was 40 feet deep. One of its most beautiful and enduring architectural features was the tunnel-vaulted Chapel Royal of St John the Evangelist, rising impressively through the upper floor above a crypt and sub-crypt. Yet religion was always subservient to the military functions of the Tower; chaplains were vastly outnumbered by the resident garrison.

The Tower's position had been carefully chosen to command the eastern approaches by land and water and enjoy full surveillance of the passage of ships. The Thames was the city's lifeline, its bustling wharves handling ceaseless traffic of imports and exports, maintaining England's reputation as a great trading nation and providing work for large numbers of people from merchants to mariners. Those who toiled along its banks in the second half of the eleventh century had only to look up to read the unspoken message embodied in the Tower: the Normans had come to stay.

From the start, the Tower of London was a place of detention, torture and execution. Many prisoners who disappeared inside its walls were never seen again. It should be remembered that the battle of Hastings in 1066 saw the defeat of King Harold and his army, but not the surrender of the whole country. London at first refused to acknowledge its new ruler, and there was stern resistance elsewhere. Exeter only capitulated after a long siege, Hereward the Wake stirred up trouble in the Fens and the Conqueror had constant trouble with the old Anglo-Danish aristocracy in the north. There was also rebellion within his ranks. The revolt of the three earls in 1075 showed that William did not enjoy uncritical support from his magnates.

His problems were not confined to England. He was still Duke of Normandy and had to enforce his rule there, keeping the French and their allies at bay and coping with the two successive revolts led by his eldest son, Robert Curthose. Throughout his reign, he was beset by enemies. On the occasions when he stayed at the Tower, he was never able to enjoy leisure: there were always hostages to hold, spies to interrogate and captured foes to execute.

Ranulf Flambard

As the years passed, the scope of the Tower site was gradually extended and the fortifications strengthened. By the accession of Henry I in 1100, there had been many internal improvements as well. But Ranulf Flambard, who had been a trusted friend of the first two Norman kings, was in no position to admire them, because in an abrupt switch of fortunes he was taken to the Tower as a prisoner – and is thought to have been the first state prisoner there.

It was a harsh interruption to a glittering career. An acute financier and an industrious scribe, Flambard had played an important part in the compilation of the Domesday Survey instigated by the Conqueror at his Christmas court in 1085. Although a clerk by profession, Flambard became chaplain to Maurice, chancellor and bishop of London. When William Rufus succeeded his father as William II in 1087, the ambitious Flambard worked closely with him as a chief minister, devising ingenious methods of extorting money from all classes of society. He profited from the tyranny of Rufus, farming for the king a large proportion of the ecclesiastical preferments which were illegally kept vacant, and in 1099 obtaining the wealthy see of Durham. It was not just his financial depredations that earned him the hatred of leading lay and ecclesiastical subjects. His private life was scandalous: shunning celibacy, he was a practised lecher who fathered at least two bastard sons.

The death – some thought assassination – of Rufus gave his enemies the chance to voice their opposition and disgust. Acting under pressure, the new king Henry sent the bishop of Durham to the Tower, allowing him many privileges and keeping him in relative comfort. Flambard was permitted to retain his own servants and to have a supply of food and wine brought in. It was the latter which aided his escape. Befriending his guards, he plied them with rich wine until they were dulled, then seized his opportunity. Legend had it that he descended from his cell on a rope concealed in one of the casks of wine, and was met by friends with horses below.

Taking refuge in Normandy with Robert Curthose, the fugitive became one of his advisers and was rewarded with the see of Lisieux. When he was reconciled to Henry in 1106, Flambard returned to Durham and spent the remaining 22 years of his life there. He left an ambiguous legacy, but even his worst enemies could not help but admire his audacious escape from the Tower.

The Tower, the City and the Jews

The reign of Henry III (1216–72) saw significant changes at the Tower. To begin with, it was painted white, hence the name of the White Tower, but the internal changes were to be the most radical. Henry and his wife, Eleanor, had a fondness for the new Gothic architecture, and an awareness of colour and beauty. They spent so much on the interior that it was said that nobody would give them a halfpenny of credit.

In other respects, Henry's record with regard to the Tower is less impressive. Atrocious treatment was visited upon Jews there. The Jewish quarter by Cheapside – many of its inhabitants acted as bankers to the ruling classes as well as to the business world – fell within the liberties of the Tower, and thus came under its protection. The City complained rancorously that the constable of the Tower favoured the Jews in his administration, overlooking the fact that Jews were taxed exorbitantly at this time. The entire Jewish community was twice taken into the Tower for safety, but there were also occasions when mass detentions occurred and Jews were ransomed.

When Edward I came to the throne in 1272, the Crown's need for the financial support of the Jews was dwindling. In an attempt to gain the support of the City, always hostile to Jewish infiltration, Edward imprisoned 600 Jews in 1278 on trumped-up charges of coin-clipping. Two hundred and sixty of the Jews were executed, and many of the others died from neglect or starvation. The delightful royal residence of Henry III was now bathed in blood; it had witnessed an act of naked anti-Semitism.

Henry had extended the fortifications, but it was left to his successor to complete the work. Edward built an outer curtain wall, completely enclosing the inner wall and creating a concentric double defence. He filled in the existing moat and had another dug around the perimeter of the new outer wall. The Tower was bigger, stronger and more forbidding than ever. To the eternal chagrin of the City, which longed for control of the Tower, it stayed in royal hands. Edward I, one of the greatest warriors in Europe, would yield up nothing easily. The Tower was a coveted part of his inheritance.

Henry III had been responsible for many of the additional towers that had been built to strengthen the fortress and provide increased accommodation. Each of these towers was to serve as a prison in its time. Halfway along his new curtain wall, Edward I placed a colossal tower that later became known as the Beauchamp Tower. Although built for defensive purposes, it was often used as a prison for people of rank: one prisoner, in a later reign, was even a member of the Beauchamp family. Individual houses were built within the Tower and these, too, sometimes held prisoners.

The princes' fate?

During the Wars of the Roses (1455–85), the Tower was in regular use by whichever party was in the ascendant, employed as a stronghold behind whose walls prisoners could be kept, tortured or despatched into the next world. After becoming king, Edward IV availed himself of the opportunity of getting rid of Henry VI, his rival and predecessor, by having him discreetly murdered in the Tower in 1471. Edward's duplicitous brother, George, Duke of Clarence, paid for his betrayal by being imprisoned there and then drowned in a barrel of malmsey wine.

The most notorious event that occurred in the Tower is still a mystery that is hotly debated. It concerns the death or disappearance of the two sons of Edward IV, the young princes with a hereditary right to the crown. Richard, Duke of Gloucester, their uncle, denied them their inheritance by claiming that his brother, Edward, was not the legitimate son of Richard, Duke of York, and had not been legally married to the queen, the princes' mother. While Gloucester seized the throne in 1483 by eliminating the opposition, his position was still threatened as long as his princely nephews, Edward and Richard, were alive. This threat had to be removed.

What actually happened to the boys is a matter for conjecture. Were they killed at the behest of the king? Did they die of one of the virulent diseases that sometimes swept through the building? Or were they spirited away to lead obscure lives elsewhere? A charter in the National Archives, recording the grant of the title Duke of Norfolk to Lord Howard in 1483, could be interpreted as suggesting that Richard III knew that the younger prince – who had been granted this title in 1477 – was dead (c 53/198). We may never know and, in the absence of documented fact, rumour and supposition will continue to fill the void.

It is interesting to look at the role of the constable in the affair. Robert Brackenbury was a close associate of the future Richard III and had acted as the treasurer of his household. When Gloucester became king, Brackenbury received a number of appointments, among which was the lucrative post of constable of the Tower of London. His duties involved maintaining the buildings, paying the garrison and looking after the prisoners:

> You are to guard them securely in the prison of our said Tower in such
> a way that you shall answer for them body for body … Fail in no part of
> this on pain of forfeiture of life and limb and all the property you hold in
> our realms.

In Thomas More's *The History of King Richard the Third*, albeit a biased account, Brackenbury is presented as a decent, honest, gentle man of integrity. When first asked to kill the princes, the constable replied that he would sooner die than obey the royal command. More claims that the king sent Sir James Tyrrell to the constable to ask for all the keys of the Tower 'to the end that he might accomplish the king's pleasure'. If this was the case – and it is uncertain – Brackenbury certainly yielded them up. Many honours were heaped upon him, including his promotion to the role of master of the mint. He became a very wealthy man under Richard III and was knighted in 1485. Was he being rewarded for condoning the death of the princes or was a loyal servant simply receiving his just deserts? Whatever really happened, it is clear that the position of constable was one that brought great kudos along with awesome responsibilities.

The bloody Tudors

The Tudor dynasty was accompanied by some of the bloodiest episodes in the Tower's history. One man saw much of it: William de la Pole was accused of plotting against Henry VII and consigned to the Tower in 1502. He remained there for 37 years to witness the full force of royal might and an endless parade of executions.

Anne Boleyn, one of the Tower's most famous occupants, occupies a unique place in the Tudor story because she was instrumental in the break from Rome and hence in the English Reformation. When Henry VIII fell in love with Anne, he was already married to Catherine of Aragon and had also had a dalliance with Mary Boleyn, Anne's sister. Anne herself refused to become his mistress, and only a promise of marriage could secure her presence in the king's bed. Henry finally consented, first living with her at Greenwich Palace – to the horror and resentment of his subjects. By Easter 1533 it became known that the couple had been secretly married since January and that Anne was pregnant.

The pope had already refused to sanction a divorce between the king and his first wife, thus precipitating the events that led in 1535 to Henry's assumption of the title of Supreme Head of the Church of England. In the wake of the secret wedding, and in an attempt to legitimize the union and its offspring, Archbishop Cranmer declared that the marriage between Henry and Catherine was null and void. Three short years later, when Anne had failed to produce a male heir and when Henry's attentions were already fixed on another woman, the archbishop pronounced that the king's second marriage was also null and void, though, to his credit, he tried to save the discarded wife from execution.

Anne was arrested in May 1536 and charged with committing adultery with four men, one of them her own brother. Though these charges were never satisfactorily proved, she was condemned to death and, ironically, spent her last night alive in the same room in the Tower that she had occupied on the eve of her coronation. As no English executioner was capable of decapitating her with a sword, a Frenchman was brought over to perform the deed on Tower Green. Anne's brief and inglorious reign as queen came to a swift end.

Prisoners of conscience

Henry VIII was prepared to sacrifice not merely a wife to execution. If they resisted him, he was ready to send to the Tower some of the most holy and learned men of the day. As lord chancellor since 1529, Thomas More had been one of his most able ministers, a brilliant scholar, lawyer and administrator. He also had great personal charm, and was renowned for his wit and for his ability to carry his erudition lightly. More resigned his office in 1532 because he felt unable to support the king's acrimonious battle for divorce from Catherine of Aragon, and was dismayed by its damaging effects on the Church.

In March 1534 the Act of Succession was passed, requiring subjects – if commanded by the king – to swear an oath recognizing the act as well as the king's supremacy. While he was willing to accept the new queen, More refused to take the oath because he did not believe that any parliament had a legal right to repudiate papal supremacy. Charged with high treason, he was imprisoned in the Tower, to the distress of the court. The Spanish ambassador, Eustace Chapuys, wrote to Charles V:

> It is feared the King will put to death the bishop of Rochester and Mr. More, late chancellor, who, as I lately wrote, are confined in the Tower with others for refusal to swear. The Scotch ambassadors laugh at this King with good reason for imagining to strengthen his cause and his laws by this oath violently extorted, for it rather tends to show that they are worth nothing, since they require such help to maintain them.
>
> *Letters and Papers, Henry VIII* vol. 7:1534 no. 530

More's wife and children petitioned for his release, arguing that he was 'in great continual sickness of body and heaviness of heart' and that his offence arose from a 'long-continued and deep-rooted scruple as passeth his power to avoid and put away' – but to no avail (*L & P Henry VIII* vol. 7:1534 no. 1591). More spent the time awaiting his trial writing his devotional *Dialogue of Comfort against Tribulation*.

The trial was held at Westminster. As befitted a lawyer of European renown, More defended himself with consummate skill – but was nevertheless condemned to death. He met his fate with characteristic dignity and courage, protesting that he was 'the king's good servant but God's first'.

More was executed at the Tower in July. A fortnight earlier, another man whose conscience would not allow him to take the oath had been beheaded at the same spot. John Fisher, Bishop of Rochester, had a long and distinguished record of royal service. As early as 1501 he was chaplain, then confessor, to Lady Margaret Beaufort, the mother of Henry VII, persuading her to endow professorships of divinity at Oxford and Cambridge and two new colleges at his beloved Cambridge, a university of which he had been made chancellor for life.

On the death of Henry VII in 1509, Fisher preached the funeral oration, doing the same for his dear friend the Lady Margaret a few months later. In the ensuing reign, his reputation as a theologian and a devout churchman steadily grew. In 1529, acting as a counsellor to Catherine of Aragon, he incurred the wrath of Henry VIII by stating that the marriage could not be dissolved by any power, human or divine. In convocation he protested strongly against the king's new title of Supreme Head of the Church and inserted the important qualification 'so far as the law of Christ allows'. Henry promptly objected, and the phrase was struck out.

Fisher refused to take any oath that resulted in the diminution of the pope's power. The passing of the Treason Act in 1535 turned his position into a treasonable one, and he was arrested. What enraged the king even more was the fact that the pope declared his intention to make Fisher a cardinal. At his trial, Fisher was condemned to be hanged, drawn and quartered, but the sentence was commuted, and he was beheaded. During his time in the Tower, he was incarcerated in the upper chamber of the Bell Tower, which was to welcome many others who had offended, challenged or in some way resisted Tudor sovereigns.

A woman racked

Anne Askew is the only woman on record to have been tortured in the Tower of London. Forced to marry Thomas Kyme when she was only 15 years old, she refused to adopt his surname. It was an uneasy marriage. A woman of strong Protestant beliefs, Askew went to London to preach against the doctrine of transubstantiation, acquiring a reputation as a tenacious debater. When her husband turned her out of the house, she tried to obtain a divorce, citing Scripture to argue that he was not a true

Christian. She continued to deliver sermons and distribute books that had been banned.

Anne Askew was eventually arrested in 1545 on a charge of heresy and taken to the Tower. She was ordered to be tortured so that the names of other extreme Protestants could be extracted from her; it was also believed that she might have crucial evidence that could be used against the queen, Catherine Parr, Henry VIII's sixth wife and a holder of advanced religious views. Sir Anthony Kingston, constable of the Tower, obeyed the command to put Anne on the rack. When he saw her being tortured, however, he found the spectacle so revolting that he refused to continue the process, claiming that it was illegal to torture a woman, especially one from a noble family.

Henry VIII pardoned the constable's breach of discipline, but he did not stop the interrogation. Instead, he put the lord chancellor, Thomas Wriothesley, and the solicitor-general, Richard Rich, in charge of it. According to the victim, these men turned the screws themselves. All that they succeeded in doing was giving her hours of excruciating agony. Unable to walk, she was still able to use her hands and wrote letters to her friends explaining what was happening:

> Then they did put me on the rack, because I confessed no ladies or gentlewomen to be of my opinion, and thereon they kept me a long time; and because I lay still, and did not cry, my lord Chancellor and Master Rich took pains to rack me with their own hands, till I was nigh dead. Then the lieutenant caused me to be loosed from the rack. Incontinently I swooned, and then they recovered me again. After that I sat two long hours reasoning with my lord Chancellor upon the bare floor; where he, with many flattering words, persuaded me to leave my opinion. But my lord God (I thank his everlasting goodness) gave me grace to persevere, and will do, I hope to the very end.
>
> *L & P Henry VIII* vol. 21 part 1:1546 no. 1181

Askew also wrote an account of her ordeal and her beliefs, published as the *Examinations* by Bishop Bale and, much later, by John Foxe in his *Acts and Monuments*, known as the *Book of Martyrs*, in which she was hailed as a Protestant martyr.

Anne Askew was burned at the stake at Smithfield on 16 July, 1546, her suffering abbreviated by the fact that bags of gunpowder were hung about her. She was 25 years of age.

Lady Jane Grey

Lady Jane Grey was, as Lady Jane Dudley, the Queen of England for a mere nine days in 1553. A gentle, amenable, beautiful and highly intelligent young woman, she became a helpless pawn in the hands of the unscrupulous John Dudley, Duke of Northumberland.

As the great granddaughter of Henry VII, Jane had royal blood, and there had been the suggestion that she marry Edward VI, who had succeeded to the throne in 1547. Northumberland had other plans for her. Seizing political power after the fall of Protector Somerset, he decided to alter the succession and secure the throne for his son, Guildford Dudley. Much against her will, and after severe parental chastisement, Jane was forced to marry Guildford Dudley in May 1553. Northumberland then set about persuading the dying king Edward to eliminate Princess Mary and Princess Elizabeth from the succession and name Lady Jane Dudley as his successor. Fearing that Mary, a staunch Catholic, might succeed him and harass her Protestant subjects, Edward agreed to 'devise' the crown to his first cousin, a hapless and helpless teenage girl.

At the death of the young king, Jane was informed by the Council that she was now queen. Her reign lasted from Sunday 9 July to Wednesday 19 July 1553. During this time, she lived in the Tower, and through the motions of royal ritual, receiving the Regalia, making a few appointments and signing a handful of documents as the rightful monarch. What she refused, in spite of her mother-in-law's hectoring, was to let her husband be made king.

Resistance to the new order was quick and decisive. Strong forces rallied around Mary to press her claim to the throne. The usurpers were put to flight, and Jane's accommodation became a prison. She must have complained of the airlessness of the conditions; the Privy Council wrote to the Lieutenant of the Tower, allowing him to permit prisoners including Cranmer and Lady Jane Grey 'to have their liberty of walk within the garden of the Tower' (see plate 2; PC 2/7). On 12 February 1554 the erstwhile Queen Jane and her husband were executed.

Lacking royal blood, Guildford Dudley was beheaded outside the precincts of the Tower. As his wife was being led to the block, she saw his headless body being brought back into the Tower in a cart for burial there. Northumberland was arrested that summer, tried and convicted of treason. On the scaffold, he proclaimed that he was a Catholic. His desperate bid for power had led to the travesty of the nine-day reign and the execution of an unfortunate and wholly innocent young woman. The Tower from which Jane had fleetingly reigned also became her tomb.

Mary and Elizabeth

Mary was the third child of Henry VIII and Catherine of Aragon, and the only one to survive infancy. Born in 1518, she was only two when she was promised in marriage to the newly born dauphin in France. When that was broken off, she reached the age of six to learn that her intended husband was now Emperor Charles V, a man in his early twenties. In fact, he later chose another bride, so Mary was then offered to James IV of Scotland and later to Francis I of France. From an early age, therefore, she realized that an English princess was at the mercy of dynastic and diplomatic considerations.

Rocked by her father's determination to secure a divorce from his first wife, Mary's Catholic sensibilities were further outraged by the turn of events. In 1531 she was separated from her mother and forbidden to write to her. Mary never saw Catherine of Aragon again. There were additional blows to come: when Anne Boleyn took her place on the throne, Mary was deprived of her title of Princess of Wales, and after the birth of Anne's child, Elizabeth, Mary was declared a bastard and cut out of the succession altogether. Her household was broken up at once, and she was stripped of all the trappings of royalty.

Mary was a strong-minded young woman, and her father resolved to break what he contemptuously called her 'Spanish pride'. She was compelled to agree to the royal supremacy and to acknowledge her own illegitimacy. One can only guess the horror she felt when she saw her father send two of his wives – Anne Boleyn and Catherine Howard – to the scaffold, and preside over a country from which all papal power had been excluded. In 1544 Mary was at least restored to the succession, but she was disappointed that her turn would come after Edward, only seven at the time.

While Mary had suffered many upheavals in her life, her half-brother's life was not without difficulties either. His mother, Jane Seymour, died soon after his birth; his first stepmother, Anne of Cleves, was divorced before he was three; and his second, Catherine Howard, was beheaded for adultery. Like Mary, he had a bewildering inheritance.

Edward was as fanatical about Protestantism as Mary was about Catholicism, but his reign ended before he was able to implement his more extreme policies. Expecting to succeed him, Mary was shocked when she heard that she had been supplanted. Instead of taking flight, she gathered her supporters at Framlingham and proclaimed herself queen. The nation was impressed by her courage and rallied around her. Lady Jane Dudley was swept aside and, when Mary entered London early in August, she did so in triumph.

The Tower now really came into its own. Henry VIII had been the last monarch to use it as a palace before showing a preference for Whitehall. It now became primarily a royal gaol, so that there was hardly a chamber that did not hold a prisoner. Torture and execution were part of the natural order. All over the country Mary's religious persecution was felt, but it was at the Tower that it was at its most intense. The list of her victims is a depressingly long one.

John Foxe's *Book of Martyrs* recorded the sustained ferocity of the attack. It was such a terrifying account of what a Catholic queen could do that Queen Elizabeth later ordered that a copy of the work should be placed in every church. In 1554 Elizabeth herself was imprisoned in the Tower for two months because of her alleged involvement in Wyatt's Rebellion, despite efforts to forestall this with a letter asking Mary to reconsider: 'I am by your Council from you commanded to go unto the Tower, a place more wonted for a false traitor than a true subject' (SP 11/4/2). Mary did not respond, and Elizabeth was sent to the Tower the following day. It was a chilling experience for an impressionable young woman, and one that she never forgot. She would have witnessed prisoners being taken to the scaffold on Tower Green or being dragged off to Tower Hill to be burned at the stake.

Having lived precariously through her half-sister's reign, Elizabeth knew the value of the Tower as a means of suppressing dissent. Since 1303 it had housed the crown jewels and the Royal Mint, but the new queen, like her predecessors, regarded it as the premier royal prison. While she displayed more religious tolerance than Mary, she could not ignore the threat of Roman Catholic plots against her.

The principal task of Sir Thomas Walsingham was to ferret out such conspiracies, and he dedicated himself to the work, using his own money to maintain a small army of agents in England and in foreign courts. Thanks to his secret service, many other potential dangers to the Crown were successfully obliterated or deflected. All this was achieved against a background of continuous argument with the queen and her chief minister, Lord Burghley. Notwithstanding her occasional outbursts of fury at her spymaster, Elizabeth was the first to admire his efficiency and recognize his importance. Until his death in 1590, Walsingham was responsible for a multitude of arrests and for sending many prisoners to the Tower for interrogation.

Robert Southwell

The fate of Robert Southwell is not untypical of what happened to many Jesuit priests caught in England in this period. Brought up in a family of Catholic gentry, Southwell went to France and, after a two-year novitiate, joined the Society of Jesus in 1580 at the age of 19. He was made prefect of studies at the Venerable English College in Rome, and was ordained priest in 1584. At his own request, he was sent to England two years later as a missionary along with Henry Garnett.

In making this journey, the two men were risking their lives. They were both keenly aware of what had happened to Edmund Campion, another Jesuit missionary, only three years earlier. Caught and taken to the Tower, Campion had been examined before Elizabeth herself, and refused the pardon she offered in return for his attendance at Anglican services. He was racked three times and at his subsequent trial – a travesty of justice – he did not even have the strength to raise his hand to plead that he was not guilty. Campion was hanged before an enormous crowd at Smithfield in December 1581.

Southwell bravely continued the work of Campion and his fellow Jesuits, moving from one Catholic house to another to administer the rites of his Church. In 1589 he became chaplain to the Countess of Arundel, operating from her house in the Strand. He wrote many treatises urging Catholics to protest vehemently against the policies of the government. Southwell contrived to have them printed and distributed in secret, but they came to the attention of the authorities. He was eventually arrested in 1592 at the home of his friend, Richard Bellamy, where he regularly celebrated Mass and where he instructed the sons and daughters of the family.

It was one of the daughters, Anne Bellamy, who was forced into betraying him. Arrested and imprisoned in the Gatehouse of Holborn, she was examined by the arch-interrogator and torturer Richard Topcliffe, a man whose reputation as a cruel monster was enough in itself to persuade many prisoners to cooperate. Anne Bellamy confessed that there was a priest-hole in the family house, and a trap was set by Topcliffe. The person caught in it was Robert Southwell. The delighted torturer wrote to the queen that 'I never did take so weighty a man if he be rightly used' (*Correspondence of Richard Topcliffe*).

By way of 'rightly use', Topcliffe at first employed his own house in Westminster as prison and torture chamber, having instruments there that could inflict unspeakable pain. He once boasted that, compared to the rack he had devised in his home, the one at the Tower was 'child's play'. The brutal torture failed to elicit the names that were sought. Southwell was then transferred to the Gatehouse, a gaol so foul and disgusting that his father begged the queen to release his son. Elizabeth ordered him to be transferred to the Tower, where Southwell was allowed books, clothes and a few visitors. But his troubles were far from over. Thirteen times he was examined by members of the Privy Council and tortured on ten occasions. Spared the rack, he was instead subjected to new forms of punishment involving fire and iron spikes. The odious Topcliffe was in his element, administering unbearable pain to every part of an already broken body. His appalling treatment of prisoners like Southwell excited so many complaints from Catholics and Protestants alike that Topcliffe was arrested and imprisoned on a charge of having exceeded his instructions. He was soon released.

Southwell, meanwhile, was tried and convicted of treason. In February, 1595, he was dragged to Tyburn on a hurdle to be hanged, drawn and quartered. Customarily, traitors were released from the noose before they had expired so that they could suffer the pain and public humiliation of disembowelment. On this occasion, Lord Mountjoy took pity on the prisoner and refused to let the hangman cut him down until Southwell was clearly dead.

Guy Fawkes

One of the most notorious episodes in the Tower's history is the torture of Guy Fawkes. The story of the Gunpowder Plot in 1605 is well known: a group of Catholics conspired to assassinate the king and the Protestant aristocracy by blowing up the Houses of Parliament at the state opening on 5 November 1605. A secondary aim was to kidnap the royal children, establish Catholics in positions of power and incite revolt.

When the plot was discovered, Guy Fawkes – not the main plotter but the man responsible for ensuring the explosion – was found with matches and touch paper in a gunpowder-filled cellar beneath the Houses of Parliament. He was taken to the Tower and interrogated under torture. This required the permission of the king, or his Privy Council; in an undated letter thought to be written around 6 November, James I stated that: 'If he will not otherwise confess, the gentler tortures are to be first used on him, *et sic per gradus ad ima tenditur* [and so by degrees until the ulimate is reached], and so God speed your good work' (sp 14/216/17). Famously, when Fawkes' confession 'to blow up the King with all his nobility about him in Parlament' was eventually made to Sir William Waad, Lieutenant of the Tower, Fawkes' signature at the foot of the resulting document, so weak as to be almost invisible, gave eloquent proof of the effects of torture (sp 14/216/54).

While Fawkes awaited execution, he was moved to inferior accommodation in the Tower as men like the Earl of Northumberland and Lord Montague came to give evidence. Such figures could expect to inhabit the royal prison in high state, living much as they did outside its walls, and Sir William Waad was running out of suitable accommodation.

The last of the principal conspirators to be executed, Fawkes had to be helped up the ladder to the gallows; the drop was long enough to break his neck, so he escaped the full horror of his sentence of being hung, drawn and quartered.

Sir Walter Raleigh

Another figure named in connection with the Gunpowder Plot was already living in the Tower. Sir Walter Raleigh – soldier, sailor, explorer and royal favourite – was first briefly imprisoned there in 1592 for seducing Elizabeth Throgmorton, one of the queen's maids of honour. The couple were later married. When James I became king in 1603, Raleigh was arrested on a charge of being implicated in a plot 'to surprise the king's person' and place Arabella Stuart on the throne in his stead.

Convicted of high treason, he was condemned to be executed, then reprieved. Raleigh spent 14 years in the Bloody Tower in comparative comfort. He made a home for his wife, children and servants, and was even permitted to turn a hen house into a kind of laboratory. When another son was born, the party was moved to better accommodation in the Tower. From these quarters, Raleigh was able to write poems, letters and his famous *History of the World*, a work that revealed his deep religious convictions.

Raleigh was released in 1616 in order to join an expedition in search of the fabled El Dorado on the condition that, in the event of failure, he would return. The expedition was a catastrophe, and he honoured his promise to come back to England. At his execution in 1618, one of the most brilliant and independent men of his day met his long-delayed end. Several accounts survive; one by a clerk called Mr Henley reads:

> Then he called for the Executioner who, kneeling down, he laid both
> his hands upon his shoulders, heartily forgiving him and demanding his
> Axe, he [the executioner] looked wildly and fearfully about him, why,
> quoth Sir Walter, do you think I am afraid of it, who being commanded
> so to do gave it into his hands, then Sir Walter taking and trying with
> his thumb the sharpness of the edge, Here is, quoth he, a Physician that
> can cure all diseases and so re-delivering it again, prepared himself for
> the Block … Then the headsman asking whether he should not cut his
> waistcoat, because it came too high up into his neck, to which Sir Walter
> answered, must thou [you must] cut my flesh, and do you fear to cut my
> waistcoat. Then laying his head on the block after his general Adieu at
> the first stroke he was quite dead, yet there were two blows given.

> (CRES 40/18)

Raleigh was the last major link with the court of Queen Elizabeth and with a Tudor dynasty that washed out the Tower on a regular basis with buckets of blood. Henceforth the Tower would never again be used so strenuously as an instrument of oppression.

The Clink

The Clink was the oldest prison in London after the Tower, and its name has become a synonym for any English gaol. It was part of a residence built by William Gifford, Bishop of Winchester, and completed after twenty years in 1127. It stood on the river bank in Southwark on land that was part of the liberty of the see of Winchester, and was a convenient residence for the prelate when attending parliament. On the south side was a great park and gardens; on the north side flowed the Thames beneath a river terrace. This magnificent palace also included a series of cells and, from the evidence of regulations drawn up in 1161 for their control, it is clear that they were in continuous use.

This was hardly surprising given that Southwark was one of the most unsavoury parts of the city, filled with brothels, disreputable taverns and gambling dens. What villains and outlaws found even more attractive than these was the fact that, as part of a Church holding, the liberty offered sanctuary from the civil law. The bishop licensed and supervised the brothels, deriving a vast income from doing so. Prostitutes were identified so closely with the area that their generic name was Winchester geese; their clients were often criminals who had fled to the district for safety.

First-hand descriptions of London in the twelfth century are rare. One of the most notable is that of William FitzStephen, who, in *The Life of Thomas Becket*, written about 1170, depicts a city that is 'ennobled by her men, graced by her arms'. The citizens are portrayed as people who are respected 'above all others for the elegance of their manners, dress, table and discourse'. In FitzStephen's account, there is no mention of crime and decadence.

It was his contemporary, Richard of Devizes, who delivered a corrective. A monk from Winchester, he was frankly aghast at what he saw in London, and his visit to Southwark remained uppermost in his mind:

All sorts of men crowd there from every country … each bringing its
own vices and customs. None lives in it without falling into some sort
of crime. Every quarter abounds in grave obscenities. The greater the
rascal, the better man he is accounted … Do not associate with crowds
of pimps; do not mingle with the throngs in eating-houses; avoid dice
and gambling, the theatre and the tavern … the number of parasites
is infinite. Actors, jesters, smooth-skinned lads, flatterers, pretty-boys,
effeminates, pederasts, singing and dancing girls, quacks, belly-dancers,
sorceresses, extortioners, night-wanderers, magicians, mimes, beggars and
buffoons … inhabit the streets.

J. T. Appleby (ed.), Richard of Devises Chronicle

Even allowing for exaggeration, this colourful account gives us some
insight into a cosmopolitan city that was tainted by vices of every kind
– and could provide plenty of prison fodder.

In the fourteenth century, the prison disappeared when the building
in which it was housed was replaced by a huge Gothic palace. A new,
larger Clink was constructed in the cellars. As a result of a statute passed
in 1352, creditors could now have those who owed them money imprisoned, and the Clink quickly became known as a debtors' prison.

Ransacked twice by rebels, the prison brought in a sizeable income
for successive bishops of Winchester until Henry VII closed the brothels in 1504 because he feared the spread of syphilis. As the bishop of the
time had spent so lavishly, a year with no golden eggs being laid by his
Winchester geese produced a financial crisis. The palace fell into disrepair, and the Clink became nothing more than a common gaol.

It was left to the next bishop of Winchester, the resourceful Stephen
Gardiner – who was also archbishop of Canterbury – to rescue the
fortunes of the Liberty. Liking to wallow in carnal pleasure himself, he
befriended Henry VIII by providing him with a supply of high-class
whores. When the monasteries were dissolved and church property was
seized all over the country, Gardiner kept the liberty and restored the
palace to its former glory.

Later imprisoned in the Fleet by Edward VI, Gardiner seemed on
the point of losing his palace and his prison – but the king died in 1553
and the new queen, Mary, not only released Gardiner from custody, but

made him her lord chancellor. He was given a duty that was close to his heart – that of pursuing and punishing Protestants, an activity in which the Clink played a leading part as both a prison and a torture site.

Under Elizabeth, the Clink was still the principal prison for religious offences, but it also served as a gaol for local law breakers and for debtors.

In 1626, a year after the succession of Charles I, the Privy Council ordered a search for recusant priests. The door of the Clink was unmanned and obligingly left open. Inside it, the raiders found four priests who had created a library, set up two altars for the celebration of Mass and accumulated a large amount of money. Also discovered were the prison keeper's financial records and accounts, showing that a priest had been acting as an accountant at the Clink. Before further action could be taken, the search was called off and no arrests were made.

During the Civil War, Winchester House was requisitioned as a lodging for Royalist prisoners. After the Restoration of 1660, it went into serious decline. According to the census of 1772, it held only two prisoners, a far cry from the days when it was brimming with deep-dyed villains, rowdy prostitutes, corrupt innkeepers, pitiful debtors and religious dissenters.

The Marshalsea

The Marshalsea got its name from the fact that it held prisoners tried at the Marshalsea Court run by the Lord Steward and Knight Marshal of the king's household. Built in the late fourteenth century, for many years it ranked second in importance to the Tower. Like the Clink, it stood in the unruly area of Southwark – and managed to provoke hostility from the start. In 1377 a riot broke out there when the marshal imprisoned a man deemed by the City of London to be privileged. Four years later, reviled for its brutal regime – its keeper was described as a 'tormentor without pity' – it was destroyed by Wat Tyler and his men, then broken into again by Jack Cade in 1450.

In 1504 conditions in the Marshalsea were so atrocious that a mass breakout took place. Many of those recaptured were hanged. Escape or rescue must have been a constant feature of a prison that was so badly built, and manned by keepers who let some prisoners walk outside the walls in return for money. A degree of comfort could be purchased by wealthy prisoners, but the vast majority endured squalor and degradation. During the Reformation and its aftermath, Catholics and Protestants were roughly handled. The lowest and worst dungeon became known as Bonner's Coal Hole, named after the last Catholic bishop of London, who, under Edward and Elizabeth, was himself a guest at the Marshalsea and died there of natural causes in 1569.

Civil debtors made up the bulk of the prison's inmates. It has been estimated that in 1641 as many as 10,000 people were imprisoned for debt in England and Wales, many of them for periods of years, even though the amount they owed was relatively small at the time of arrest. Behind bars, of course, they were building up further debts that had to be discharged before they could be released. Poverty was thus a vicious circle: creditors were hounding people into the one place where they were unlikely ever to settle their debts.

It was part of the Marshal's role to deal with anyone judged to be in contempt of royal authority. In 1597 the playwright Ben Jonson was put into the Marshalsea for his part in writing *The Isle of Dogs*, a satire for the stage 'containing very seditious and slanderous matter'.

The following year, Jonson was in prison again – this time in Newgate – for killing a man in a duel. He escaped execution by pleading benefit of clergy, and was instead branded as a felon.

The poet Christopher Brooke was imprisoned in the Marshalsea for witnessing the secret marriage of Anne More to John Donne in 1601; the bride had failed to obtain her father's consent to the match (p. 47). Another poet to inhabit one of the ramshackle buildings that comprised the Marshalsea was George Wither, who in 1613 wrote his best poem, *Shepherd's Hunting*, there. Wither's crime had been to attack the lord chancellor in his satire *Abuses Stript and Whipt*.

Newgate

London's gatehouses were built to defend the city, but the capital was seldom under threat, and as there was so little property that could serve as a prison, buildings such as Newgate were used to accommodate felons inside their thick walls. Built around 1130, it was not until over fifty years later that Newgate could rival its neighbour, the Fleet prison. In

1187 adjoining land was bought so that the gaol could be extended. As its size grew, there was a corresponding increase in its importance, and it began to handle suspects accused of serious crimes. Minor criminals and debtors tended to go to Ludgate.

Newgate was a royal prison administered by the sheriffs, and they sold the management of the institution to successive keepers. These were usually men who maintained corrupt regimes, housing their charges in dreadful conditions while abusing them and extorting money from them. Escapes, riots and bouts of gaol fever marked the prison's history. So much scandal was attached to it that Dick Whittington, the mayor, made a bequest 'to re-edify the gaol at Newgate'.

Work began in 1423, and a new five-storey, custom-built prison eventually greeted visitors who entered the city through that particular gate. Inevitably, it was known as Whittington's Palace, or the Whit. A dining hall was included, and separate accommodation provided for those holding the freedom of the city. Less fortunate prisoners were held in dark, underground cells that were secure and solid. Old abuses, however, continued in the new prison. In 1449, for instance, keeper William Arnold was arrested for raping a female prisoner. Blackmail, torture and fees for affixing or removing irons were among the ways that keepers could make profits.

None of the money accumulated was spent on the fabric of the building. When a portion began to decay, prisoners were simply moved to another area, making the overcrowding even worse and rendering the inmates more vulnerable to outbreaks of gaol fever. Criminals of all kinds were thrown together: harmless debtors were forced to rub shoulders with killers, and female recusants shared the same roof as brazen whores. An indication of the sort of inmates who came to the prison can be found in the work of Henry Goodcole, the first of the ordinaries of Newgate to publish accounts of what went on there.

In 1620 he wrote *Heaven's Speedie Hue and Cry Sent after Lust and Murther*, a description of the arrest and imprisonment of a prostitute, Elizabeth Evans, and her partner, Thomas Shearwood. Evans would entice drunken clients to a place where Shearwood could kill them. In his confession, Shearwood supplied information about 'many base persons of his condition, and the dispersed places of secret harbouring of

such unprofitable obnoxious members unto a state and commonwealth'.
Like Richard of Devizes, Goodcole was shocked by what he learned
about the underworld.

Interestingly, at this time Catholics imprisoned in Newgate for refusing to take the oath of allegiance were allowed considerable freedom, even
to the extent of being allowed to celebrate mass. Keeper Simon Houghton
was married to a Catholic convert, and sustained this tolerant regime for
nine years. When the truth came to light in 1621, he was prosecuted for
gross neglect of duty, and replaced by a keeper who believed in the traditional virtues of strict control, random brutality and a starvation diet.

During the Great Plague of 1665, all trials were suspended, so even
more inmates were crammed into the limited space. The next year, the
Great Fire of London destroyed most of the city, cleansing it of the
disease. Newgate, on the edge of the fire zone, was badly damaged, and
its prisoners were hastily transferred to the Clink. It was time to rebuild
the prison again.

The Fleet

First recorded in 1170, this London prison was built on the eastern bank
of the River Fleet, off Farringdon Road. It was fortified and moated,
a stronghold in itself, and used principally to house those who owed
money to the Crown and those committed by the King's Council and
the Court of Chancery. The post of keeper was hereditary and from 1197
to 1558 it was held by the Leveland family. Two of the early keepers were
women, widows who inherited the post from their husbands. Keepers
enjoyed the privilege of receiving the customs dues levied on the Fleet
and charging the prisoners fees for food, lodging and irons. Fees were
said to be the highest of any prison. A wealthy inmate could even
purchase temporary freedom without any bail.

The Fleet consisted of a prison proper, where debtors were kept, a
prison precinct of about an acre surrounded by the moat, and 'the rules',
a string of houses built outside the moat. It was rebuilt in the reign
of Edward III, then razed to the ground in 1381 during the Peasants'
Revolt. When it was rebuilt again, the moat was filled in because it had
become a glorified latrine; so much offal was dumped into it by slaugh-
terers working nearby that, it was claimed, people could walk across the

water. The perpetual stink had been one more horror that generations of inmates had had to endure.

From the reign of Henry VIII until 1641, prisoners convicted by the Court of Star Chamber were sent to the Fleet. Many famous people came to know its rigours. Sir Thomas Wyatt, the poet, was held there in 1542 on a charge of treason, before being released. John Hooper, Bishop of Gloucester and Worcester, was another Protestant martyr sent to the Fleet in 1555 to await execution. John Donne spent a brief time there after his elopement with Anne More. In 1638 John Lilburne, champion of individual liberty and leader of the Levellers, who believed in freedom of conscience and of the press, faced the Star Chamber in the first of many trials. He was sentenced to a massive fine and also to be whipped from the Fleet prison to Westminster and there pilloried, and to be kept behind bars until he conformed to the law. William Prynne, the Puritan pamphleteer, suffered a similar fate and lost both ears.

Destroyed by the Great Fire of 1666, the Fleet was subsequently rebuilt.

Other London prisons

As there was an ever-increasing supply of criminals in London, many other gaols sprang up. Each of the two sheriffs had his own prison, rented out to a keeper. The Bread Street Compter and the Poultry Compter were busy establishments, catering for debtors, whores and petty offenders. When the Bread Street gaol was closed in 1555, its inmates were transferred to the Wood Street Compter, where the same abuses of neglect, exploitation and cruelty operated.

The playwright Thomas Dekker, imprisoned for debt in the Poultry in 1598, recalled its clamour in *Dekker His Dreame* in 1620.

> jailors hoarsely and harshly bawling for prisoners to their bed, and prison-
> ers reviling and cursing jailors for making such a hellish din. Then to hear
> some in their chambers singing and dancing, being half drunk; others
> breaking open doors to get more drink to be whole drunk. Some roaring
> for tobacco; others raging and bidding hell's plague on all tobacco.

Those who avoided the compters might find themselves in the Tun, the Gatehouse in Westminster, the King's Bench prison in Southwark or in any of the many other places of confinement. There might be architectural differences between them but, for the most part, their regimes were frighteningly similar.

Outside London

By 1500 most municipal communities, whether they were boroughs or not, had a prison that was governed locally and acted as a receptacle for offenders convicted in their courts. The duty to build a prison was often part of a charter of incorporation. In Coventry, for instance, one of the four largest cities in 1345, the following clause appeared in its charter:

> And also that a certain gaol shall be had and made in the same vill within the tenure of the said mother, for the chastising of malefactors there apprehended, as the manner is, of which certain prison and the prisoners therein, from whatever cause it shall happen that they shall be there taken, the aforesaid Mayor and Bailiffs for the time being shall have the custody and care as is aforesaid.

Cities and towns built around medieval castles already had a prison, but the growth of a community often meant that an additional gaol was needed to cope with the drunks, ruffians, pimps, whores, debtors and vagabonds who were short-term occupants. Keepers were no more humane in the provinces than in the capital. In the course of his peregrinations, George Fox, founder of the Society of Friends, was imprisoned in gaols from Carlisle to Cornwall. His *Journal*, which he kept until 1676, is a remarkable autobiography, detailing the brutal persecution suffered by Quakers and the harsh treatment received behind bars.

Fox's contemporary, John Bunyan, spent 12 years in Bedford county gaol in Silver Street. Indicted for blasphemy and preaching without a licence, he was incarcerated in 1660, refusing to promise that he would discontinue his fiery sermons. Bunyan's conscience would not allow him to give that undertaking, so he remained in custody, taking the opportunity to educate himself and to write, among many other things, *The Pilgrim's Progress*. The county gaol was typical of many around the country, offering poor food, constant noise, foul smells and little comfort. But it did at least grant Bunyan the freedom to write one of the masterpieces of English literature.

Released in 1672 under the Declaration of Indulgence, Bunyan preached in London as well as Bedford. Three years later he was arrested again and imprisoned this time in Bedford town gaol on the stone bridge over the River Ouse. (In 1660 it had been in such a state of disrepair that he could not be accommodated.)

Wakefield prison

By an Act of parliament in 1576, justices of the peace were required to establish houses of correction in places under their jurisdiction. Their function was to provide work for the poor and to correct, by imposing hard labour, the behaviour of vagrants, harlots, idle apprentices and anyone else in need of stern reforming discipline. As a result of this Poor Law legislation, Wakefield prison first came into being as the West Riding House of Correction. Records suggest that it was not built until as late as 1597. Appropriately, its first keeper was 'Maister Key'.

Vagrancy had been a serious problem for centuries. If justices followed the letter of the law and imprisoned all vagrants, the burden on the rates would be immense. In Wakefield as elsewhere, therefore, it was easier to have them whipped by the beadle and sent on their way. The only way to deal with an insoluble problem was to shift it on to the next town. A whipping might have been preferable to being locked up in a damp cell with disagreeable companions, kept on a miserable diet and forced to take on laborious tasks.

The court records of the West Riding quarter sessions give a clear picture of the sort of miscreants who were sent to the House of Correction, and they repeat a story that was happening all over the country. To bring about some reform of those in prison, a prisoner had to remain in such an institution for a length of time. But, for financial reasons, short sentences were the norm, and the deterrent aspect then took precedence. Those entering Wakefield house of correction – and the prison that it later became – were treated in such a way that they would think twice before committing further offences.

In sentencing people to imprisonment, justices felt that they had discharged their duty; they felt no real obligation to concern themselves with the physical, mental and moral welfare of the inmates. Wakefield prison was as bare, cheerless, overcrowded and insanitary as other county gaols. Inspections were carried out, but few improvements were made, because magistrates drew back from spending public money on the scum of the community. Those taken into the prison for short periods had no hope of rehabilitation. When they were released, they were bitter, vengeful, underfed wretches who had often been fleeced by an unscrupulous keeper and battered by a strict regime. It was only in the wake of John Howard's visit in 1774 that even basic improvements were finally made.

* * *

Both in London and the provinces, prisons proved an inadequate response to the ever-rising tide of crime. Instead of taming offenders, prison was far more likely to create them, by acting as schools for crime. Debtors, whose only fault might have been to lose their jobs or suffer an injury that made them unable to work, could be tutored by professional thieves, confidence tricksters and cardsharps. Petty offenders could be lured into more serious crime, and hitherto decent men could be tempted to ease their suffering by resorting to the strong drink, tobacco and sexual contact that was readily on sale for those able to pay.

When she published *Malice Defeated* in 1680, Elizabeth Cellier, known as the popish midwife, described the shocking conditions and gross malpractices she had witnessed as a prisoner inside Newgate. Her comments could also apply to other prisons in and outside London:

> There have been many cruel things acted in that Mansion of Horror, as the story they tell of Captain Clarke, who being a prisoner only for debt, was locked up in a little dark hole for two days and two Nights, having no other company but the Quarters of two Executed Persons, the extream stench of which perhaps had kill'd him, had he not took the miserable relief of holding a foul Chamber Pot to his Nose.

Newgate had been rebuilt in 1672 and much of the enormous cost of this had been spent on the sumptuous exterior with its Tuscan pilasters and massive statues symbolizing Peace, Security, Plenty and Liberty. Those inside the prison could not see its most attractive features – nor could they expect any peace, security, plenty or liberty. To prisoners in early English gaols, such concepts were mere phantoms.

CHAPTER TWO

The State of
Eighteenth-century Prisons

Here are but thirteen poor wretches of us on the Common Side, and twelve of 'em were brought in upon the tally account. If Providence show us no more mercy than our creditors, here they will keep us as examples of their cruelty, to frighten others in their books to turn either whore or thief to get money to be punctual in their payments. This many of us have been forc'd to do to my certain knowledge, to satisfy the hungry demands of those unconscionable usurers.

Ned Ward, *The London Spy*, 1703

Nobody in this period could be entirely unaware of the horrors that lurked on the other side of the prison walls; released prisoners often spoke feelingly about their respective ordeals. Debtors, in particular, like the woman quoted above that satirical writer Ned Ward met in the Poultry Compter, were loud complainers. They were not felons, but they could be imprisoned on the word of a creditor for a trifling debt. If they could not pay up, they might be held in custody for years, suffering all the miseries and dangers that were concomitant with prison life. The brutalities in such infamous gaols as the Marshalsea, the Fleet and Newgate were so outrageous that the lord mayor was forced occasionally to intervene by issuing dire warnings against abuse of prisoners. Once he had done so and retired from the scene, the scandals quickly resumed.

In the last decade of the seventeenth century, a veritable flurry of books, pamphlets and tracts sought to inform the public of the routine savagery practised behind prison gates. One of the most disturbing accounts was *The Crye of the Oppressed from Prison*, written by Moses Pitt in 1691 when he was imprisoned in the Fleet. In spite of resistance from the authorities, Pitt later had the text published at his own expense; detailed, precise and authoritative, it was thrown into sharper focus by its vivid illustrations.

Pitt wrote in support of a petition to parliament for the relief of indigent debtors. One of the abuses he described was unique to the Fleet, and related to a law by which a creditor had the right to a writ of habeas corpus. This enabled him to have any prisoner moved to the highly expensive Fleet from another prison, thus putting the debtor in even more dire financial straits. Its staff offered inducements to creditors to take out writs against certain individuals and have them transferred to the Fleet, where fee-paying prisoners could be mercilessly deprived of any money they still had.

Pitt's research was not confined to London. By speaking to other inmates, he gathered first-hand accounts of the villainies occurring in provincial prisons. Some of the illustrations are harrowing. One shows a starving prisoner catching mice to eat. In another, a debtor is dragged along on a crude hurdle because he had the gall to ask the keeper to account for money entrusted to him to buy leather so that the prisoner could earn money at his craft. In a third illustration, a row of debtors lie dead from starvation and blood poisoning. A fourth shows debtors covered with ugly 'Boyles, Carbuncles and Botches', signs of venereal disease contracted in a prison where there was no segregation of the sexes and promiscuity was rampant.

Durham gaol provided one of the worst examples of official depravity. The keeper, who was known for his cruelty, locked nine debtors in a cell three feet square with no access to the privy; the stench was so nauseating that inmates complained: 'we are almost poisoned with our own Dung'. There is an eyewitness account of how this same drunken keeper 'Murthered one Mary Barnard a Prisoner who was under his Custody … by knocking her on the head with the Gaol-Keys'. Almost as grotesque is an illustration showing a debtor chained to the wall with iron billhooks round his neck, so that he is unable to move his head without gashing himself. His hands are joined in front of him with thumbscrews, and he is suspended from the ceiling so that his toes barely touch the floor. Here was a torture worthy of Richard Topcliffe.

Only a man as determined as Pitt could have persisted with this work, because he was baulked at every stage. When he finally secured the sympathetic interest of members of the Lords and the Commons, he was summoned to parliament to present his petition. The keeper of the Fleet did everything in his power to stop Pitt from going. Fearing the loss of his position, and the fees and chamber rents that went with it, he had already been intercepting Pitt's correspondence, even withholding some of the letters from parliament. As a punishment for daring to speak out, Pitt was thrown in with the wretches forced to beg through the bars for alms.

But the keeper was thwarted. A messenger was sent from parliament to fetch the prisoner and, in spite of the keeper's protests, he took Pitt off to the Commons. Although many consciences were pricked by what he revealed, no major reforms followed the petition. Published later in the form of a book, *The Crye of the Oppressed from Prison*, it had a much wider influence, and its illustrations aroused pity and anger. The work of Moses Pitt foreshadowed the radical changes in the prison system that came over a century later.

Newgate

Imprisonment in Newgate was an equally hideous experience. In 1700 the Lord Mayor and Aldermen were shocked by the revelation that William Robinson, the deputy keeper, was using the site as a brothel, allowing prostitutes to spend the night there. Robinson charged male prisoners sixpence to enter women's cells, and female prisoners were often eager for these visits because pregnancy – pleading the belly – would mean a stay of execution. They therefore competed zealously with the whores imported into the prison.

The prison also featured in *An Essay towards ye Reformation of Newgate and Other Prisons in and about London*. Written in 1702 by Dr Thomas Bray, founder of the Society for the Promotion of Christian Knowledge, it showed what a den of iniquity Newgate was. Prisoners swore, blasphemed, drank heavily and fought each other. Religious worship was badly neglected, and the staff connived with the inmates instead of trying to control their excesses. Bray was not one for empty complaint: in 1727 he got involved with relief work at Whitechapel gaol, working tirelessly with others who recognized the need for urgent reform of prisons.

One of the most eloquent attacks on the system came from the anonymous author of *The History of the Press Yard or, a Brief Account of the Customs and Occurrences that Are Put into Practice in that Ancient Repository of Living Bodies called Newgate.* Written in 1717, it may well be the work of Daniel Defoe; it certainly has his eye for detail. A graphic description is given of condemned prisoners living in a filthy, malodorous, cockroach-infested, underground hold as they faced the prospect of execution. Many were kept in chains in the dark. If they wanted a candle to fend off the gloom, they had to pay for it. There was no privacy. While condemned men made their last poignant confessions to the prison chaplain, other inmates and visitors would be listening at the grille.

Those awaiting trial sought ways to escape conviction or, at the very least, to soften their sentences. In 1708 *The Memoirs of the Right Villainous John Hall, the Late Famous and Notorious Robber. Penn'd from his Mouth Some Time before His Death* was printed. It gives an intriguing account of how prisoners helped each other.

> In the boozing ken … the students, instead of holding disputes in philosophy and mathematicks, run altogether upon law; for such as are committed for house-breaking, swear stoutly they cannot be cast for burglary, because the fact was done in the day-time; such as are committed for stealing a horse-cloth, or coachman's cloak, swear they cannot be cast for felony because the coach was standing still, not stopp'd; and such as steal before a man's face, swear they value not their adversary, because they are out of the reach of the new act against private stealing. Thus with an unparallel'd prudence every brazen'd faced malefactor is harden'd in his sin because the law cannot touch his life.

According to Hall, many prisoners spent hours conducting mock trials, learning how to cope with cross-examination and how to confound witnesses offering evidence against them. There were over 200 offences on the statute book bearing the death penalty, the vast majority relating to theft of, or damage to, property. As a large proportion of those sent to prison could be executed if found guilty, they would go to any lengths to avoid the hangman.

The Windmill

The total lack of hygiene in Newgate was conducive to the spread of gaol fever and other diseases. As a result of bad sanitation and severe overcrowding, an epidemic could sweep through the prison and the adjoining Sessions House. In 1750 Newgate was filled to capacity. An infectious disease broke out, attacked the prisoners and was carried on clothes and bodies into the Court of the Old Bailey at the May session.

The fever took hold of everyone indiscriminately. More than sixty people died, including jurymen, barristers, court clerks, the lord mayor, under-sheriff and the former lord mayor. Newgate was washed down with vinegar and so were any prisoners due to appear in court. As a precaution, judges developed the habit of carrying a nosegay of flowers to ward off the stench of the prison. They and the city authorities urged that immediate improvements had to be made at Newgate to prevent another tragedy.

One obvious suggestion was that houses at the rear of the sessions house should be knocked down, creating an open area where prisoners could exercise in the open air; this was undertaken when Newgate was rebuilt in 1762. Another idea was that a windmill should be constructed on the roof of the gatehouse, to act as a ventilator and draw off poisonous air. The plan was put into effect and seems to have had some success.

The keeper was paid £13 a year to maintain the windmill's condition. After four months in operation, it was inspected and a report was written which noted that only seven people had died since the introduction of the machine, compared to sixteen in the same months of the preceding six years. Statistically, it was argued, nine lives had been saved – but the whirring sails did not dissipate the abiding stink or draw off all of the poison in the air. The only way to get rid of the pestilential atmosphere was to burn Newgate down, a feat that was accomplished in 1780 by those caught up in the Gordon Riots protesting against the Papists Act of 1778. Though they were not prompted by medical motives, the rioters unwittingly did future inmates a huge favour.

Transportation

Throughout the seventeenth century, transportation to the colonies in North America or the West Indies had been a convenient alternative to hanging. It removed troublesome prisoners and prevented them becoming martyrs on the scaffold. Catholics, extreme Protestants and other religious offenders were banished overseas, along with thieves, thugs and rebellious Scotsmen. The authorities were quick to spot the additional advantages of transportation: it was cheaper than imprisonment and furnished the colonies with indentured slaves who could be put to hard work.

Courts could sentence offenders to periods of seven or fourteen years abroad. Destinations like Virginia and Maryland were the most popular. Prisoners were taken overseas by contractors who charged a flat fee of £5 a head; when this fee was later waived, contractors could still make a tidy profit by selling their stock of prisoners to their new owners.

The lowest fees were for women; in the West Indies, women were not at all wanted. This caused a problem, because the gaols were packed with females arrested on coining and clipping charges: if they could not be sent abroad, they would have to be hanged. Male convicts were acceptable in the West Indies because they could work on the plantations and, in the event of attack, could help to defend a property. There was a great deal of wrangling about taking female convicts to destinations like Jamaica, and this went on interminably because of the time it took for letters to be exchanged. Some women imprisoned in Newgate and sentenced to transportation found the wait intolerable and, in 1700, a number of them tried to escape by shinning down a rope. They were swiftly recaptured.

When the Leeward Islands eventually agreed to take 50 women, the government paid them £8 per head.

Transportation was a workable system until 1776, when the War of American Independence stopped the practice dead in its tracks. From

1615 until that date, it is estimated that as many as 40,000 convicts were shipped overseas from gaols all over England. A typical example of transportation may be found in *A true list of all the prisoners taken from the Counties of Hertford, Essex, Kent, Surry and Bucks and shipped on board the* Dorsetshire ... (T 53/38)

Of the 30 prisoners, seven were female. Appended to the list is a statement made by William Loney, commander of the vessel:

> I humbly certify to whom it may concern that the prisoners above named
> being in number 30 are received by me on board the *Dorsetshire* from
> the keeper of the several Gaols above mentioned by order of Mr Jonan
> Forward of London, merchant, to be effectually transported to Virginia,
> as witness my hand 25th Dec.1736.

So even on Christmas Day felons were shipped abroad.

Having lost the option of transportation, parliament swiftly passed an act in 1776 that authorized courts, for a limited period, to pass sentences of three to ten years on men who would otherwise be shipped to the colonies. Prison hulks – rotting ships moored in the Thames and elsewhere – were used to house the convicts. The hulks will be explored in the next chapter, but it is important to note that, like transportation, they were not a state-controlled punishment. The hulks were delegated to a private contractor who had formerly been involved in shipping convicts to America.

Executions

Retribution and deterrence were the guiding principles of criminal law in the eighteenth century. The punishment for every felony was death, and neither youth nor old age could save the offender. Women were subject to the same harsh statutes, and took their turn on the scaffold. Soft-hearted judges – and there were a few – sometimes commuted a death sentence to a fine, a whipping and a stay in the pillory, but there was still plenty of work for the country's hangmen. In London, a mystique grew up around their work: an execution was not just a barbaric spectacle, it was a festive occasion attended by thousands and lending the criminal a specious glamour.

Preparations for the fatal day were carried out with great care. In 1698 Henri Misson, a sharp-eyed Frenchman, produced *Memoirs and Observations in His Travels over England*. Those who read the English translation of 1719 would have admired the accuracy of his comments on the ritual that preceded a meeting with the hangman:

> He that is to be hanged or otherwise executed first takes care to get himself shaved and handsomely dressed, whether in mourning or in the dress of a bridegroom. This done, he sets his friends at work to get him leave to be buried, and to carry his coffin with him, which is easily obtained. When his suit of clothes, or night-gown, his gloves, hat, periwig, nosegay, coffin, flannel dress for his corpse, and all those things are bought and prepared, the main point is taken care of, his mind is at peace and then he thinks of his conscience.

To pay for their coffin, settle their prison debts or bequeath money to their families, some condemned men sold their memoirs, justifying their crimes and signing off their human existence with an act of bravado. More repentant prisoners used their memoirs to warn readers of the consequences of a criminal life. But it was only the notorious murderers, pirates and highwaymen who commanded high prices for their works; humbler offenders had nothing to sell.

Prison officials stood to gain most from any execution. The ordinary of Newgate (its prison chaplain) had a salary of £35 a year, but this was supplemented by what he could earn from the sale of accounts, confessions and dying words of criminals. Selling in their thousands, these would cost anything between threepence and sixpence. Nobody but the chaplain had such exclusive access to prisoners, spending long hours alone with them, hearing their final confessions and accompanying them to the gallows.

John Allen, the resident ordinary in 1700, had a further means of making money. He built up a thriving funeral business and was rumoured to have offered reprieves to condemned men in return for sizeable sums. Allen was a vulture, feeding off the dead, and he was by no means the only predator to secure the position at Newgate. His successor, the Reverend Paul Lorrain, a Huguenot refugee, published over 200 pamphlets containing confessions from various prisoners, and made a substantial profit in doing so. Under the guise of offering spiritual comfort, such unprincipled men could take the utmost advantage of prisoners when they were at their most vulnerable.

The procession

The journey to the gallows was an important part of the execution ritual. Prisoners were brought into the Press Yard and, in front of a crowd of spectators, had their chains struck off. When the gates were flung open, the carts transporting the condemned rolled out into a street lined with excited onlookers. The procession was led on horseback by the city marshal and the under-sheriff; they were flanked by constables and other peace officers, armed with staves so they could beat off any attempt to rescue the prisoners. A strict order of precedence existed among the carts, with those guilty of the most serious crimes leading the way. Rich men could buy the privilege of travelling in their own coach. Traitors were dragged backwards on a hurdle, pelted with missiles and jeered at.

The procession stopped at the church of St Sepulchre's, where, in accordance with ancient custom, the bellman rang his bell twelve times before making his declaration.

> All good people pray heartily unto God for these poor sinners, who are now going to their death, for whom this great bell doth toll. You that are condemned to die, repent with lamentable tears; ask mercy of the lord for the salvation of your soul through the merits, death and passion of Jesus Christ, who now sits on the right hand of God, to make intercession for as many of you as penitently return to Him. Lord have mercy on you! Christ have mercy upon you!

The bellman then handed each prisoner some flowers and a cup of wine. In many cases it was not the prisoner's first drink of the day. To dull their brain during the ordeal, some prisoners had usually already drunk themselves into near-oblivion and had no idea what the bellman was saying.

After moving on down Snow Hill, the cavalcade turned sharp left at the bottom and crossed the Fleet Ditch. It went up the hill to High Holborn and slowed in the narrow and well-populated streets near St Giles.

The final stage of the journey took them along Oxford Road to Tyburn (see plate 3). Crowds lined the whole route, but it was here that they were at their thickest, wildest and most dangerous. Riots were not unknown; people could be crushed to death in the mêlée. At Tyburn itself, the scene often verged on chaos. Prisoners were deafened by the clamour; they were reviled or cheered by the crowd as they were confronted with the sight of the gallows. No quick release awaited them: hangmen were rarely proficient, and sensible victims paid their friends to hang on to their legs while they were suspended, to attempt to break their necks and cut short the agony.

Mingling with the seething mass around the scaffold were pickpockets, prostitutes, thieves, drunkards, and people selling ballads, hot pies, gingerbread and other treats. While prisoner after prisoner entertained the crowd with grisly death, purses were being stolen and assignations made; food was being gobbled down, drunkards were being obstreperous and ballads were being sung about those still dangling from the gallows. Watching the spectacle was not a male preserve; whole families turned up to revel in the fairground atmosphere. A visit to Tyburn was a public celebration in which the guests of honour were hanged.

The bodies of executed men were believed to have mystical qualities. Because of this, grotesque scenes regularly took place at the gallows. Mothers held their children against the hands of hanged men, in the mistaken belief that it was a guarantee of good health. Others pressed forward in the hope that the mere touch of a dead felon would cure their diseases. Ropes used on the scaffold were also surrounded by superstition, and hangmen could sell pieces of them to the baying crowd; the more notorious the criminal, the more his death rope would fetch.

One last indignity awaited those executed. The anatomists who trained surgeons in the art of dissection were allowed 10 free bodies a year from among the hanged, and would pay handsomely for any additional corpses. Naturally, they preferred younger, healthier bodies, rather than those of diseased old men, on which to demonstrate. First, however, they had to lay hold of the bodies, and this was never an easy business. Dissectionists were loathed, and the crowd would often join the victim's family in protecting a corpse. It was another excuse for a brawl, and readily seized; respect for the dead was never even considered.

The *Newgate Calendar*

This was originally a monthly bulletin of executions, produced by the keeper at Newgate. The title was then appropriated by hawkish publishers who turned out chapbooks about illustrious criminals such as Eugene Aram, Dick Turpin and Jonathan Wild. Collected editions started to appear, and in 1774 a standard version was issued in five volumes. It contains descriptions of the crimes, arrests, trials and deaths of men who had, in some cases, acquired mythical status. Each case ends with a solemn and portentous homily. Indeed, there is a moralizing note throughout that would have been largely unheeded at the time of publication; the majority of readers wanted to satisfy either a natural interest in the trials of certain criminals or a ghoulish fascination with the details of their execution.

The Malefactor's Register, to use its other title, offered details of all capital trials for bigamy, burglary, felony, forgery, highway robbery, high treason, murder, petit-treason, piracy, rape, riots, street robbery, unnatural crimes and various other offences. A perennial favourite was Captain Kidd, the pirate, tried at the Old Bailey and hanged at Execution Dock in East Wapping in May 1701. After the traditional procession from Newgate, Kidd was hanged on the gallows – but the rope snapped and he fell to the ground. Exhorted by the ordinary to repent, Kidd is supposed to have 'professed his charity to all the world and his hopes of salvation through the merits of his redeemer'. After he was successfully hanged, his body was left suspended until it was washed by several tides. The account of Kidd concludes with a warning: 'The story of this wretched malefactor will impress on the minds of the reader the truth of the old observation, that "Honesty is the best policy".'

In the case of John Smith, hanged in 1705 for house-breaking, the same self-righteous finger-wagging was impossible because, after fifteen minutes of swaying in the wind at the end of a rope, Smith was cut down and found to be alive. He was christened Half-Hanged Smith and was lucky to avoid being sent back to the gallows on two other occasions. The *Register* struggled to find a moral in the story:

> History scarce affords a more extraordinary case than this of Smith: but let no one who reads this account of his triple escape from the gallows

indulge a moment's inclination to the pursuit of illicit practices: since in almost every instance but the present, the ways of vice assuredly lead to destruction.

The Jacobite rebellion of 1715 gave work to a number of hangmen. The *Register* reported that five of the rebels were hanged at Manchester, six at Wigan and 11 at Preston. Most of them were brought to London and 'suffered the utmost rigour of the law', though two of them, the earls of Winton and Nithisdale, had managed to escape from the Tower. In the following year, John Hamilton was found guilty of murder and executed in Edinburgh by means of the Maiden, a form of guillotine. He was the last man in Scotland to be beheaded by this means.

Laurence Shirley, the Earl of Ferrers, was the only peer to be hanged for murder. Violent, drunken and deranged, he treated his wife abominably and once kicked her unconscious. She obtained a legal separation by act of parliament and, being short of money, borrowed £50 from Johnson, the steward of the household. Ferrers was so enraged that he shot Johnson in the head, then taunted him for several hours as he bled to death. He was tried by the House of Lords in Westminster Hall. Conducting his own defence, Ferrers pleaded insanity, but he was found guilty.

As a peer of the realm, Ferrers could have been beheaded, but this option was denied him. Instead he was sent to Tyburn in May 1760, travelling there in his own landau and wearing his wedding attire, an embroidered silver suit. Thousands of people turned out for the execution, and the procession through the crowded streets took three hours. As a gesture of gratitude, he gave the hangman and the chaplain five guineas each. Ferrers was the first man to be executed with the aid of a trap door, a device that later became a standard part of the scaffold. The *Register* recorded what happened next:

> After hanging an hour and five minutes, the body was received in a coffin lined with white satin, and conveyed to surgeon's-hall, where an incision was made from the neck to the bottom of the breast, and the bowels were taken out, on inspection of which the surgeons declared that they had never beheld greater signs of long life in any subject which had come under their notice.

Criminal registers

A more official record of crime and punishment had its origins in this period. Registers of all persons indicted for criminal offences in London and Middlesex – whether found guilty or not – were kept from 1791. It was not until 1805 that other counties kept annual records. The registers make interesting reading: the file on Sarah Douglas notes that she arrived at Newgate in July 1791 at the age of 63. Her crime was 'Stealing table linen, Mr Ibbetson's', and she was transported for seven years. Alexander Elder's offence is also recorded in the register. A former seaman, he was sentenced to death for 'Stealing stays &c., Mr Fletcher's', and was hanged at Newgate in May 1793 (HO 26/56).

The registers were the first step towards a national system of recording crime and imprisonment – a reform milestone – but today they make shocking reading as we encounter individuals receiving punishments which seem completely disproportionate to the crime.

Henry Fielding

Fielding became a justice of the peace for Middlesex and Westminster in 1748 and made an immediate impact. His interest in crime and punishment was long-standing. When his career as a playwright was rudely halted by the passing of the Licensing Act of 1737 – a response by Prime Minister Robert Walpole to Fielding's satirical attacks on him on stage – the author turned to pamphlets and novels. In 1743 he produced *The Life and Death of Jonathan Wild the Great*, about the famous thief-taker who had already appeared in works by Swift, Gay and Defoe.

Wild was an incorrigible criminal who turned bounty hunter, catching thieves in return for rewards and, in some cases, setting up burglaries so that he could 'solve' them. On behalf of the government, he sent well over a hundred men to the gallows, many of them from his own gang. He was in the ideal position to remove rival gangs and become the ruling figure in the London underworld. When he broke up the Carrick gang and served them up to the hangman, he collected almost £1,000 in bounty. His own criminal activities continued, and his Office for the Recovery of Lost and Stolen Property was a lucrative enterprise, selling property back to its owners that had been stolen by Wild's own thieves. By the time he was convicted and hanged in 1725, he had a reputation for daring and shrewdness that lived on in the popular imagination. To the general public, he was a romantic hero.

In Fielding's vicious satire, Wild symbolized the corrupt Great Man, admired for his avarice and cruelty. His victims were often the simple and the good. Detesting hypocrisy, the author made this Wild's defining characteristic as he lied, cheated and bullied his way through life. The novel comments powerfully on the deplorable state of law and order in the capital.

> Whoever indeed considers the Citties of London and Westminster, with the late vast Addition of their Suburbs, the great Irregularity of their Buildings, the immense Number of Lanes, Alleys, Courts and Bye-places; must think that, had they been intended for the very Purpose of Concealment, they could scarce have been better contrived. Upon such a view, the whole appears as a vast wood or forest, in which a Thief may harbour with as great Security, as wild beasts do in the deserts of Africa and Arabia … It is a melancholy truth that, at this very Day, a Rogue no sooner gives the alarm, within certain Purlieus, than twenty or thirty armed Villains are found ready to come to his Assistance.

As chief magistrate, Fielding tried to address this problem by founding the Bow Street Runners in 1748. A mere eight in number, they were attached to the Bow Street magistrates' office and paid with funds from the central government. They did not patrol but served writs and arrested offenders on warrants issued by the magistrates. Runners were prepared to travel all over the country in pursuit of wanted men. When Fielding retired in 1754, he was succeeded by his brother John, the Blind Beak, whose lack of eyesight did not prevent him from refining the Runners into the first effective police force.

Henry Fielding was also interested in prison design. Aided by an architect, Thomas Gibson, he devised a plan for a combined prison, house of correction and workhouse, capable of holding a total population of 6,000. It comprised a series of courtyards, surrounded by narrow accommodation blocks with tall ground-floor arcades. This bold scheme never came into being.

Jonas Hanway

Jonas Hanway, by contrast, lived to see his ideas take shape. He was a merchant whose travels took him as far as Russia and Persia. The story of his adventures, *Historical Account of British Trade over the Caspian Sea, with a Journal of Travels,* published in 1753, brought him some fame.

Hanway was also a philanthropist and social reformer who was distressed by the plight of the thousands of women forced into prostitution and by their high fatality rate as a result of venereal disease. In 1758 he and his partner Robert Dingley founded a Magdalen house in Goodman's Fields and took in a first batch of eight women. Within three years, there were almost a hundred former prostitutes there. By 1758 almost 2,500 had passed through the house, and the overwhelming majority of these never returned to the streets. A frugal regime was maintained and the women spent their time reflecting on the evil and danger of their lives before they were rescued.

In 1776 Hanway published *Solitude in Imprisonment: With Proper Profitable Labour and a Spare Diet.* On the evidence of what he saw in the Magdalen house, he advocated total separation as the most humane and effective way to rehabilitate prisoners. Given time for contemplation, and isolated from fellow-prisoners even when in chapel, convicts would have time to see the error of their ways. In the system that Hanway proposed, promiscuity, drunkenness, violence, idleness, the planning of future crimes and all the other abuses of prisons would be swept away. When an inmate returned to society, Hanway believed he or she would be sober, law-abiding and ready to take up honest work. 'The walls of his prison will preach peace to his soul,' he declared, 'and he will confess the goodness of his Maker, and the wisdom of the laws of his country.'

Hanway was not alone in pressing for the isolation of prisoners and the use of hard labour. Houses of correction had long tried to cure idleness by imposing daily labour and a mean diet. Yet they allowed association in their institutions. What Hanway and others were contending was that enforced solitude would turn a prison into an agent of divine justice, replacing the gallows as the inevitable punishment for all convicted felons. Such proposals for reform were deemed to be too expensive and unreliable to be taken up by the government but some individuals responded more positively.

The duke of Richmond was the most notable. When the duke had the Sussex county gaol rebuilt at Horsham in 1776, he experimented with a number of measures put forward by reformers. The prison was well-situated and built on arches to allow a constant circulation of air. Each prisoner had a separate cell, equipped with bed and blankets. Felons were washed on entry and given a uniform. They were allowed only water to drink while debtors were allowed a quart of strong beer or a pint of wine a day, a distinction thereby being made between the criminal and the poor. All fees were abolished. Like the keeper, the chaplain had a regular salary, giving a sermon once a week and saying prayers once a day. Religion and isolation went hand in hand. Horsham was a comparative success but few tried to emulate it.

Hanway, who died in 1786, was ahead of his time, and his ideas would be at their most influential in the 1830s. An Italian aristocrat, Cesare Beccaria, found rather more disciples in 1767, when his *On Crimes and Punishments* was translated into English. He contended that the best way to reduce crime was to make punishment selective and proportional to the offence. Sentences should be imposed as soon after any crime as possible. Furthermore, they should be designed to influence the mind of the malefactor rather than his body, deterring him from being tempted to commit any additional crimes by showing him how harshly he would be treated as a result.

Beccaria opposed torture. He favoured corporal punishment for assaults, but thought that hanging was too barbaric to be used so widely. It should be kept, he felt, for criminals who were a danger to society. Beccaria succeeded in promoting a lively debate about a subject largely ignored, and his ideas had a direct influence on the greatest of all prison reformers – John Howard.

John Howard

Howard (see plate 4) was almost 30 when his first wife died in 1755. As a means of getting over her death, he decided to tour Portugal – but his ship was captured by French privateers and he was held prisoner. For some weeks he endured miserable conditions and learned how painful the loss of liberty could be: it gave him sympathy for all those under lock and key. In 1756 he took steps to alleviate the plight of captured seamen with charitable donations, but it was another 17 years before he took any real interest in the state of English prisons.

In 1773 Howard was appointed high sheriff of Bedfordshire and was startled to discover a rank injustice in Bedford gaol: when a prisoner was acquitted after months on remand in gaol, he could be locked up again if he was unable to pay the correct fees to the keeper. Those fees, authorized by the justices, were appreciable. Every prisoner charged in a civil action paid an entrance fee of two shillings. For his chamber and for the sole use of his bedding and sheets, the fee was two shillings and sixpence a week. If two prisoners shared a bed, they were charged one shilling and threepence apiece. On release every prisoner had to pay fifteen shillings and fourpence. If a man had incurred other debts during incarceration, then the total amount owed might well be beyond his purse. Simply being confined in a prison could be a step towards bankruptcy. Innocent of the felony, the prisoner was found guilty of being in debt.

It was a situation that Howard found insupportable, and he reacted swiftly. He applied to the county justices to provide the keeper with a regular wage, so that he would not have to extort money from the prisoners. At a stroke, he was trying to remove an abuse that had operated in the county gaol for centuries. But before they would grant the money, the bench demanded a precedent.

This was the spur that sent Howard off on his exhaustive tour of prisons. As well as journeying around England, Wales and Scotland, he went to all the European countries, including Russia. He covered an estimated 50,000 miles in all, mainly travelling on horseback over bad roads in all weathers, impelled by a vision of a fairer and more humane penal system – 'The work grew upon me insensibly. I could not enjoy my ease and leisure in the neglect of an opportunity offered me by providence of attempting the relief of the miserable' (*The State of Prisons*). To pay for his indefatigable touring, he spent £30,000 of his own money – a remarkable act of philanthropy.

Howard rarely encountered resistance from prison officials. He was allowed to visit every part of an institution, inspecting cells, dungeons and torture chambers and making a point of talking to the inmates even if he needed an interpreter to do so. One fact was evident: in all the countries visited, the role of prison staff had evolved in much the same way.

It was the Dutch who impressed Howard most: their prisons were so clean and quiet that he was astounded. In contrast, English prisons like Newgate, the Fleet and the Marshalsea were known for their squalor and eternal din, and provincial gaols were also grimy and strident.

In 1774 Howard attended the House of Commons to give evidence in support of legislation drafted by Alexander Popham, MP for Taunton. Having already visited a number of prisons by this time, Howard spoke with authority and passion. The encouraging result of this was that two Acts were soon passed. The Discharged Prisoners Act 1774 abolished charges for a prisoner's release, and replaced them with payments from the rates up to a maximum of thirteen shillings and fourpence for each inmate.

The Health of Prisons Act 1774 was the first attempt to improve conditions that were filthy, unhygienic and demoralizing. The walls and ceilings of cells and wards were ordered to be scraped and whitewashed once a year. They were to be washed regularly and ventilated properly. Sick prisoners were to have separate rooms, and baths were to be introduced. Every gaol was to have an experienced surgeon or apothecary. All provisions of the Act were to be painted on a board and conspicuously displayed so that keepers would know what their duties were.

Unfortunately, it was much easier to pass legislation than to implement it and some, if not all, of the orders were often ignored. Even if the provisions of the Act were on display, they were meaningless to the many prisoners who were illiterate and who, in any case, had no means of forcing their gaolers to comply with the rules. But small advances had nevertheless been achieved. The fingerprints of John Howard were on the statute book for the first time.

Howard's findings were published in 1777 as *The State of Prisons in England and Wales*, with revised editions in 1780, 1784 and 1791. It was the first detailed, objective, comprehensive study of British prisons. Howard's name was on the title page, but it is possible that he had assistance from like-minded friends. His notes, for instance, appear to have been edited by someone else. This does not detract from the fact that he compiled a work that was to revolutionize prison reform.

Howard's recommendations

Sickened by many sights encountered on his travels, Howard praised what he saw as best practice and made a note of it for the benefit of everyone involved with prison administration. One of the key sections of his book was entitled 'Proposed Improvements in the Structures and Management of Prisons'. It was intended as a guide for members of parliament and justices of the peace.

Any new gaol, he recommended, should be built on an airy site, perhaps on a hill. Flooding was a problem in many old prisons, so Howard urged that, although the site should be near a river or brook that could provide fresh water, there must be no danger of flooding.

The right architecture was a crucial component. Howard had seen far too many dilapidated buildings hardly fit to keep animals. Prisoners deserved much better. 'A Plan for a County Gaol' was supplied. It consisted of a series of square or rectangular blocks with separate accommodation for male and female felons, male debtors and young criminals. Each category of inmate was to have his or her exercise yard. Kept apart from hardened criminals, juvenile delinquents would be saved from corruption. Isolated in their own quarters, women would be in no danger of sexual assault.

The keeper had to be a good, sober, reliable man who lived in the prison and was constantly at home. Like him, the chaplain and surgeon should receive a salary so that there was neither need nor temptation for anyone to extort money from the inmates. The keeper's house was to be sited at the centre of the prison and would contain accommodation for debtors, always numerous in any gaol. The chapel and infirmary would be at the rear of the building, so that spiritual and medical assistance was always available. The whole building, with the exception of the central block containing the keeper's house, had vaulted open arcades on the ground floor. As well as providing exercise areas during inclement weather, these would improve the circulation of air.

Having experienced the noisome stink and stifling atmosphere of many institutions, Howard was keen to let fresh air blow through the whole gaol. To this end, he advocated that sewers were to be located beneath the paved yards and not the buildings themselves. 'No stable, hogcote or dunghill should be suffered in any court.' The Dutch influence was strong here: Howard wanted to achieve the same neatness, cleanliness and order he had witnessed in Holland.

Howard's main recommendation was that prisoners should sleep in individual cells. This would entail major changes in prisons: because of the expense involved, there were few examples of cellular accommodation in England. At Newgate, the condemned cells were rebuilt in the Press Yard in 1762 and held a series of individuals before execution. What Howard wanted had already been achieved by Robert Hooke in 1675, when he designed Bethlem hospital to cater for 120 patients in separate cells. In that case, however, most of the inmates remained in their cells 24 hours a day and were not allowed 'the liberty of the gallery'. Howard did not approve of such permanent confinement for prisoners; regular exercise was a vital part of their regime.

Underlying Howard's recommendations was the belief that prison should be used as a substitute for the death sentence that any felon could expect. Traitors and murderers might merit hanging, but execution was a disproportionate sentence for someone who might have stolen a cheap scarf or a few items of food. Detention should be a punishment in itself. Unlike Hanway, who wanted prison to have a spiritual function, Howard merely demanded that it should clean, healthy and well-managed, an ordered environment that contrasted starkly with the social chaos from which most prisoners came. Hanway sought to instil Christian virtues in inmates. Howard had no such programme, believing that good prisons would inevitably have a beneficial effect on the characters of their inmates.

Bodmin county gaol

Horsham gaol had been the first fully cellular prison constructed in England, and the Duke of Richmond was understandably proud of it. A second prison inspired by the ideas of reformers such as Howard and Hanway was built in Cornwall in 1777. The design for the Bodmin county gaol was actually dedicated to Howard by its architect John Call, a magistrate and a former military engineer. An act of parliament provided £5,000 for the building of the gaol, the remaining £6,000 being raised by local justices of the peace.

Call's design bore a close resemblance to Howard's plan for a county gaol. It had the same ground-floor arcades that could be used as workrooms, and the keeper's house was sited at the heart of the establishment. Howard's recommended chapel and infirmary were also included. There were, however, differences: Bodmin gaol was more compact and symmetrical; its courts were smaller and its cell block larger, to cope with a bigger population.

The gaol's design overcame the problem of being situated on a relatively steep hill, and was both clean and hygienic. Single cells gave the inmates privacy at night. Alcohol was banned from the premises, and so all of the evils associated with it were completely absent.

When he visited the gaol, Howard was very impressed with it and praised it in the 1780 edition of *The State of Prisons*. Horsham and Bodmin would be important parts of his legacy, visible proof that his ideas were both feasible and progressive.

William Blackburn

The end of transportation put enormous pressure on the existing prison system. A national solution was needed and, in 1779, an Act was passed authorizing the building of a pair of large penitentiaries for male and female inmates. Hard labour, solitary confinement at night and religious instruction were to be the watchwords of the new order. In 1784 William Blackburn won the competition to design the male prison and, although the concept of a national penitentiary was not realized until the building of Millbank in the next century, a brilliant penal architect had been discovered.

Inspired as it was by Howard's work, Blackburn's ambition was to use a combination of space and stone to mould human nature. His belief was that architecture could both confine and improve inmates. By incorporating separate cells into his highly symmetrical designs, Blackburn controlled the dangers of infection that bedevilled prison life throughout the country. Mental contamination was also heeded; by categorizing prisoners and keeping the different groups apart, it was impossible for the new prisons to operate as unsupervised universities of crime.

Howard's favourite architect matched his brilliance with application. He laboured incessantly and, in the late 1780s, was working on 16 different prisons. Some were local houses of correction, but the bulk of them were large, urban gaols in places like Oxford, Liverpool, Stafford, Ipswich, Gloucester and Salford. He also designed Limerick gaol, and was in charge of alterations to Newgate gaol in Dublin. Where he was not directly employed as an architect, Blackburn was often used as a consultant.

In 1790 he died of a paralytic stroke while travelling to Glasgow to discuss plans for a prison there. John Howard died in the same year, killed by typhus contracted during a visit to a Russian gaol. Their joint contribution to the English penal system is immeasurable. Howard's name lives on in the League for Penal Reform, founded in 1866, but, sadly, Blackburn's work has been largely obliterated.

Sent to Australia

While counties like Sussex and Cornwall were ready to build new prisons in the 1770s, others were less enthusiastic, believing that transportation would soon resume and that national penitentiaries would house prisoners instead of local gaols that drained the rates. A sudden rise in crime marked the early 1780s, caused by widespread unemployment, a trade depression, an increase in food prices and a decline in wages. The return of many demobilized soldiers exacerbated the problem.

In 1784, during the Younger Pitt's first ministry, Home Secretary Lord Sydney observed that:

> The great Number of Felons under sentence of Transportation who are now in confinement in this Kingdom, have rendered the condition of the Gaols extremely alarming ... All our gaols are overglutted ... and half the British navy, converted into justitia galleys, would scarce suffice to contain all our English penitents.
>
> J. Almon and J. Debrett, *The Parliamentary Register (1780–96)*

Responding to general concern, parliament passed the Transportation Act 1784, even though it had no firm destination in mind. It was not until 1786 that Australia was chosen and that the notion of a convict colony became reality.

The first fleet of 11 British ships set sail for Botany Bay in 1787 under the command of Navy Captain Arthur Philip. Thanks to his choice of sound vessels and his insistence on a good supply of food and medicine, only

32 deaths were recorded on the voyage out of a total of 1,000 passengers. Philip allowed convicts up on deck for exercise and they were given fresh food at every port of call. The fleet reached Botany Bay in January 1788.

The second fleet set sail in 1789–90. In July 1789, 11-year-old Mary Wade was one of over 200 female prisoners aboard the *Lady Juliana* on its year-long voyage to Australia. The Recorder of London, James Adair, had recommended a conditional pardon for Mary and other women sentenced to death (HO 47/9). Spared the gallows, Mary was instead banished for life. She had the first of her 21 children at the age of 14, and lived to the age of 80.

Some of her fellow prisoners were not as lucky: the fleet had a horrendous voyage, losing a quarter of its passengers to disease. Following this, an effort was made to improve conditions on convict vessels, and shipping contractors were paid according to the number of prisoners who reached the colony alive. Naval surgeons were appointed to each ship, and captains who ran healthy vessels were offered gratuities. Captains were forbidden to engage in private trade or to carry cargo. Their sole concern was to ensure the health and safety of their convicts. As a result of these changes, a voyage to Australia became far less dangerous.

Transportation relieved the pressure on prisons in England until the outbreak of the war with France. It was then checked. The resulting convict surplus was reduced in two ways: prisoners were either pressed into service in the army or navy, or they were forced to work on the docks and live in the hulks. During the war only a few hundred convicts were shipped off to the colony in New South Wales.

The immediate need for new national penitentiaries capable of holding large numbers of prisoners had vanished. Howard's work was greatly admired and Blackburn's prisons were monuments to sound penal principles, but it was almost half a century before there was any nationwide building scheme to rival that of the 1780s. Protecting the realm and defeating Napoleon were considered more important than promoting the welfare of criminals.

Prisons in literature
Prison was not merely a subject for discussion among reformers and members of parliament. It provided plots and themes for many authors.

In a century when the novel first came into its own, its possibilities were exploited to the full. Published in 1719, Daniel Defoe's *Robinson Crusoe* depicted a man held captive on an island and, even though he was effectively its governor, he was still being held there against his will. Jonathan Swift's *Gulliver's Travels* (1726) also showed its hero imprisoned in an alien world, and the image of Gulliver being captured and restrained by the Lilliputians remains one of the most powerful in the novel.

Those wanting an insight into prison conditions in England received it in Defoe's *Moll Flanders* (1722), a picaresque novel about a heroine who is born in Newgate, spends a dozen years as a whore, another dozen as a thief and eight as a felon before she acquires great wealth and repents of her evil ways. Imprisoned in Newgate under sentence of death, Moll reflects on her life and shows true remorse. Instead of being executed, she is transported to Virginia, where she continues her lifelong search for happiness and married prosperity. Her outrageous adventures caused shock and amusement, but they also revealed something of the true nature of imprisonment.

Henry Fielding's *The History of Tom Jones, a Foundling* (1749) is another picaresque novel in which prison plays a decisive role. Its impetuous but engaging hero ends up in the Gatehouse, but this ultimate crisis turns out to be a prelude to pure joy. When his true parentage is revealed, Tom is united with the woman he loves and has the pleasure of seeing his persecutors getting their just deserts. Moll's crimes were real. Tom's misadventures arise out of the fact that he is too thoughtless, impulsive and unversed in the ways of the world.

Tom Jones might be Fielding's best novel, but his *Amelia* (1751) enjoyed more success at the time. Injustice is its theme, and most of the novel is spent inside Newgate. Amelia's husband, imprisoned for debt, is an archetypal victim of corrupt laws and experiences all the miseries of the penal system. The novel ends happily when it is revealed that Amelia has been defrauded of her inheritance by a crooked lawyer, who is despatched to Newgate to await execution. An interesting feature of *Amelia* is the presence of the London mob, used by the author as a warning against the imposition of unjust laws. Unless there is a fair and open legal system, Fielding contends, anarchy and mob rule will be a lurking menace.

Tobias Smollett found it difficult to write a novel in which prison did not have at least some place. *Roderick Random* (1748), *Peregrine Pickle* (1751) and *Humphrey Clinker* (1770) all portray the pain and ugliness of imprisonment, but they lack the reforming zeal that pervades Oliver Goldsmith's *The Vicar of Wakefield* (1766). When first published, Goldsmith's novel achieved instant success and became one of the most beloved books of its time.

The Reverend Dr Charles Primrose is both hero and narrator. When the vicar and his charming family are committed to the county gaol in wintry weather, their fortunes seem at their lowest ebb. Out of their misery, however, comes something extraordinary. The benevolent vicar conducts worship, preaches to the inmates and endures their jests with good humour. In less than a week, 'some were penitent and all attentive'. Primrose sets the prisoners to work, establishes a system of fines and rewards and introduces harmony into the gaol. Goldsmith, the social reformer, speaks out.

> It were to be wished then that power, instead of contriving new laws to punish vice, instead of drawing hard the cords of society till a convulsion come to burst them, instead of cutting away wretches as useless, before we have tried their utility, instead of converting correction into vengeance, it were to be wished that we tried the restrictive arts of government, and made law the protector, but not the tyrant of the people. We should then find that creatures, whose souls are held as dross, only wanted the hand of the refiner; we should then find that wretches, now stuck up for long tortures, lest luxury should feel a momentary pang, serve to sinew the state in times of danger; that, as their faces are like ours, their hearts are so too; that few minds are so base that perseverance cannot amend; that a man may see his last crime without dying for it; and that very little blood will serve to cement our security.

Literature in the eighteenth century, then, was asking all the right questions about imprisonment – but it was a very long time before any satisfactory answers were given.

CHAPTER THREE

Rat-infested Prison Hulks

Dear Father and Mother I have taken The Earliest Opertunity of writing these few Lines to you Hopeing to find you in good health as it Leaves me at Present Thank God for it and I received your kind Letter witch you sent me and I was very Hapy to hear from you Dear Parents my poor Brother Solomon is no more he died last Monday weak at half past one in the morning, and the Good Captain let me see him on Sunday when he was alive and he also let me go to his Funeal.

Letter from the *Euryalus*, 15 April 1829

John Edwards was only nine years of age when he and his brother, Solomon, aged 11, were sentenced to transportation for stealing a chain – worth five shillings – from a cart in a marketplace. While they were in the hulks awaiting transportation, the elder boy died. Writing to his parents, John Edwards adopts a tone of careful deference, referring to the 'Good Captain' even though masters of such vessels were usually known for their unremitting harshness. The letter is depressingly typical of many written by semi-literate prisoners in the hulks. The tender age of the Edwards brothers was not an extenuating factor; in the previous century they would have been hanged. For Solomon Edwards, confinement in the disease-ridden hulks was a death sentence in itself. (See also the *Euryalus* ship's register in HO 9/10.)

A society needing solutions

The prison hulks were just one manifestation of powerful social and political upheaval in the late eighteenth and early nineteenth centuries. Improvements in public health partly triggered by the Industrial Revolution meant that there was a sharp rise in population over the period 1760 to 1850: from over six-and-a-half million to over twenty-one million. Inevitably, there was a marked increase in the volume of crime. The effects of industrialization and war, as well as events like the Corn Laws and the return of soldiers after Waterloo in 1815, were severe: unemployment, low wages and high food prices. These privations created criminals out of the law-abiding, as hungry people turned to begging and stealing, or even to protest. For example, during the Luddite Riots in 1811 and 1812 unemployed workers smashed the stocking frames, steam-power looms and shearing machines that had put them out of work.

The Peterloo Massacre of 1819, when a peaceful meeting in Manchester in favour of parliamentary reform was broken up by a cavalry charge from the militia, showed how nervous and repressive the government had become. Eleven people were killed and 500 injured; this aroused immense public indignation, but nothing whatever was done to appease this.

Instead, the response from the authorities was the infamous Six Acts. Meetings for military training were prohibited, warrants were issued for the seizure of arms, meetings to draw up petitions were limited to 50 local people, magistrates could seize what they felt was seditious and blasphemous literature and stamp duty was imposed on certain pamphlets, making it expensive to print and distribute them. The procedure for bringing cases to trial was also streamlined.

Opposition to these and other restrictive laws was ruthlessly put down. The Industrial Revolution may have impoverished some people, but it enriched others, and they became tempting targets; the property-owning classes howled for more protection from the law.

The founding of a Metropolitan Police Force in 1829 could not begin to control the rapidly expanding criminal population of the capital. It did, however, steadily increase the number of convictions, and the hulks became an ever-more convenient destination for offenders.

The first hulks

In their encyclopaedic study of *The Criminal Prisons of London and Scenes of Prison Life* (1862), Henry Mayhew and John Binny noted a clause in an act that turned ships into floating prisons:

> And for the more severe and effectual punishment of atrocious and daring offenders, be it further enacted, That, from and after the First Day of July, one thousand seven hundred and seventy-nine, where any Male Person…shall be lawfully convicted of Grand Larceny, or any other crime, except Petty Larceny, for which he shall be liable by Law to be transported to any Parts beyond the Seas, it shall and may be lawful for the Court…to order and adjudge that such Person…shall be punished by being kept on Board Ships or Vessels properly accommodated for the Security, Employment, and Health of the Persons to be confined therein, and by being employed in hard Labour in raising Sand, Soil and Gravel from, and cleansing, the River Thames, or any of River Navigable for Ships of Burthen.
>
> 16th Geo.III, cap 74

This act regularized a practice that had begun in 1776 when events in America curtailed transportation. It condemned thousands of convicts to miserable lives or early deaths. The vessels used had been taken out of service because they were old, decayed and no longer seaworthy. They were cold, dank, smelly and ill-equipped to cope with large numbers of men in cramped conditions. But they seemed at the time to be a viable substitute for transportation or, when it resumed, useful as holding prisons for those about to be shipped overseas.

Security, employment and health – the descending order is significant. It was imperative that prisoners were securely imprisoned and forced to work hard. Only then was their health considered. In fact, the nature of the confinement and the gruelling labour had a deleterious effect on the physical condition of the convicts: life in the hulks was far more rigorous than in most of the country's gaols.

The first two prison hulks were the *Justitia*, a retired Indiaman (a vessel that traded with India), and the *Censor*, a frigate deemed unfit for ocean-going voyages. Treasury Board Papers relating to the two vessels for the period between 6 January 1778 and 11 February 1778 (T 1/539) make interesting reading. Both ships were moored in the Thames, and their respective inmates were marched off under armed guard each morning to raise gravel from the river, monotonous and fatiguing work that occupied the whole day.

Between them, the two ships took 369 convicts on board, the *Censor* having almost twice the number of the *Justitia*. The convicts came from as far apart as London, Devon, Norfolk, Guildford, Chelmsford, York, Lancaster, Salisbury, Westmoreland and Horsham. During this period of little over a month, seven prisoners died on the *Justitia* and four on the *Censor*. Nine were pardoned.

The management of these early hulks was in private hands. Duncan Campbell, the contractor, had already had experience of transporting criminals. It is his name that is signed at the bottom of the Treasury return:

> The convicts in the within return have been since the last report constantly employed when health and weather permitted, in raising gravel from Barking and Woolwich Shoals, in wheeling the same to cover and raise the surface of the ground and contiguous to a new Proof Butt of a large extent of which they are now erecting, and in making a wide and deep entrenchment round the additional part of the Warren, under the direction of the Board of Ordnance.
>
> I have much satisfaction in saying that the ships are now very healthy, every means in my power has been, and shall be, used to promote so desirable an end having ever considered the same as the principal object of my duty.

Campbell's stated concern to create a healthy environment for the convicts would be touching if it were remotely true – but it was not. He was essentially a businessman who treated the prisoners as a source of profit. Out of the £38 a year he was paid by the Treasury for each man, he had to supply, equip and staff the two ships and provide food, clothing and discipline for his charges. Good accommodation and decent sanitation were never items on his agenda. Cleanliness was non-existent; infested with rats and other vermin, the ships were veritable hell-holes. In the public press, they were given the sardonic nickname of 'Campbell's Academy'.

Prisoners were crammed in below deck every night, given a hammock and left to their own devices. Violent argument and gross sexual interference were inevitable. On the *Justitia*, only one warder was on night duty. Whatever happened on the lower decks, he would not open the hatches until the following morning. Duncan Campbell's professed commitment to the health of his vessels has no statistical basis. Of the 132 prisoners taken on board the *Justitia* between August 1776 and March 1778, almost a quarter died.

Campbell, however, stood to gain nothing from the work done by the prisoners. Governmental projects were supervised by the Home Department and it retained full control. There was one speck of light in the darkness of the prisoners' lot. Like those transported, they were given an amount of cash on discharge with which to begin a new life. The gratuity came in two parts: the first on actual release, and the second payment some months later – but only if the discharged man could present a letter attesting to his good conduct and signed by a clergyman or respectable citizen. He thus had a financial incentive for turning his back on crime.

A temporary expedient

The prison hulks were an immediate response to a crisis and were never intended to last for more than a few years. However, when transportation resumed in the 1780s with Australia as the new destination, the hulks were kept in use. They were busier than ever in the 1790s when transportation was again interrupted by warfare. As the nation began a long, uncertain and expensive struggle against France on land and at sea, the government dismissed all thought of building the national penitentiaries that had been discussed. Any available money was diverted to the war effort.

Not only were the hulks kept in service, they were increased in number. Most convicts who would otherwise have been transported to Botany Bay in the late 1790s were held in disused ships moored at Plymouth, Portsmouth, Sheerness, Chatham and in the Thames at Woolwich. Males predominated; the only female convicts held on board a prison hulk were those on the *Dunkirk* at Plymouth in 1784, and the experiment was discontinued after seven years. Conditions that killed untold numbers of men would surely have claimed even more victims among women.

Criticism of the hulks was loud and continuous. It came from lawyers, prison reformers, parliamentarians, anxious clergymen, newspaper editors, families of inmates and members of the general public. The waterborne communities not only represented a visible scandal; they were repulsive to the nose as well, because the stench from the ships was carried on the air. When the shirts of the prisoners were hung on the rigging, they were so infested with vermin that they were a mass of black spots.

The temporary expedient of the hulks was still in operation in 1850, prompting W. Hepworth Dixon to write in *The London Prisons*:

> The hulk system was continued, notwithstanding its disastrous consequences soon became patent to all the world; and it still flourishes – if that which only stagnates, debases and corrupts, can be said to flourish – though condemned by every impartial person who is at all able to give an opinion on the matter, and this because the labour of the convicts is found useful and valuable to the government – a very good reason for still employing convicts upon useful public works, but no reason at all for continuing the hulks in their present wretched condition.

Prisoner of war vessels

The hulks were not used solely for civil prisoners. In 1811 the Select Committee on Penitentiary Houses was highly conscious of the fact that at least 20 ships were being used for prisoners of war. During the Seven Years War (1756–63), the *Royal Oak* was moored at Plymouth to receive an intake of foreign prisoners. It was later moved to Portsmouth. The American War of Independence necessitated the use of a few additional vessels, but prisoners of war really began to pour into England during the conflict with France, and many more ships were pressed into service. Retired old men-of-war like the *Sandwich*, *Nassau* and *Belliqueux* took on a less honourable role.

Some of the vessels had been captured from the enemy. The *Vryheid*, for instance, had been Admiral de Wynter's flagship at the battle of Camperdown in 1797; it served a different purpose at Chatham.

On his release from captivity, Captain Charles Dupont, a French prisoner of war, sent a report to the French government:

The Medway is covered with men of war, dismantled and lying in ordinary. Their fresh and brilliant painting contrasts with the hideous aspect of the old and smoky hulks, which seem the remains of vessels blackened by a recent fire. It is in these floating tombs that prisoners of war are buried alive – Danes, Swedes, French, Americans, no matter. They are lodged on the lower deck, on the upper deck and even on the orlop deck...Four hundred malefactors are the maximum of a ship appropriated to convicts. From eight hundred to twelve hundred is the ordinary number of prisoners of war heaped together in a prison ship of the same rate.

quoted in W. Branch Johnson, *The Prison Hulks*

Those in command of these hulks were, according to foreign prisoners, the dregs of the navy. This was overstating the case, but there were certainly many instances of deplorable conduct. Commissioner Boyle inspected some vessels in 1813 and was critical:

Lieut. Harley of the *Suffolk*, I find extremely drunk at ten o'clock, and I understand that is generally the case with him. Lieut. Peding, 2nd of the same ship, is also a most Drunken Character. Lieut.Voller, 2nd of the *Guildford*, who is absent on leave, I should recommend to the Board to be immediately discharged for reasons unnecessary to point out in a Public Letter but which I will communicate on my return.

English Prison Hulks

Milne, the commander of the *Bahama*, was a disgrace, according to ex-prisoners held by him. While his human cargo was locked below in shocking conditions, Milne was in the habit of holding wild parties on deck. During one of these, he contrived to set fire to the ship and gave an order that the prisoners should be shot rather than be allowed to save themselves. Hulks for civil prisoners had bad commanders but none sank to this level.

Medical care was poor, and surgeons often left the work to their less qualified assistants. In 1811 a truly appalling incident occurred at Portsmouth. The *Vengeance* received 30 French prisoners, who, having been in Spanish hands, were like walking skeletons. Only a third had the strength to crawl on board, the rest being left in an open boat. The surgeon refused to accept them and the commander of the *Pegasus* hospital ship would only take them if they were washed. So, on the order of the surgeon of the *Vengeance*, the prisoners were thrown into the sea. By the time they were hauled aboard the *Pegasus*, most of them were dying.

Boredom was the major problem on the hulks. All that prisoners of war could do to relieve the enforced idleness was to read, chat, bicker, fight, play cards or other games and improve their command of English. Escape was a constant temptation, and the most popular method was to cut a hole in the ship's hull above the water line and squeeze through it. As able-bodied soldiers or sailors, prisoners were quite capable of swimming some distance to safety. In 1809 a French general tried to escape from the *Brunswick* in Chatham in a boat that sold vegetables to the prisoners. In 1810 some 32 prisoners left the *Vigilant* at Portsmouth and three-quarters of them were never recaptured. Tom Souville escaped from captivity four times, usually with the aid of smugglers. His biographer described him as *Un Corsair de Calais*.

Public protest

Voices were raised against the hulks from the start. John Howard visited them several times. At Plymouth he saw the *Chatham* and its replacement, the *Dunkirk*, writing of the latter:

> The prisoners were all in total idleness, except six or seven who were making a boat for the captain. One ingenious man had made a small inkstand (which I have by me) out of a bone of his meat; but his knife has been taken from him. I saw some with Bibles in their hands; but there is no chaplain, nor any religious service. Here also the keepers, by their profaneness, set a bad example to the prisoners.
>
> *The State of Prisons in England and Wales*

Howard was saddened to find ten-year-old boys at Gosport on the *Lion*. On the *Ceres* he discovered sick prisoners too numerous to be sent to the hospital ship – 'Several had gaol fever or petechia. Six out of ten that went from Bedford were dead and two of the others are sickly and dispirited' (*The State of Prisons*). In a footnote, Howard added that a gaoler at Reading told him in July 1788 that of the 11 convicts he delivered to the hulks the previous April, only three were still alive. Such grim statistics stoked the fires of protest against the hulks.

Patrick Colquhoun, a magistrate, one of the most eloquent critics, described the hulks as 'seminaries of profligacy and vice'. Prison ships, he argued, 'vomit forth at stated times upon the public a certain number of convicts, who having no asylum, no home, no character and no means of subsistence seem to have only the alternative of adding strength to the criminal phalanx' (*Treatise on the Police of the Metropolis*, 1797). Figures produced by Colquhoun were even more damning. Between 1779 and 1795 almost 6,000 convicts served their sentences on board the hulks. One in three of them died in custody.

Complaints were regularly made in parliament and in the press, but no action resulted. One of the most well-informed detractors was James Hardy Vaux, a gentleman-thief on board the *Retribution*, a captured Spanish vessel. His *Memoirs* (1819) are a terrible indictment of the system:

> If I were to attempt a full description of the miseries endured in these ships, I could fill a volume; but I will sum up all by stating that besides robbery from each other, which is as common as cursing and swearing, I witnessed among the prisoners themselves during the twelve-month I remained with them, one deliberate murder for which the perpetrator was executed at Maidstone, and one suicide; and that unnatural crimes are openly committed.

John Henry Capper

Criticism of the hulks embodied in the report of the 1811 Select Committee on Penitentiary Houses led in time to the appointment of a new Superintendent of the Convict Establishment. John Henry Capper took up the post in 1814 and was to hold it for the next 33 years. His predecessor, Aaron Graham, a lawyer, had shown a tolerant attitude to the patent miseries of life aboard the hulks, admitting that the system had defects but pointing out that the ships provided an important service.

Capper was employed to make that service more efficient and more humane. He implemented the recommendations made in 1811, particularly those relating to the division of vessels into cellular units. But he lacked drive, imagination and any real concern for the prisoners he controlled. Though he gave half-yearly reports to the home secretary, he doctored them so that he always appeared in a good light, presiding over well-run vessels in which the conduct of officers and convicts had been above reproach. While successful escapes were glossed over, those that failed were credited to the vigilance of the system.

The new superintendent was paid £400 a year, a generous salary by the standards of the day. There was also an allowance of £131 for using his house as an office. Even after he acquired a room at the Home Office, he made sure that he kept this. In 1823 Capper persuaded the Home Secretary that he needed a clerk and employed his nephew, Robert, at a salary of £270 a year from governmental coffers. Robert Capper was pleased that the job did not interfere with his grocery business in the Strand.

While giving an impression of reliability, the superintendent was lax in his duties and poor at keeping records. Employing convicts to undertake work for him, he deliberately forgot to pay them. As Capper grew older – he was 40 at the time of his appointment – he handed more and more work to his nephew, though Robert had no experience or aptitude. Yet ministers continued to retain Capper in office and regard him as a good and faithful servant. It was not until 1847 that this illusion was shattered.

In March of that year, Thomas Slingsby Duncombe, a radical dandy, made a speech in the House of Commons attacking the hulks. Particular venom was reserved for Peter Bossy, Principal Medical Officer at Woolwich, who was accused of treating prisoners alive or dead in a manner that was disgraceful in a Christian country.

Capper tried to rebuff the criticism, but Sir George Grey, the Home Secretary, was not satisfied. Captain William John Williams was therefore asked to conduct an inquiry into the treatment of convicts at Woolwich.

The inquiry was thorough, and its findings exploded the official complacence surrounding the hulks. Every aspect of them was heavily criticized, from their poor ventilation to their daily barbarities. Of especial horror was the treatment of dead prisoners. Robbery of the corpses was habitual, with convicts fighting over meagre possessions. Bodies were carried in a dung cart and dumped in the marshes overnight until they could be buried on the following day. Inquests were held in a public house in Woolwich, and no evidence was ever admitted from convicts. After postmortems, parts of dissected bodies were sometimes left in pails in a shed for several days.

Dr Bossy, it was revealed, had outside interests that interfered with his work in the Convict Establishment. He had bought a business and, with his brother, had a flourishing private practice in Woolwich and its neighbourhood: 'His emoluments are further increased by taking apprentices, an advantage which he admits is ascribable to the office he holds, from its affording great facilities for the study of the medical profession.' (*Report and Minutes of Evidence Taken upon the Inquiry into the General Mistreatment and Condition of the Convicts in the Hulks at Woolwich*, 1847)

Prison officers were described in the report as:

manifestly incapable of performing their duties satisfactorily, in consequence of age and infirmity, others as so tainted by long habit with the
vicious system of employing convicts to work for themselves, and other
irregularities, and the evidence develops against other cases of such a
suspicious character, I feel I can do no less than advise a thorough re-
organisation of their whole body.

There were immediate consequences: Bossy was dismissed, John and Robert Capper allowed to resign. Others left the service voluntarily. There was an immense amount of huffing and puffing in parliament and in the newspapers. Reforms would follow and yet – in spite of their wholesale condemnation by the inquiry – the prison hulks remained.

All manner of prisoners
Until transportation was conceived as an alternative to execution, all felons would have been hanged. From 1776 onwards, many had their

sentence commuted to hard labour in the hulks. Prisoners came from all walks of life. A Return of Employment of Prisoners in the Defence Hulk for the Week Ending 16 December 1853 gives a clear idea of the wide difference in abilities and skills among the inmates (HO 8).

Over 500 convicts are listed as providing labour. The return notes four carpenters, one smith, one tinker, one painter, one sawyer, one cooper, two ropemakers, one bookbinder, four shoemakers, six tailors, twelve washers and four cooks. The mass of prisoners – 329 – were drafted into working parties that removed and stacked timber, discharged mud, loaded and unloaded stores, cleaned out sheds, cleaned shot and shell at the arsenal, carted sundries, dug gravel, did 'odd jobs not measurable', made and repaired grommits and wads, assisted tradesmen and cleaned out drains.

Convicts had to work for 10 hours a day. The *Defence* was moored at Woolwich along with the *Warrior* (see plates 5 and 7), another vessel of deteriorating condition. Both ships are mentioned in the Report of the Directors of Convict Prisons on the Discipline and Management of the Hulk Establishment (1854). This claimed that:

> the men generally have worked willingly and with good effect, consider-
> ing the disadvantage inseparable from their being occasionally mixed
> with, or in the neighbourhood of, numbers of free labourers and others
> – a circumstance which requires, for the sake of security, consider-
> able restraint to be placed on their freedom of action. Punishments for
> idleness, though always inflicted where the offence is proved, have been
> by no means of frequent occurrence.

Mayhew and Binny (*The Criminal Prisons of London*) observed that the so-called willingness was more likely to be the result of resignation or fear of being punished. As it was much easier to escape from an outside working party than from a prison cell, convicts on shore were controlled by guards with loaded carbines and fixed bayonets. If a felon were allowed to escape in such a well-populated area, there would be adverse publicity for the hulks; a policy of strict supervision was there-fore enforced.

There were bound to be those who resisted this supervision. Escapes were attempted from the hulks themselves or from working parties. Mayhew and Binny discovered that 17 attempts at escape had been made from the *Defence* workforce in one year, and only three were successful. Five attempts were made in 1854, but four of them failed. As part of their duties, warders searched under the waistcoats and neck cloths of the convicts to see if they had secreted any clothing that would enable them to disguise themselves and mingle with the free labourers before slipping away.

There were even sporadic mutinies, wild protests against the intolerable conditions in which convicts were forced to live. In 1850 there was a riot on the *York* and a revolt on the *Stirling Castle*. The following year saw a mutiny on the *Warrior* at Woolwich. All these disturbances were firmly suppressed. As there was no separation of prisoners relative to their ages or the seriousness of their crimes, the young were in with the old and the weak with the strong. Hardened criminals soon corrupted those guilty of a single, thoughtless offence. There was no hope of reform. Within the convict community, all manner of crimes were committed, ranging from petty theft and assault to coin-forging operations. Even in the demeaning squalor of ships like *Defence* and *Warrior*, there were those who knew how to contrive an advantage. The only law they knew was that of the jungle. They had to survive – by any means – or perish.

Two prisoners on record

In the days before photography came into general use in the police and penal systems, care was taken to identify prisoners by other means. For example, when Joseph Clayton (alias Cary) was a prisoner on board *Cumberland*, moored at Chatham in 1831, his records give quite a full picture of the man: he was 21, came from Nottingham, and had been sentenced to seven years after stealing an ass. His gaoler described him thus – 'Character bad. Been convicted before. Connections indifferent' (ADM 6/418).

Clayton was described as having dark brown hair, black eyes, dark eyebrows and lashes, a nose and mouth of average size and shape, a dark complexion, a round visage and a stout 'make' or frame, five feet five-and-a-half inches tall. He was a single man, living at his parents' address, illiterate, and a sweep by trade.

The most telling detail comes under the heading of 'Remarks', which describes that on Clayton's breast was a tattoo saying 'Do not dispute a Thief if he steal to satisfy his soul when hungry'. Printed on his right hand were the initials GRN and JCN, and a star. He had rings on the first, second and fourth fingers. On the back of his left hand was a tattoo of a rope and anchor. He had two rings on this hand. There were other marks on both of his arms. Such details would make Clayton very distinctive. Surprisingly, he was allowed to keep his rings, items that could be used for barter in a hulk.

Another prisoner described in Prison Commission files, Dennis Trenfield, catches the eye because he was a married man of 54, worked as an attorney at law and was described as having superior literacy. Arrested in Gloucester in 1858, he was convicted of forgery at the Assizes and sentenced to 10 years' penal servitude. He joined the other prisoners at Chatham on the *Defence*. A man of previously good character and a respectable middle-class background would have felt totally out of place among the sweepings of the gutter inhabiting the hulk. It was noted that his distinguishing mark was a bad wound on the right side of the neck 'from pistol shot attempting self-destruction' (PCOM 2/131).

Mayhew and Binny on the *Defence*

When Mayhew and Binny embarked on their investigation into the prisons of the capital, they were characteristically thorough, arriving at five o'clock on a chilly morning to inspect the *Defence*. This leaky hulk had formerly been a 74-gun ship. It now held over 500 convicts.

> As we run up the gangway of the silent hull, and survey the broad decks and the massive 'galleys' and hammock-houses, in the misty light, the only sounds heard are the gurgling of the tide streaming past the sides of the black-looking vessel, and the pacing of the solitary warder-guard – the silence and stillness of the scene in no way realising the preconceived idea of a prison hulk. Yet as we pass to the ship's galley, at the fore-part of the vessel, and see the copper sheathing glistening on the floor round the cook's fire, with the large black boiler above it, and the sparkling yellow fire shining through the broad bars, the sight reminds us that there are hundreds of mouths to feed below...

On reaching the top deck we found it divided, by strong iron rails (very like those in zoological gardens, which protect visitors from the fury of wild beasts) from one end to the other, into two long cages, as it were, with a passage between them. In this passage a warder was pacing to and fro, commanding a view of the men, who were slung up in hammocks, fastened in two rows, in each cage or compartment of the ship. There was also a little transverse passage at the end of each ward, that allowed the officer on duty to take a side view of the sleepers, and to cast the light of his bull's-eye under the hammocks, to assure himself that the men are quiet in their beds.

The daily round

At half-past five, the two authors watched the prisoners being turned out to begin another day. They rose, washed and rolled up their hammocks. Breakfast was served at six o'clock. By seven-fifteen the labour force was ready to get into boats to be rowed ashore. The prisoners then landed, marched to their working ground and stayed until noon, when they and the officers had dinner. An hour later they were mustered and marched back to work, finishing at five-thirty. They were marched back to the vessel and, by six o'clock in the evening, had washed and prepared for supper.

Evening prayers followed, and some convicts were given schooling. Others repaired clothing or did other necessary jobs on board. At eight-thirty the order was given to sling hammocks, and they were all in bed by nine. This routine was strictly observed throughout the year, with slight variations according to the amount of daylight. In summer the whole process took fifteen and a half hours. It was an hour less in winter when bad weather conditions could make the outdoor work impossible.

When the prisoners were mustered in the morning, they had to remain silent while every name was checked against a register to ensure that nobody was absent. The messmen of the various wards were summoned to fetch the breakfasts. They went to the galley in single file and returned, each man carrying 'a large beer-can filled with cocoa'. Baskets of bread were brought in and served by the officers at the ward-doors. Throughout the meal, warders were constantly yelling for silence.

After breakfast the doctor came on board and an officer would go to all the wards, shouting out 'Any men to see the doctor?' If a case was considered at all serious, a trapdoor was opened and the patient was passed down into a separate room below and given a bath before examination. Mayhew and Binny noted that 'nine-tenths of the calls for medical assistance, however, are dismissed as frivolous, such calls being looked upon with great suspicion, as generally evincing a desire to avoid a day's labour in the arsenal'.

Diet on board

Convicts on the *Defence* existed on a frugal diet. Each man was given 12 ounces of bread and a pint of cocoa for breakfast. Dinner consisted of six ounces of meat, one pound of potatoes and nine ounces of bread. A pint of gruel and six ounces of bread sufficed for supper. Mondays, Wednesdays and Fridays were Soup Days when dinner comprised a pint of soup, five ounces of meat, one pound of potatoes and nine ounces of bread. These amounts were weighed with scrupulous care.

Prisoners on the sick list were put on a gruel diet and had to subsist on a pint of gruel and nine ounces of bread for each meal. Those on punishment diet were given only bread – one pound a day – and water. Heavy manual work made men hungry and thirsty but they were never allowed to go beyond the prescribed diet. Tight control of food provisions enabled the overseer to make a profit; prisoners serving long sentences would eat the same unvarying diet year after year. None of them was ever troubled by obesity. On release from the hulks, men might lack the prison pallor that distinguished their counterparts elsewhere, but they had the same gaunt appearance.

Men of discipline

The arrival of the hulks and the building of convict prisons called for a new type of warder. Keepers in former times had been able to rule the roost in their respective gaols and indulge in all types of corrupt practices. That was no longer the case. Warders were recruited to control large numbers of convicts, some of whom were violent and desperate. As stern discipline was required, many of the officers came from the army or navy where everything was done on command.

Like the convicts, the warders were governed by the clock. Only a few of them remained on board the *Defence* overnight. The rest were picked up at seven o'clock: if they were not at the landing-steps on time, the boat would return to the ship without them. As it made its way back 'it was crowded with the glazed caps and dark uniforms of the officers, relieved by the fresh white guernseys of the convict rowers'. As soon as they came aboard, there was an officers' parade on the quarterdeck to check that they were all sober and fit for duty.

A guard then came on deck, consisting of four men with carbines, their cartouche boxes slung behind them on a broad black belt. Holding their weapons at the ready, the quartet stood near the gangway as the convicts filed towards them. Officers for duties ashore were called over by the chief warder in the presence of the deputy-governor of the hulk. Their names were checked. 'Twelve extra guards, composed chiefly of soldiers from the Crimea, and some wearing clasps upon their warder's uniform (an uniform, by the way, exactly resembling that of Pentonville officers) stood ready to supervise the loading of the long boats.'

The military precision of the whole operation impressed the visiting authors:

> it is an exciting sight to see the never-ending line of convicts stream across the deck, and down the gangway, the steps rattling as they descend one after another into the capacious boat, amid the cries of the officer at the ship's side 'Come, look sharp there, men! Look sharp!'

These were not the unpaid warders of yesteryear who extorted money from the prisoners, but a group of well-trained men on a regular wage, hired for their ability to impose an austere and unyielding regime on convicted felons.

Hard at work

Penal servitude was a sentence that was enforced to the letter. Some of the convicts from the *Defence* were made to load timber on the quay. Most of them were marched off to Woolwich arsenal, where they were engaged in a number of laborious tasks. One gang dug out shot, then scraped it clean. In the stone-yard, other gangs broke granite, punishing and repetitive work that was assigned to the stronger convicts: each man had to break up so many bushels a day, and the stones were measured in a wooden machine to make sure that they were the requisite size.

Mayhew and Binny describe a scene of much activity:

> Through fields of cannon lying in rows – here black as charcoal, there red as rust – past stacks of wheels and wheelless wagons, by sheds where the air was impregnated with turpentine from the freshly-worked timber, under heavy cranes, through mud and sawdust and shavings – here hailing a gang turning a wheel, and there a gang clearing rubbish – deep down a grove of conical heaps of rusty shells, where the men were filing and polishing them, we made our round of the convict working parties. All of them were busy. The officer takes care of that; for he is fined one shilling every time one of his men is caught idling, while the escape of one entails his dismissal.

The presence of so many free men created a problem. Almost 15,000 were employed there in 1861, and they had been taken on without any assessment of their character or history. Ex-prisoners or friends of the convicts could well have been among them. The very sight of free labourers would have stirred up the envy of the prisoners and sharpened their urge to escape. The governor of the *Defence* reckoned that his men worked twice as hard as the free labourers and this must have fostered resentment among the convict working parties. Mayhew and Binny report that two men tried to flee through a drain that led from the arsenal to the marshes, but they were caught at its mouth by the Plumstead road.

When the visitors were taken across the marshes, they came to an area where the ground was disturbed: they were standing on the Convicts' Burial Ground. Death stalked the hulks from the moment of their inception. Inmates could perish from disease, old age, accident or even murder that went unseen and unreported. Cholera epidemics that could decimate a hulk population came from drinking contaminated water. Panic often set in. So frightened was the chaplain of catching the disease that, when the dead bodies from one epidemic went ashore, he conducted the burial service from a mile away, standing on the poop of the ship, waving his handkerchief when it was time to lower the corpses into their graves.

Religion and schooling

As in convict prisons like Millbank and Pentonville, attention was given to the spiritual and educational needs of the hulk convicts. Many were totally illiterate. Mayhew and Binny give a Tabular Statement of School Progress at the *Defence* hulk during the Year 1852, showing that many prisoners were taught to read and write and that those designated as 'well educated' on reception made 'considerable advancement in arithmetic and the lower branches of mathematics'.

School was held in the chapel, a square room even with the middle deck. The pulpit was at the stern end between two decks, and thus rose above the main body of the chapel. Prisoners came in batches of just over 50, washed and brushed, and wearing rough shirts and trousers, blue and white neckerchiefs and grey stockings barred with red stripes, to take their places at the black desks. School always began with two psalms and a prayer:

> Then the clerk reads a chapter of St Luke; next the schoolmaster cites a
> verse from a psalm and the men go stammering after him. It is a melan-
> choly sight. Some of the scholars are old bald-headed men, evidently
> agricultural labourers. There, amid sharp-featured men, are dogged-
> looking youths, whom it is pitiful to behold so far astray, and so young.

There was little enthusiasm for learning, but attendance at school at least got the convicts out of their wards. A library of almost 1,100 books was set against the side of the pulpit. The juxtaposition was deliberate: the majority of the books aimed at the moral improvement of their readers. As many of the works were too difficult for the convicts to read, their preference was for less demanding fare such as *Chambers' Miscellany, The Leisure Hour* and *Papers for the People*. The chaplain on the *Defence* had refused to permit a copy of Dickens' *Household Words* to join the library.

Church services were held on Sundays and attendance was compulsory for all convicts. As well as hearing prayers, psalms and readings from the Bible, the men had to listen to a sermon that chided them for their evil deeds and exhorted them to lead more honest and God-fearing lives when they were discharged. Those who could read well enough were allowed Bibles of their own to study. As with the school, the only attraction of the services for most convicts was that it was a welcome break in their working routine.

The hospital ship

Moored next to the *Defence* was a 36-gun frigate captured from the French. The *Unité* had been converted into a hospital for sick convicts from the *Defence* and the *Warrior*. It was a fine vessel and in much better condition than some of the rotting British hulks that were over half a century old, riddled with decay and poorly maintained. The *Unité*, by contrast, had large, airy decks along which iron bedsteads were placed so that there were gaps between them.

Nine warders, an infirmary warder, a surgeon and the principal of the vessel ran the establishment. They were aided by 20 healthy convicts – including boatmen, cooks and washermen – who must have built up a degree of trust to be employed on the ship. The work was infinitely preferable to breaking stones at the arsenal or shifting timber on the quay.

The hospital ship was kept clean by healthy convicts, while some of those convalescing acted as nurses for other patients. One of the convalescents who could be entrusted with shears and razors also acted as resident barber, an important job on a ship that usually numbered at least 50 patients, and where hair had to be kept very short.

In the course of 1854 some 675 men were admitted to the ship. Twenty-five of them died, two were pardoned on medical grounds and another two were invalided to the *Stirling Castle* for further treatment.

There was always a steady turnover of patients, many suffering from such common ailments as asthma, influenza and gastric enteritis. Venereal disease was prevalent. Dysentery was also widespread, caused by drinking brackish water. As a result of mishaps among working parties, broken limbs occasionally needed to be reset.

Almost all of those transferred to the *Unité* were infested with vermin and covered in grime. They only ever washed their hands and faces, so their bodies and feet were filthy. As no regular supply of body linen was issued, some had been in the same festering underwear for over a month. Sheets were in short supply on the hospital ship and each man was limited to one. Bibles and Testaments were placed at the head of each bed, but more practical items such as combs and towels were not. As new cases were admitted to the hospital ship, they occupied beds or hammocks recently vacated and left with dirty sheets that sometimes bore obvious blood, urine or semen stains.

Though some care was taken to provide ventilation and, in winter months, to maintain a warm temperature, the ship was still unwholesome, and the stink from the neglected water closets was revolting. Patients were given only basic treatment and, as felons, were not felt to merit anything more. On their tour of the vessel, Mayhew and Binny saw a man suffering from phthisis, a form of pulmonary tuberculosis. Coughing uncontrollably, the patient had chloride of lime all round him to destroy the odour of his expectoration. Another patient, with heart disease, had been spitting blood and they could see it on the pillow.

The diet varied from that on board the prison hulks. For their breakfast, convalescents had four ounces of bread, a quarter of a pint of milk and two ounces of oatmeal gruel. At dinner they were served with eight ounces of bread, eight ounces of raw mutton, one pound of potatoes, half an ounce of salt, half a pint of porter and a pint of soup. Their supper was four ounces of bread, one sixth of an ounce of tea, half an ounce of sugar and a quarter of a pint of milk. Patients in a serious condition might be allowed such additional items as eggs, arrowroot, wine, oranges, sago pudding and even brandy – but these were rare privileges.

For the typical patient, the hospital ship was a refuge from the hard labour, the continual supervision and the packed wards of the hulks. But relief was only temporary. As soon as they were deemed to be well enough, they were sent back to the foul accommodation where they had contracted their diseases in the first place. It is not surprising that so many prisoners died before their sentences had been completed. Given the obvious limitations of the hospital ships and official indifference to the state of health of criminals, the wonder is that the number of fatalities was not substantially higher.

1. (*above*) The Tower of London
(photographed in 1899; COPY 1/442/2).

2. (*right*) Privy Council register recording Lady Jane Grey and
Thomas Cranmer's protests at the lack of air in the Tower of London (PC 2/7).

3. (*top*) An execution at Tyburn, around 1680 (WORK 16/376).

4. (*left*) Prison reformer John Howard (1726–1790).

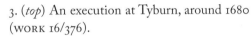

5. (*below*) The *Warrior* convict hulk at Woolwich, from the *Illustrated London News*, 1846 (ZPER 34/8).

An ACCOUNT of the Number of Convicts Victualled on board the *Bellerophon* Hulk, and of Clothing issued to them, between the First Day of January and Thirty First of March 1818.

No. on S. B.	ENTRY.	NAME.	Discharge.	No. of Days Victualled.	CLOTHING.								Bedding.		
					Jackets.	Waistcoats.	Breeches.	Shoes.	Shirts.	Stockings.	Handkerchiefs.	Hats.	Beds.	Blankets.	Irons.
22	Jan.y 1	Robert Gibson		90						1					
36	"	James Nuttall	Jan.y 26	26				1	1	1					
42	"	Squire Battersill	d.o	26	1			1	1		1				
44	"	James Mills	Jan.y 29	29				1							
47	"	William Entwistle	26	22				1		1					
46	"	James Entwistle	d.o	26					2	1					

6. (*top*) Record of clothing issued to convicts on the *Bellerophon* convict hulk, 1818 (T 38/310).

7. (*above*) The *Warrior* washroom (ZPER 34/8).

No.	NAME	Age	TRADE	Degree of Instruction	Name and Address of Committing Magistrate	Date of Warrant	When received into Custody	Offence as charged in the Committment.	When tried.	Before whom tried.	Verdict of the Jury.	Sentence or of the Court.
					IN THE BOROUGH GAOL & HOUSE OF CORRECTION AT LEICESTER.							
1	James Robinson	27	F.W.K.	Imp	Joseph Underwood, Esq., Mayor, Leicester.	Dec. 31st, 1857.	Dec. 31st, 1857.	Feloniously receiving a gold watch, value £5, and a gold chain, value £3, the property of Thomas Green Crofts, on the 25th December, 1857.	26th Feb., 1858.	John Mellor, Esq., Q.C., Recorder.	Guilty of larceny from the person.	Imprisonment, for 18 months, in the rough House of Correction, at Lei
2	William Forster	41	Labourer	Well	James Hudson, Esq., Southfields, Leicester.	Jan. 26th, 1858.	Jan. 26th, 1858.	Stealing 28 dozen pairs of stockings, and 6 dozen pairs of socks, the property of William Kempson and another, on the 18th January, 1858.	Ditto	Ditto	Guilty of larceny after previous conviction for felony.	4 years' penal ser
3	William Jarvis	24	F.W.K.	R. Imp	Ditto	Jan. 27th, 1858.	Jan. 27th, 1858.	Stealing 5 watches, 2 spoons, and a sugar crusher, the property of John Th... 767 D.	Ditto	Ditto	Pleaded guilty of breaking and entering a shop, and larceny therein, after previous conviction for felony.	3 years' penal ser
4	Mary Smith, alias Smith								Ditto	Ditto	Pleaded guilty of larceny, after a previous conviction for felony.	3 years' penal ser
...	Ditto								Ditto	Ditto	Not sentenced.	
...	Ditto								Ditto	Ditto	Not sentenced.	

8. (*top*) Calendar of Leicester assizes and quarter sessions, 1857–8, showing the harsh sentences that even in the nineteenth century were given for offences like stealing stockings (PCOM 2/306).

9. (*above*) Male prisoners from Pentonville's photograph albums, 1877–1882 (PCOM 2/100).

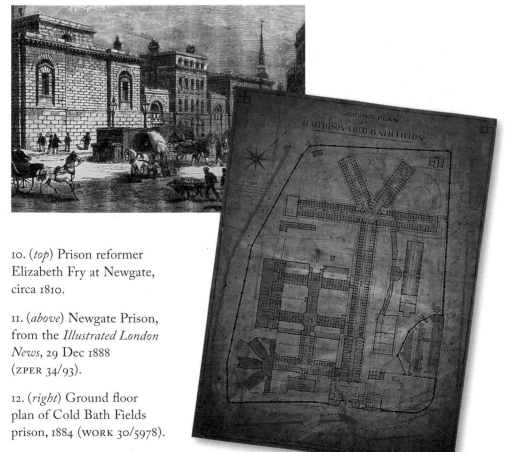

10. (*top*) Prison reformer
Elizabeth Fry at Newgate,
circa 1810.

11. (*above*) Newgate Prison,
from the *Illustrated London
News*, 29 Dec 1888
(ZPER 34/93).

12. (*right*) Ground floor
plan of Cold Bath Fields
prison, 1884 (WORK 30/5978).

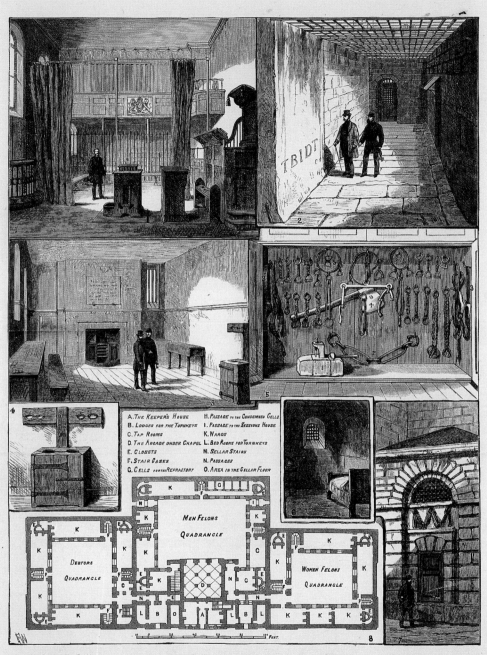

A. The Keeper's House	H. Passage to the Condemned Cells
B. Lodges for the Turnkeys	I. Passage to the Sessions House
C. Tap Rooms	K. Wards
D. The Arcade under Chapel	L. Bed Rooms for Turnkeys
E. Closets	M. Sellar Stairs
F. Stair Cases	N. Passages
G. Cells for the Refractory	O. Area in the Cellar Floor

MEN FELONS QUADRANGLE

DEBTORS QUADRANGLE

WOMEN FELONS QUADRANGLE

1. The Chapel (looking South).
2. The "Bird-Cage Walk": the Murderers are buried under the flooring, and on the left is a piece of the old Roman Wall.
3. The Flogging Ward (looking North).
4. The Flogging Block.

5. The Chain Cupboard: inside are—1. The Anvil for working out Rivets. 2. Chains from which Jack Sheppard freed himself. 3. Pinions. 4. Axe, formerly carried before Prisoners at Executions, another version being that it was made for the Cato-street Conspirators but not used. 5. Old Irons. The rest are modern and in use.

6. The Condemned Cell.
7. Gateway over which the Scaffold was erected for Executions.
8. Ground Plan.

NEWGATE PRISON, INTERIOR VIEWS AND PLAN.

13. Inside Newgate, from the *Illustrated London News*, 29 Dec 1888 (ZPER 34/93).

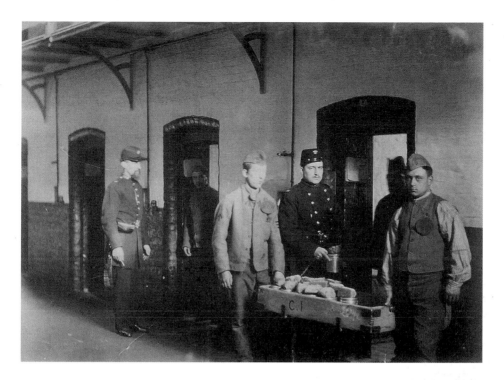

14. (*top*) Feeding prisoners at Wormwood Scrubs, 1895 (COPY 1/420/2).

15. (*above*) The treadmill at Preston prison, 1902 (COPY 1/455).

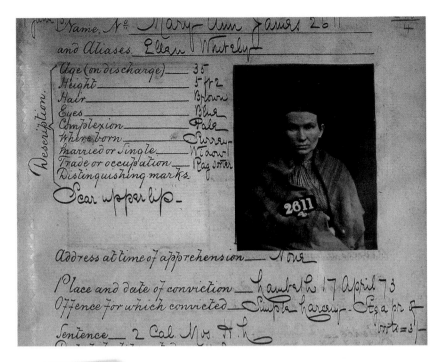

Name, N°. *Mary Ann James* 2611
and Aliases *Ellen Whitely*

Description.

Age (on discharge) ___ 35
Height ___ 5 ft 2
Hair ___ Brown
Eyes ___ Blue
Complexion ___ Pale
Where born ___ Surrey
Married or Single ___ Widow
Trade or occupation ___ Rag sorter
Distinguishing marks.
Scar upper lip —

Address at time of apprehension ___ None

Place and date of conviction ___ Lambeth 17 April 73
Offence for which convicted ___ Simple Larceny — Stg a pr of
boots = 5/—
Sentence ___ 2 Cal. Mos. H.L.

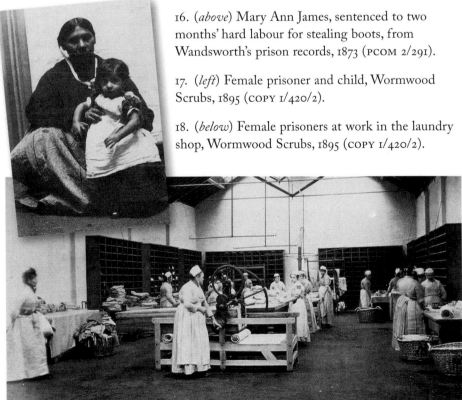

16. (*above*) Mary Ann James, sentenced to two months' hard labour for stealing boots, from Wandsworth's prison records, 1873 (PCOM 2/291).

17. (*left*) Female prisoner and child, Wormwood Scrubs, 1895 (COPY 1/420/2).

18. (*below*) Female prisoners at work in the laundry shop, Wormwood Scrubs, 1895 (COPY 1/420/2).

Sailing to Bermuda

Sailors who had visited Bermuda often spoke of it as a paradise – but no convict sent to the hulks there would have endorsed this view. To them the name denoted a kind of hell: their descent into it began on the long, dangerous, tempest-tossed voyage there. The first hulk to be stationed there was the *Antelope* in 1824; she was joined in the next few years by the *Dromedary*, *Coromandel* and *Weymouth* (HO 7/3). At any one time, these four hulks together accommodated between 1,200 and 1,400 men. The dilapidated *Weymouth* was replaced in 1836 by the *Medway* and the hospital ship *Tenedos*.

The most undisciplined convicts were sent to Bermuda to create a safe distance: they were brutal, desperate men who needed the closest supervision. Occasional mutinies took place and had to be put down with gunfire. Those feared most were kept in chains throughout the entire voyage.

What the convicts found in Bermuda was a warm, moist climate that exacerbated the tubercular conditions from which many of them suffered. Poor ventilation was an added hazard. As the Reverend J. M. Guilding noted with sympathy in 1859:

> in the close and stifling nights of summer, the heat between the decks
> is so oppressive as to make the stench intolerable, and to cause the
> miserable inmates to strip off every vestige of clothing and gasp at the
> portholes for a breath of fresh air.
>
> quoted in *The Prison Hulks*

Dysentery was rife, and the seamen's bane of scurvy also cut a swathe through the convicts. A new, frightening affliction was added to all the diseases that could be contracted: because of the bright glare from the sun as it was reflected by the sea and the limestone rocks, many prisoners were half-blinded by ophthalmia. The scourge of the islands, however, was West Indian fever, and it could reap a rich harvest. There were severe epidemics in 1837, 1843 and 1844 but the worst struck the hulks in 1853. Moored in mud in hot weather and swarming with vermin, the ships were a perfect breeding ground for the fever. Some 160 convicts died, and many more were so afflicted that they never recovered their health.

Nominally under the supervision of the governor of Bermuda, the hulks were controlled from London – but John Henry Capper was too far away to exert any meaningful influence. When an illicit trade grew up between prisoners and Bermudans, nobody could stop it. Warders were often dismissed for being involved in the practice, and convicts caught smuggling rum aboard were moved away from the islands – yet the trade in tobacco, sugar, tea and other items continued to flourish.

The same regime of cruelty, maladministration, bad food, poor living conditions, corruption, violence and desolation that existed in England was repeated on the other side of the Atlantic. It was a tale of intense and unrelieved suffering. In all probability, those sent to Bermuda would have preferred to shiver below deck on the Thames rather than sweat to death in paradise.

Transportation

Though the hulks were originally employed to hold prisoners prior to transportation, some served their whole sentence on board a vessel moored in England. Those shipped off to Australia endured a triple ordeal. They first joined the convict slave-labour in the hulks, then underwent an interminable voyage through treacherous waters, and finally finished up in the penal colonies of Sydney, Van Diemen's Land or, later on, the dreaded Norfolk Island. The psychological fear of travelling into the unknown was an added source of misery.

Convicts destined for Australia came from a wide spectrum. Edward Gibbon Wakefield, imprisoned in Newgate in 1827 for abducting a young heiress, noted the decline in the work for public hangmen: 'The administration of capital punishment is a solemn mockery of truth. The judges, the prisoners and the public are convinced that the sentence will not be carried out in more than one case in eight' (*Facts Relating to the Punishment of Death in the Metropolis*, 1831). Crimes such as murder, forgery, rape, piracy, arson, burglary, sacrilege, mutiny and even treason no longer carried a mandatory death sentence. Saved from the gallows, those who committed such crimes instead packed the hulks.

There were anomalies. Although the old and infirm were supposed to be winnowed out, Hannah Beckford was transported in the first fleet in 1787 when she was 70. She had been convicted of stealing Gloucester cheese to the value of four shillings from one Henry Austen. When found guilty of perjury in the same year, Dorothy Handland (alias Gray) was 82 years old. Such prisoners had to undergo a voyage that might take from seven to twelve months.

The records of the *Ganymede*, a hulk operating in the 1830s, list the occupations of the prisoners and the destinations to which they were sent (HO 9/12). The convicts hail from all over the country, but there are disproportionate numbers of labourers, hawkers and unemployed men. Thomas Barlow of Huntingdon, a hawker and fiddler, was sentenced to seven years' penal servitude in 1837 for stealing a silk handkerchief. Single, illiterate and of 'bad character', he sailed to Van Diemen's Land on the *Coromandel*. Another labourer, Geoffrey Watson of Derby, a married and literate man, was sentenced to 15 years for sheep-stealing, and transported to New South Wales on the *Lord Lyndock* in 1838.

Some crimes were unusual. The Reverend Stephen Aldhouse was transported for bigamy; James Prideaux, aged 70, was shipped to Australia in 1843 for bestiality with a donkey; and Lieutenant Robert Gates committed the unique offence in 1850 of striking Queen Victoria with a cane. Over 100 Chartists were transported, including John Frost, a wealthy draper from Newport, Gwent, and its former mayor. The seven Tolpuddle Martyrs were convicted of administering unlawful oaths, a felony dating back to 1797. In trying to form a workers' union in Dorchester in 1834, they inadvertently acquired legendary status.

Once inside the hulks, such convicts were treated the same as all the others, braving hostile conditions and needing good health to survive life in a penal colony. James Hardy Vaux was transported three times and lived to write his *Memoirs*. Transferred to the *Retribution* to await his second visit to Australia, Vaux never forgot his initial repugnance:

> There were confined in this floating dungeon, nearly six hundred men, most of them double-ironed; and the reader may conceive the horrible effects arising from the continual rattling of chains, the filth and vermin naturally produced by such a crowd of miserable inhabitants, the oaths and execrations constantly heard among them; and above all the shocking necessity of associating and communicating more or less with so depraved a set of beings.

Decade after decade of condemnation of the hulks finally bore fruit. The *Defence* caught fire at Woolwich in July 1857 and had to be scuttled. Its convicts, along with those from the *Unité*, finished up on land in Lewes prison. The *Sterling Castle*, the only remaining hulk in England, was closed in 1859. One of the most scandalous and punitive episodes in penal history had at last come to an end.

CHAPTER FOUR

A Most Victorian Zeal

We shall never forget the mingled feelings of awe and respect with which we used to gaze on the exterior of Newgate in our schoolboy days. How dreadful its rough heavy walls, and low massive doors, appeared to us – the latter looking as if they were made for the express purpose of letting people in and never letting them out again. Then the fetters over the debtor's door, which we used to think were a bona fide set of irons, just hung up there, for convenience sake, ready to be taken down at a moment's notice and riveted on the limbs of some refractory felon! We never tired of wondering how the hackney-coachmen on the opposite stand could cut jokes in the presence of such horrors, and drink pots of half-and-half so near the last drop.

Charles Dickens, *Sketches by Boz*, 1836–7

Writing on the cusp of the Victorian age, Dickens went on to become our most reliable literary guide to another of London's ancient gaols: the Marshalsea, which had been rebuilt in 1811 at a cost of £8,000. It had two sections: one for Admiralty prisoners under court martial and the other for debtors. John Dickens, the novelist's father, was sent there as a debtor in 1824, because he owed forty pounds and ten shillings.

It was a shattering blow for the 12-year-old Dickens, and he could never pass the Marshalsea without a shudder. The prison featured in his first novel, *The Pickwick Papers* (1836–7), and in his autobiographical work *David Copperfield* (1849–50) – but it is in *Little Dorrit* (1855–7) that the most comprehensive portrait is given. William Dorrit has been an inmate so long there that he has acquired the unsought title of 'The Father of the Marshalsea'. His humiliation is intensified by the fact that his daughter, Amy (Little Dorrit), views him through adoring and uncritical eyes, not understanding the terrible shame of imprisonment for debt. Prisoners would often take their families in with them so that wives and children were not left to struggle on outside on charity, with all the concomitant shame. Whole communities sprang up in debtors' prisons. When the Fleet was closed in 1842, some debtors were found to have lived there for forty years.

Crime and punishment are threads that run constantly through Dickens' novels, showing how prominent a place they occupied in the Victorian mind. *Oliver Twist* (1837–8) exposed the evil of juvenile gangs, and demonstrated how easily homeless children could be seduced into crime. *Barnaby Rudge* (1841) looked back on the Gordon Riots of 1780, and featured the attack on Newgate. Another historical novel, *A Tale of Two Cities* (1859), includes scenes set in the Bastille during the French Revolution, and there are countless other instances of the author's obsession with law and law-breakers.

Charles Dickens' writings reflected the changing face of the penal system during the Victorian period. The many thousands who gathered to watch the notorious Jack Sheppard being hanged in 1724 would have been bemused by the appearance, function and administration of prisons as they existed at the death of Dickens in 1870. Order had replaced chaos; silence had ousted pandemonium. Separate cells had taken over from common wards, and male and female prisoners were segregated. Hygiene was at last considered. Architecture was used as a means of detention and, some hopefully dreamed, positive reform.

The national picture
When Queen Victoria came to the throne in 1837, the prison system was confused and heterogeneous. Prisons for counties, boroughs and legal liberties existed in 200 English towns and 20 Welsh towns. Every local authority had the right to maintain a prison and the responsibility to run it efficiently. Because there was a perplexing mixture of jurisdictions, there were no fixed standards. The design of individual prisons

was diverse: of the county and city prisons covered by the 1823 Gaol Act, 30 per cent had radial plans, another 30 per cent had a quadrangular layout and a further 10 per cent were of polygonal design. The remainder – old prisons with extensions added and renovations made over the years – had highly irregular plans.

There were also marked variations in the severity of their respective regimes. People convicted in one part of the country might fare much better or worse than in gaols elsewhere. Geography ruled; the system was a lottery.

The lack of uniformity across all aspects of prison life was glaring. The Whig administration of 1831 had tried to address the problem by appointing a select committee of the House of Commons to investigate the situation: it recommended solitary confinement and hard labour, aspects of the silent system practised at Auburn prison in New York.

Punishment remained a matter for parliamentary concern. In 1835 a select committee of the House of Lords looked into the question of prison discipline, and there was broad agreement with the earlier recommendations. Under the chairmanship of the Duke of Richmond, the select committee urged the adoption of the silent system and claimed that 'Entire Separation, except during the Hours of Labour and of Religious Worship and Instruction, is absolutely necessary for preventing contamination, and for securing a proper System of Prison Discipline' (House of Lords Committee on the State of the Gaols and Houses of Correction, 1835).

The recommendations were enshrined in the 1835 Prisons Act. Also included was a clause requiring all prison rules to be submitted to the Home Secretary for his approval. Inspectors were appointed to visit and to produce annual reports on every prison in the land. The first important moves towards a uniform system were being taken. And under the new queen things would be very different.

The population continued to grow in the capital city, just as it did all over the country. Around a million people lived in London in 1800. By the death of Queen Victoria in 1901, there were six times that number, pushing out London's boundaries in all directions. The original prisons had all been cheek by jowl on both sides of the river. But building land at the heart of the city was extremely difficult to find and expensive to buy in the nineteenth century, so sites for new prisons were therefore sought in the outer suburbs – healthier places, away from the smoke and fog of a major industrial community.

Victorians had an unassailable confidence: they believed that every problem had a solution. With the arrival of railways, they saw that the problem of moving prisoners any distance was immediately solved. To cope with the inexorable rise in crime and the eternal problem of the poor, they increased the numbers of police and built more prisons and workhouses. Size was given priority. Instead of the plethora of small gaols that had grown up over the centuries, they opted for vast buildings of daunting solidity that could house large numbers of inmates. These new convict prisons were an architectural statement of intent. The Victorians believed they were taking a serious problem seriously.

Millbank

The first new prison to be built in the nineteenth century was the one on the left bank of the Thames in Pimlico. Designed by William Williams in 1812, it conformed to the utilitarian principles laid down by Jeremy Bentham. It was a modification of his Panopticon, a radial design that enabled someone standing in the central hexagon to have a clear view of the interior of the six pentagons attached to it. (In Bentham's original scheme, a circular building with a domed roof, it was possible to see every single cell from a central position.) After experiencing changes of architect and recurring difficulties in construction, the General Penitentiary at Millbank was only fully opened in 1821, five years behind schedule.

To passing traffic on the Thames, the forbidding new prison looked like a fortress, a huge, ugly, unyielding mass of stone and brickwork built to defy any attackers and frustrate any escape attempts. Conceived as a home for 600 convicts, it was eventually able to take 1,000. Millbank was a rabbit warren, its three miles of passages so full of sudden angles, identical rows of cells and winding staircases that warders used to chalk up directions on the walls in order to find their way around. Built on an unhealthy marshland site and plagued by damp, it soon had cracks appearing in its walls. Epidemics of scurvy and cholera swept through it in 1822 and 1823.

Some of the theories that informed its regime proved unsuccessful in practice. The first part of a prison sentence was spent in seclusion, except for those times when inmates were working at the treadmills (see plate 15) or water-machines, or were taking exercise. On these occasions, it was impossible to prevent conversation or covert contact between prisoners as they passed each other.

After eighteen months or two years, convicts began the second part of their sentence. They now laboured side by side, and the result, in the opinion of Mayhew and Binny, was disastrous:

> The evil tendency of this regulation soon became apparent and, as in the
> case of Gloucester, the governor and chaplain remonstrated against it,
> alleging that the good effects produced by the operation of the discipline
> enforced in the first class, were speedily and utterly done away with on
> the prisoner's transfer to the second class.
>
> *The Criminal Prisons of London*

After a decade of failure, the system was changed in 1832 so that effective separation of the inmates was maintained throughout their stay.

Mayhew and Binny were also critical of the clergyman who was the governor of Millbank at the time, a well-meaning man who:

> placed an undue reliance on the efficacy of religious reforms. The prison-
> ers, independently of their frequent attendance at chapel, were supplied,
> more than plentifully, with tracts and religious books and, in fact, taught
> to do nothing but pray. Even the warders were put to read prayers to
> them in their cells, and the convicts taking their cue from the reverend
> governor, with the readiness which always distinguishes them, were not
> long in assuming a contrite and devout aspect, which, however, found no
> parallel in their conduct.

The running of Millbank was thus handicapped by the naivety of its governor. Believing that he could bring the inmates to a state of repentance, he did not realize that 'the most desperate convicts in the prison found it advantageous to complete their criminal character with the addition of hypocrisy'. When inspectors visited in 1843, they considered Millbank to be 'an entire failure' (Arthur Griffiths, *Memorials of*

Millbank). The penitentiary was reclassified as a convict prison: a clearing house in which prisoners were detained for shorter periods before being transferred to other institutions.

In his *Handbook of London* (1850), Peter Cunningham gives this description:

> Its ground-plan resembles a wheel, the governor's house occupying a circle in the centre from which radiate six piles of building, terminating externally in towers. The ground on which it stands is raised but little above the river, and was at one time considered unhealthy ... It is the largest prison in London. Every male and female convict sentenced to transportation in Great Britain is sent to Millbank previous to the sentence being executed. Here they remain for three months under the close inspection of the three inspectors of the prison, at the end of which the inspectors report to the Home Secretary, and recommend the place of transportation.

The annual number of those shipped abroad was close to 4,000 but, contrary to what Cunningham claims, they were not all sent to Millbank (many were confined in the prison hulks).

In their detailed account of life inside Millbank, Mayhew and Binney include a table showing how much was produced in the manufactory during a nine-month period in 1854. The quantities – beginning with 24,000 military greatcoats – are remarkable. Prisoners also made jackets, waistcoats, trousers, flannel garments, jackets and trousers for the militia, belts, pouches, shirts, navy flushing jackets, shoes, navy biscuit bags, beds, pillows, hammocks, woven cloth, handkerchiefs and bagging, and over 10,000 miscellaneous articles. The clothing for almost all the institutions whose convicts were engaged in public works – Dartmoor, Pentonville, Chatham, Portland, Portsmouth and the hulks – was made there. It was unquestionably the most useful contribution Millbank made to the prison system. Closed in 1890, it was demolished in 1903. Nobody mourned its passing.

Pentonville

Pentonville – sited on the Caledonian Road in north London – was the archetypal Victorian prison, and it was intended to act as a model in every way. The person most closely involved in its construction was Captain Joshua Jebb of the Royal Engineers, one of the titans of the penal system, who was knighted in 1859. Early discussions of the plan for Pentonville involved William Crawford, a Home District Inspector of Prisons, and the Reverend Whitworth Russell, former chaplain at Millbank. Jebb's many virtues did not include tolerance, and he clashed with both of his colleagues, insisting on having his way.

When the prison was opened in 1842, in spite of angry protests from Russell, Jebb was credited as its sole architect. In 1844 he became the first Surveyor-General of Prisons and, later in the same year, he was appointed the Inspector-General of Military Prisons. From 1850 he was able to add another title to his already impressive tally – Chairman of the Board of Directors of Convict Prisons. He also found time to get involved in the design of Broadmoor hospital and Mountjoy prison in Dublin.

In 1842, the year that Pentonville opened, prisons in England and Wales held over 31,000 inmates. Those sent to Pentonville went through a demoralizing routine that was to be standardized in all institutions. Taken to the prison in a Black Maria, the horse-drawn omnibus with dirty, tiny, unventilated cells, they were handed over to a welcoming party of uniformed warders. When their names were called, prisoners had to reply by stating their offence aloud.

They then had to hand over all of their personal property. Watches, chains, collars, ties, pipes, tobacco, matches, money, handkerchiefs, keepsakes and any other items, however precious to the individual, had to be surrendered and duly recorded in the Property Book. Stripped of their possessions, prisoners were then divested of their clothing. There was no privacy. Under the eyes of the warders, they had to wait for their turn in one of the baths, using the same water as the person before, even though he might have a hideous skin disease. As some of the prisoners never bathed, the water would soon blacken and acquire a scum. The bath was also an opportunity for surreptitious urination.

As they were sentenced to penal servitude, prisoners were issued with a short, loose jacket and vest, and a pair of baggy tweed trousers with broad black stripes. On their legs they wore blue worsted stockings with red rings around them. They had low shoes and a grey and red worsted cap. All articles of clothing were stamped with the broad arrow that showed they belonged to Her Majesty. When the Fenian Jeremiah O'Donovan Rossa arrived in Pentonville on Christmas Eve in 1865, he was alarmed to find that he was offered no flannel underwear: prisoners had to endure the bitter cold without an inner layer of clothing.

The rules

A medical examination of newcomers took place before or during the issue of prison dress. It was often fairly perfunctory, its main reason being to determine whether a convict was fit for hard labour or for a lighter alternative. A few might be sent to the prison hospital. Hair was then cut close to the scalp. No combs were used; the scissors were simply laid flat on the head. Beards and whiskers also perished. Those who took a pride in their carefully cultivated facial hair found its removal spiteful and demeaning.

The final indignity suffered by the newcomers was the loss of their names. Within the prison walls, names simply did not exist. Each prisoner was reduced instead to a mere number, a bare statistic in Pentonville's records.

Once the reception procedures were over, the new intake was lined up so that one of the principal warders could read out the rules and regulations. There were far too many to memorize at a first hearing, but one fact stuck firmly in the mind: they were being enjoined to obey all the rules to the letter – or be punished. Every day of the year was subject to unvarying rules. The most disturbing dictated that a prisoner would occupy a single cell and that he would be unable to make any verbal contact with his fellows. He was entering a world of silence. It must have been very frightening.

Personal silence was offset by the general clamour as cell doors opened and clanged shut, keys jangled, footsteps pounded up and down steps or along landings and the voices of bellowing warders reminded the prisoners of the sanctity of the rules. Newcomers must have felt as if their tongues had been cut out and their ears cruelly enlarged to take in the constant, echoing, ear-splitting din that was Pentonville.

Architecture

Occupying a site of almost seven acres, Pentonville had a curtain wall with massive posterns at the front. The large, ornate entrance was designed by Charles Barry, the architect of the future Houses of Parliament. Four wings radiated from the main building, which was surmounted by an Italian clock tower. Each wing contained 130 separate cells, arranged in three storeys. The prison was thus able to hold well over 500 prisoners in solitary confinement.

Each cell measured thirteen by seven feet, and was nine feet high. Its furniture was strictly functional – a table, a three-legged stool, an open corner cupboard on which the prisoner's hammock was stored during the day and a shaded gas-burner. In the door was an eyehole through which warders could inspect the occupant at any time. High up in the wall, the barred window of ground glass did not open, so ventilation had to be supplied through a series of flues in corridor walls. Foul air was extracted through a vent near the floor, diagonally opposite the one providing fresh air. Pentonville also had a complex heating system.

The overall impression was one of light, cleanliness and order, a complete contrast to the gloomy, soiled, stinking prisons of earlier centuries or, indeed, to the disgusting conditions of the hulks. To Victorians aghast at the sharp rise in crime, the new model prison of Pentonville seemed like a positive response to the problem.

Silence and separation

One of the first to experiment with a silent system was the governor of Wakefield gaol, who, in 1834, employed four extra men to act as overseers and wardsmen in every workshop to impose silence. Prisoners were restless under the new regime, and hundreds had to be punished. That same year George Laval Chesterton, governor of Cold Bath Fields, who introduced silence as the controlling feature of his prison population of over 900, claimed that it did not have 'the least symptom of overt opposition' (George Laval Chesterton, *Revelations of Prison Life*, 1856).

Chesterton was therefore dismayed when the success of his new regime was ignored, and when the prophets of the rival separation system gained more power and influence. Joshua Jebb, a keen advocate of separation, dismissed the Cold Bath experiment with faint praise.

'The separation system will,' Jebb wrote, 'by its own merits, eventually bear down all opposition' (Jebb's correspondence). At Pentonville his theory was put to the test. By embracing silence *and* separation, its regime commended itself to those who stressed the punitive element of imprisonment as well as those who believed that solitary confinement would give inmates time to reflect and experience remorse.

Even before the prison was fully built, voices were raised in protest, none clearer than that of the redoubtable Elizabeth Fry, Quaker and penal reformer. When she visited the site, she was less than impressed by the conditions and was moved to send a warning to Jebb:

> the dark cells ... should never exist in a Christian and civilised country. I think that having prisoners placed in these cells a punishment peculiarly liable to abuse ... in the cells generally the windows have that description of glass in them that even the sight of the sky is precluded ... I am aware that the motive is to prevent the possibility of seeing a fellow prisoner; but I think a prison for separate confinement should be so constructed that the culprits may at least see the sky ... My reason for this opinion is that I consider it a very important object to preserve the health of mind and body in these poor creatures; and I am certain that separate confinement produces an unhealthy state of mind and body ...
>
> Katharine Fry and Rachel Cresswell, *Memoirs of Elizabeth Fry with Extracts from Her Journals and Letters*, 1847

As she died a few years after writing the letter, Fry did not live to see how prescient her comments were. The combination of silence *and* separation broke the spirits of generations of offenders and drove some to madness. Locked in a whitewashed cell, denied conversation with any human being – including the warders – the average prisoner was completely disoriented. Even in chapel on Sunday, he was not permitted to speak. Instead he was shut in a single, high-sided cubicle that made it impossible for him to see anyone but the chaplain conducting the service.

Chaplains were not always the kind and tolerant people of myth. Some were more than ready to enforce discipline. William Lovett, the Chartist leader, was imprisoned in Warwick gaol for seditious libel. He later reported that some of his fellow convicts, having been out in a cold yard for some time, began to cough uncontrollably during service in the chapel. From his elevated pulpit, the chaplain immediately pointed them out and they were later hauled off to punishment cells.

Though supporters continued to trumpet the success of the separation system, its shortcomings were apparent to any objective observer. By 1848 even the prison commissioners had to admit in their sixth report that the Pentonville regime was not without its problems. They mentioned 'some instances of partial aberration of mind not amounting to insanity' and 'the occurrence of hysterical convulsions in some of the convicts on their first being embarked for transportation' (*Report of the Directors of Convict Prisons*, 1848). Governor Chesterton of Cold Bath Fields (see plate 12) was quick to point out that, after 18 months in Pentonville, some prisoners transferred to Millbank showed clear signs of mental disturbance as a result of the separation system.

As the number of victims mounted – the insane, the despairing and the suicidal – it was decided in 1848 that the period of solitary confinement preceding transportation should be reduced from 18 to 12 months. During the second half of the nineteenth century, the usual period became nine months. Yet even in its attenuated form, Pentonville's regime of silence and separation managed to derange many more minds and destroy countless souls.

Prison books and journals record the range of inmates at the mercy of the Pentonville regime. In May 1884, Visitors' Observations (PCOM 2/95) mention a deaf and dumb boy on the point of release who has 'made considerable progress with his education'. Another prisoner was a Birmingham surgeon found guilty of causing death by procuring an abortion:

> perhaps the most painful case it is possible to come across in a convict prison. He is a star classed prisoner named Weaver. He has been 34 years Secretary to the Society for the Propagation of the Gospel ... and led an exemplary life before his downfall.

Weaver had no complaints about his treatment but asked for 'more intellectual books' to read.

Hard labour

A sentence of penal servitude was intended to add physical pain to a convict's isolation. There was also a school of thought – not endorsed by anyone in prison dress, of course – that productive manual labour gave offenders a sense of achievement, of contributing something to a society whose rules they had flouted. None of the prison memoirs of the Victorian era talk about the liberating effect on the mind of hard labour. All of them emphasize its agony, monotony and pointlessness. To the convicts, it was organized torture.

When portrayed in a contemporaneous print, picking oakum looks like a relatively easy task. In fact, it was fiendishly difficult. Oakum was old tarred ships' ropes that were at least an inch thick. Writing about it in *Stafford Gaol and its Associations* (1887), the author W. Payne recalls that 'the very worst that can be obtained is used for prison use, and it often, in hardness and firmness, resembles wire pit ropes more than anything of a hempy or flaxy nature'. Lengths of oakum were tossed into a cell and convicts were expected to unpick them until the strands were straight and smooth. They could then be re-spun into ropes or used for caulking wooden walls.

Because it was covered in tar, oakum left the fingers extremely dirty, and it sometimes took fifteen minutes with soap and water before a convict's hands were clean. The task was also painful, especially as a prescribed amount had to be picked each day: nails broke, fingers bled and blisters appeared. Those with large, clumsy hands were at a serious disadvantage. The trick, as many discovered, was to use a nail to prise apart the strands and, during exercise, prisoners would scour the yard for a nail or something else which could make the job less onerous. It was simple, tedious, unrewarding work, despised by those involved in it, and criticized by many outside prison because it did not seem at all hard enough.

Sewing was also considered a soft option by those never compelled to do it. Prisoners found it demanding because, when they sewed mailbags or coal sacks, their needles could not easily penetrate the hard, stiff canvas. Palms and fingers were regularly pricked. Inmates with delicate hands such as Jabez Balfour, a former Liberal member of parliament convicted of fraud in 1895, feared punishment because they were so slow with the needle: 'but I suppose that through the spy-hole the warder had seen that I was doing my best, and far from being reprimanded, I was rather encouraged' (*My Prison Life*, 1901). Lord William Nevill, also convicted of fraud, knitted stockings during his nine months in solitary confinement. Mat-making was another example of work that could be carried out in a prisoner's cell.

The treadmill conformed to most people's notion of hard labour. It had been invented by William Cubitt, the civil engineer, on a visit to the gaol at Bury St Edmunds in 1818. By enlarging a wooden wheel so that it could be turned by human beings, Cubitt conceived a new type of torture. At Reading gaol, the treadmill supplied water to various cisterns. At Stafford it was used to grind wheat for consumption by the prisoners and by the occupants of two local lunatic asylums. In some cases, the treadmill simply acted as a bellows and produced nothing but draughts of air.

The wheels were large enough for a number of convicts to work side by side in separate compartments. They had to lift their leg and body up three feet each time. Once a prisoner mastered the technique, it was like walking uphill by taking long strides. The number of revolutions of the wheel varied from prison to prison, but an average stint would take six hours. In that time, convicts at York walked at least 6,000 feet on the moving gradient. The Prison Discipline Society urged that at least 12,000 feet of ascent *per diem* should be completed. It was dull, repetitive and exhausting work.

The treadmill attracted much criticism because of its dangers and inherent pointlessness. It had a decidedly adverse effect on the health of prisoners. After only a fortnight on the wheel, prisoners could hardly recognize themselves in a mirror. Accidents were common and deaths not unknown. If anyone slipped off the step, he might have a foot or a leg crushed by the force of a wheel. Yet the wheel found a champion in Governor Chesterton. He even consigned women to it at Cold Bath Fields. Without the wheel, he contended, 'the care, comfort and solid diet bestowed upon prisoners tend to strip imprisonment of much of its salutary terrors' (*Revelations of Prison Life*, 1856).

Cold Bath Fields was the home of another salutary terror. This was the crank, a wheel set against cogs that resisted pressure. In order to turn the wheel, prisoners had to put great effort into their work. Some cranks could be put to productive use – at Leicester county gaol they helped to make firewood – but most were simply grinding air. At Cold Bath Fields a cunning refinement was devised. The cranks were set up as counter-weights at each end of the axle of the treadmill. While one group of prisoners was forcing the wheel to turn with their legs, others were using their arms to turn the cranks in the opposite direction. In his *Report on the Prisons of England, Scotland, Holland, Belgium and Switzerland* (1839), the shocked M. L. Moreau-Christophe noted: 'I know of nothing harder and more degrading than this work.'

Prisoners were worked so hard at the crank that their health invariably suffered. George Bidwell (see CRIM 1/6/37), an American sentenced to life imprisonment in 1873 for fraud against the Bank of England, recalled that at Dartmoor he had to turn the crank over 1,800 times before he was allowed breakfast. Dinner was earned with another 5,000 revolutions and supper with 4,000. If a strong inmate was able to turn the crank with relative ease, the screw was tightened by a warder so that the work became much harder, a cruel practice that gave prison staff the contemptuous nickname of 'screws'.

While there was continuous protest against the use of the treadmill and the crank, both remained in use until 1895, when the Gladstone Committee recommended their removal. A third form of hard labour had fallen into disuse by this time. Shot drill was a means of enforcing military discipline which had been easily transferred to prisons. Inmates had to lift 24 or 32 pounds of round shot, hold it up to their chest, then move it to another position some paces away. They would then pick it up again and return it to its original location. This back-breaking work went on for four hours with a five-minute halt every half-hour so that strained muscles could rest and sweat could be wiped away with a forearm. In some prisons, a circle of men simply passed the shot to each other so that it went round and round. Whatever variation was used, the task was exacting, depressing and profoundly boring.

Public works

The treadmill, the crank and shot drill would have struck many Victorians as ideal punishments for long-term prisoners at Pentonville and Millbank. In fact, they were more often inflicted on those serving short sentences in local prisons. Picking oakum and sewing were more usually allotted to those in solitary confinement in the two larger establishments. After serving their nine months in the separation system, however, convicts were moved to Chatham, Portland, Portsmouth and Dartmoor, the 'public works' prisons.

Hard labour was carried out in 'silent association', though it was difficult to suppress all contact between prisoners. In his *Account of the Manner in which Sentences of Penal Servitude Are Carried Out in England*, Sir Edmund Du Cane looked back in 1882 with excessive pride on the building of the Chatham dockyard:

> The whole island has been drained and surrounded by a sea-wall and embankment 9,200 feet, or nearly two miles, in length, principally executed by convict labour. In carrying out these works, the prisoners have been employed in excavating, pile-driving and concreting, for the foundations; brick-laying, concreting, stone-dressing and setting, in connection with the construction of the basin walls and entrances; removing the earth from the area of the basin by means of wagons and incline planes; barrow roads, barrow lifts, and tipping wagons; loading and unloading materials; plate-laying; and attending standing and locomotive engines.

Since 1869 Du Cane had been Surveyor-General of Prisons, Chairman of the Board of Convict Prisons and Inspector-General of Military Prisons. Like the illustrious Joshua Jebb, he was an army man with an inflexible belief in the virtues of hard labour and stern discipline. His benign view of the construction of Chatham Docks was not shared by the convicts involved. One of them, the pseudonymous 'No.7', wrote in 1903 that, in such places, 'more human blood was spilt and more human lives lost through excessive labour than in any other prison in the country' (*Twenty-Five Years in Seventeen Prisons*).

Austin Bidwell, brother of the George mentioned above, and convicted of the same crime, was told on his arrival at Chatham: 'You were sent here to work, and you will have to do it or I will make you suffer for it.' When the prisoners marched off to work, Bidwell was 'amazed to see their famished wolfish looks – thin, gaunt and almost disguised out of all human resemblance by their ill-fitting mud-covered garments and mud-splashed faces and hands' (from his illuminating memoir *From Wall Street to Newgate*, 1895). Joining them later in the basins, he worked with a gang feeding the giant pug-mill with clay that had to be dug out. After an hour with a spade, Bidwell saw that his hands were a mass of blood-blisters and 'my left knee a dead duck'.

There were frequent injuries and occasional deaths attending such hard manual work. Convicts hewing rock from the quarries of Portland and Dartmoor were especially at risk. Some were maimed by falls of rock or blinded by fragments that shot up unpredictably into their eyes. A crushed foot was the most familiar injury among quarrymen. Kicks from horses could be fatal. And not all deaths were accidental: unable to cope with the physical and mental strain of the work, more than one prisoner tried to commit suicide with any available implement. A faked attempt at escape from an outside working party was another possible means of suicide: a bullet between the shoulder blades was sometimes considered preferable to more long and stressful years as a slave-labourer.

Six varieties of food

In the prison dietaries recommended in 1843 by Sir James Graham, the Home Secretary, only six items of food are listed – bread, meat, potatoes, soup, gruel and cocoa. Intended for county and borough gaols, his suggestions were also adapted for use in the large convict prisons. Graham separated prisoners into eight classes, four with hard labour and four without. The lines of demarcation related to the lengths of an individual's sentence. But whichever class a prisoner fell into, he would never be able to claim that he was well fed.

During his first week, a prisoner not sentenced to hard labour had to survive on a diet of bread and gruel. Bread varied from the freshly baked to the stale and inedible. The oatmeal gruel with no sugar to sweeten it was often so thick that a spoon would stand up in it. Over the years this stirabout, as it was called, did not improve. The Gladstone Committee Report of 1895 made a comment that could have applied at any time in the whole century – 'The stirabout appears to be so distasteful to a large proportion of prisoners that very much of it is rejected' (*Report of the Departmental Committee on Prisons*, 1895).

In the context of the rest of the diet, soup and meat were often looked upon as luxuries – but their quality could differ markedly. As it was repeated so often, the vegetable soup soon began to pall. And the beef soup served to William Lovett and his fellow Chartists was included in a petition of complaint to parliament on the grounds that 'there was no other appearance of meat than some slimy, stringy particles, which, hanging about the wooden spoon, so offended your petitioners' stomachs that they were compelled to forgo eating it' (William Lovett, *The Life and Struggles of William Lovett*, 1876).

The meat won few admirers. A prisoner quoted in a Howard Association report of 1872 described it as tasting more like *gutta percha* (a gum used in manufacture). Jabez Balfour considered the tough, stringy and fat meat as part of the punishment. Henry Harcourt, a convicted felon, wrote in *My Twelve-and-a-Half Years Awful Torture* that he had to hold his nose when trying to eat the meat in the 1870s. These same convicts were also served rotten potatoes or soft, spongy ones with dirt or mud still stuck to them.

Cocoa was a staple ingredient of the diet. According to Dr William Guy, medical superintendent at Millbank Prison, when he appeared before the Carnavon Committee of 1863, cocoa 'contains a good deal of that oily element which, if we could manage it, should always exist in food' (*Report of the Select Committee of the House of Lords on the Present State of Discipline in Gaols and Houses of Correction*, 1863). The problem was that prison cocoa supplied too much of it, and the oil floated on the surface. The mere sight of the miniature oil slick deterred some prisoners.

While the majority of prisoners survived on the diet, others became its victim. Diarrhoea, indigestion, flatulence and piles were noted on many medical records. In his book *Penal Servitude* (1903), Lord William Nevill remembered the enormous number of prisoners admitted to the infirmary where he worked 'suffering from indigestion in various forms – spots, boils, and rashes and other skin diseases'. The most obvious symptom of the spare diet was a dramatic loss of weight. Balfour lost two stones. Arthur Orton, the infamous Tichborne Claimant, sentenced in 1874 to 14 years' penal servitude for perjury, lost a total of seven stones in as many months.

Scurvy was also linked to diet, and an outbreak of it struck Millbank in 1823. Because of a disastrous potato harvest in 1847, Salford gaol substituted rice and saw half its inmates go down with scurvy. Potatoes – even if in poor condition – were at least a means of keeping this dreaded disease at bay.

Acute hunger drove some men to seek an alternative supply of food. They ate beetles, spiders, snails, slugs, worms, mice, grass, weeds, candles and even toilet paper. 'In our hunger,' said Austin Bidwell, 'there was no vile refuse we would not devour greedily if the opportunity occurred' (*From Wall Street to Newgate*). Inevitably, these additional items of food led to many more gastric upsets – but prisoners preferred stomach pains to the pangs of hunger.

Medical care

Daily medical care was available in Victorian prisons, and large numbers of convicts applied for it, though not always with just cause. Cheats and malingerers got short shrift from the medical staff, who wielded great power because they could decide if a man was fit for hard labour or not or even if he should be released on medical grounds. Lord William Nevill's observation was an accurate one:

> In some respects they are more powerful than the Governor or even the
> Directors, for though they have no authority over the general discipline
> of the prison, they have entire control of the men in the hospital, and
> they also have absolute discretion in all cases of punishment.
>
> WBN [Lord William Nevill], *Penal Servitude*, 1903

Prison doctors worked within strict limits. They had only a limited number of medicines at their disposal; what they prescribed most often was rest and a change of diet. Relief from hard labour would be a blessing, but the infirmaries in most prisons were stocked with few nutritious luxuries. At Reading gaol, for instance, Oscar Wilde was allowed by the doctor to have white bread instead of the coarse black or brown bread eaten by other convicts. The Tichborne Claimant was given a little boiled mutton each day. After protesting that he was being starved, Thomas Cooper, the Chartist, was allowed two boiled eggs, coffee and bread and butter.

Only the most serious cases were admitted to prison hospital to enjoy the rare delights of rest, care, relaxed discipline and decent food. Austin Bidwell was among the fortunate. During a smallpox scare, everyone in the prison was inoculated, and Bidwell's arm grew so swollen that he was allowed into the hospital – 'With nothing to do but read my Shakespeare, the cravings of hunger for the first time since my imprisonment satisfied. I was tempted to believe – that the world had few positions pleasanter than mine' (*From Wall Street to Newgate*).

Bidwell's experience differed from that of his brother, George. When taken to Woking prison hospital, George encountered a doctor who felt an 'inexpressible hatred and contempt of all prisoners who ever had the misfortune to come under his treatment' (*Forging the Chains: The Autobiography of George Bidwell*, 1988). This attitude was understandable, if not commendable: with all its drawbacks – including the danger of physical assault – prison was not an attractive workplace for medical staff. The best doctors worked for larger fees in more congenial surroundings.

Inmates kept up a regular chorus of complaint against prison doctors who were jaded, unsympathetic or even incompetent. The compassionate Oscar Wilde was appalled at the treatment he witnessed of a lunatic soldier named Prince:

> Prison doctors have no knowledge of mental disease of any kind. They are a class of ignorant men. The pathology of the mind is unknown to them. When a man grows insane, they treat him as shamming. They have him punished again and again. Naturally the man becomes worse. When ordinary punishments are exhausted, the doctor reports the case to the justices. The result is a flogging ... the result on the wretched half-witted man may be imagined ...
>
> Rupert Hart-Davis (ed.), *Selected Letters of Oscar Wilde*, 1979

In 1842 George Jacob Holyoake was sentenced to six months for blasphemy. What distressed him most in Gloucester prison was that the warders and orderlies showed little sympathy for sick convicts. When one convict had an epileptic fit and fell out of bed, his groans were ignored, and so were the cries from Holyoake and others. No medical assistance was offered to the unfortunate man.

It was no wonder that there were so many suicide attempts. While most involved hanging, Holyoake had his own method:

> There was just width enough in my cell to admit of the heavy iron bed-frame being raised at one end. By marking a circle around one of the legs, which I did with a fragment of stone, I determined the place on which the leg would fall when the frame was pulled down.
>
> George Jacob Holyoake, *History of the Last Triumph of Atheism*, 1850

Holyoake believed that the weight of the bed would drive the leg straight through his brain, causing instant death. Like so many who contemplated suicide, however, he never put his plan into effect. George Bidwell tried and failed to cut his throat with a piece of sharpened tin. Poisoning was another suicide method attempted by some, and so was a simple refusal to touch food or drink, although this could be counteracted by forcible feeding.

The high incidence of suicide attempts in the reign of Queen Victoria shows the desperation to which thousands of convicts – from the uneducated to the highly intelligent – were driven. The combination of silence, separation, hard labour, bad food, poor medical attention and a daily round of sustained misery was just too much to endure.

Discipline

Another factor that drove some to suicidal despair was prison discipline.

Pentonville, and the prisons such as Wandsworth, Leeds, Lewes and Wormwood Scrubs built with Victorian zeal to resemble it, were not merely imposing structures of brick and stone. Their very appearance gave promise of a cold, bleak, friendless, closed world where dangerous felons were caged and controlled by rigid discipline. Hanging in the cell of each prisoner – whether he could read it or not – was a copy of the prison rules. This Abstract of the Regulations Relating to the Treatment and Conduct of Convicted Criminal Prisoners showed how complete was their loss of freedom. Of the 15 rules, the twelfth had a ring of terror because it warned of severe physical pain:

The following offences committed by male prisoners convicted of felony or sentenced to hard labour will be liable to corporal punishment.

Ist   Mutiny or open incitement to mutiny in the prison, personal violence to any officer of the prison, aggravated or repeated assaults on a fellow-prisoner, repetition of insulting or threatening language to any officer or prisoner.

2nd Wilfully and maliciously breaking the prison windows, or otherwise destroying prison property.

3rd When under punishment, wilfully making a disturbance tending to interrupt the order and discipline of the prison, and any other act of gross misconduct or insubordination requiring to be suppressed by extraordinary means.

Abstract of the Regulations Relating to the Treatment
and Conduct of Convicted Criminal Prisoners

To enforce all the rules, the prison staff had to be industrious, vigilant and of strong character. Compassion was not a prerequisite. It was vital that discipline was maintained at all times and that the warders were visibly in control. An extract from the journal of the governor of Portland prison in 1849 reveals the dangers that prison staff often faced:

The prisoner No.891 J. Gallavin said at once that he had struck the officer, and on my ordering him off to close confinement he hesitated and drew back. The two officers standing by him took hold of him to take him away when he appealed to me to desire them to take their hands off him and he would go quietly. To shew him that there was no wish to treat him harshly I said 'very well then take your hands off him', and the moment they did so he struck at me but the blow reached me lightly on the face. The two officers secured him and immediately the other prisoners inside the palisade tried to force the wicket of it to come to their assistance. There being sixty-five men in this yard and only five officers present and the whole of the prisoners being on the point of coming in from labour, I sent for the military guard to assist in quelling the disturbance and went to assist Principal Warders Bowerie and

Warren who were struggling with the prisoners who were trying to force the wicket. Before it could be closed these officers were severely kicked and beaten by the prisoners inside.

PCOM 2/354

The disturbance was suppressed and the ringleaders punished. But the incident acted as a warning to other governors that showing consideration to a prisoner could sometimes lead to his taking advantage to strike out. Violence had to be met with violence. More minor offences were dealt with by the prison governor, who could order close confinement, a punishment diet or both. He accepted the word of his staff without question, allowing the more unscrupulous warders to report prisoners they disliked for offences they had not committed.

In 1852, a scandal occurred at Birmingham borough gaol that brought the subject of prison discipline to the public gaze. It was revealed at the inquest into the death of Edward Andrews, a boy of 15, that he had hanged himself because of cruel treatment received in custody. Concerned citizens petitioned the Home Secretary, Lord Palmerston, and a royal commission was set up to investigate. Present and former members of staff were questioned, and a history of severe and illegal punishments was uncovered, dating back to the time when Captain Maconochie had been governor.

His successor, Lieutenant Austin R.N., had intensified the punitive regime. His methods of restraint were stringent. Inmates were not only put into straitjackets; they were strapped to the wall of a cell with a leather collar fitted to restrict movement of the neck. For periods of four to six hours, they were kept standing in positions that caused them agonizing pain. Some prisoners who had failed to turn their cranks were restrained like this for a whole day. Lloyd Thomas, a boy of 10, was not strapped to the wall, but he was kept in a straitjacket for three whole days. His offence was ringing the bell on Sunday.

Buckets of cold water were thrown over jacketed prisoners, sometimes by the governor himself. Edward Andrews' fate was described thus by John Wood, the prison schoolmaster:

He had the straitjacket last Sunday morning, two hours. It made shriv-
elled marks on his arms and body. A bucket of water stood by him in
case of exhaustion. He stood with cold, red, bare feet on a sock soaked
in water. The ground was covered in water. He looked very deathly and
reeled with weakness when liberated … Too weak and jaded to be taught;
could only be talked to; always appeared wild. His crime, talking and
using obscene language; was also threatened with trial before magistrates.

> Royal Commission Appointed to Inquire into the Treatment and
> Condition of Prisoners Confined to Birmingham Borough Prison, 1854

As a result of the commission's findings, the governor was dismissed and
the prison surgeon, Dr Blount, resigned before he was given the sack.
The Birmingham inquiry had given a worrying insight into the brutalities that could be inflicted behind the high perimeter walls of a prison.
The fact that Andrews was only 15 made the tragedy even more poignant.
Governor Austin's regime was condemned, but a great deal of sanctioned
violence remained in the system. In Victorian courts a common sentence
was flogging to accompany a period of imprisonment.

Writing in 1856, Governor Chesterton recalled his early days in the
prison service, when judicial floggings were held in public. Tied to the
rear of a cart, a prisoner had his bare back flayed with a cat-o'-nine-
tails while he was towed slowly on. It was a scene witnessed over the
centuries and the victims were often vagrants, prostitutes and petty
offenders. The flogging of women was finally abolished in 1820, much to
the annoyance of Chesterton. While agreeing that the sight of a woman
being flogged by a man was barbarous, he believed that 'manual correction by a woman, in the presence of women only, would infuse salutary
intimidation' (*Revelations of Prison Life*).

Being flogged was certainly intimidating. Whether or not it had a
salutary element is questionable. In *An Echo from Prison* (1877), Henry
Holloway, a convicted felon, had a vivid recollection of his ordeal at
Manchester:

When I got into the great yard I saw the governor, the surgeon, the
chaplain and about forty prisoners, the latter with their faces to the wall.
When the triangle was brought out I began to shake from head to foot

... When the first was strapped he began to shout and roar like a child, but the lash was nevertheless administered with great force ... My name was called out and I in turn began to cry for mercy and pardon; but it was only like the prophets of Baal calling unto their god – no help came. On the contrary, the more I cried for mercy the more severely was the lash felt. At length I was released from the triangle, and marched slowly to my cell. On arrival there I fell down from exhaustion, and was scarcely able to lie in bed for pain.

Henry Harcourt was flogged for throwing a chamber pot at another prisoner. Unfortunately, he missed his target and hit a warder. Resolving not to weep or cry out, Harcourt underwent his punishment:

The chief officer, who was calling the strokes, gave extra instructions to the flogger, saying 'Lower down, more to the left,' and so on, knowing that the first few lashes are much more acute than those that follow, for they know that those who can bear a dozen without flinching can bear the whole number without uttering a sound. It was a great disappointment to the doctor and his friend, the governor not to hear me bellow.

My Twelve-and-a-Half Years Awful Torture

Floggings were not regular events, but a great deal of random violence was used to punish or subdue inmates. Prison memoirs bristle with indignation at remembered instances of sadistic conduct from warders. They talk of inmates being savagely beaten, chained, thrown down steel staircases, straitjacketed, made to stand in one position for long periods and generally abused. The separation system favoured the prison staff, because each man was isolated and therefore vulnerable. Where warders were vastly outnumbered, other methods of control were needed. In prisons like Chatham, Portsmouth and Dartmoor, chain gangs were often seen, and prisoners resented being stared at by the public as if they were wild beasts.

Transfer from one site to another usually involved handcuffs and embarrassment for a prisoner. Oscar Wilde, having courted attention throughout his life, was at its mercy after conviction:

From two o'clock till half-past two that day I had to stand on the centre platform of Clapham Junction in convict dress and handcuffed for the world to look at. I had been taken out of the Hospital Ward without a moment's notice being given to me. Of all possible objects I was the most grotesque. When people saw me they laughed at me. Each train as it came up swelled the audience. Nothing could exceed their amusement.

Selected Letters of Oscar Wilde

The mood suddenly changed when the crowd realized that the man they were mocking was Oscar Wilde. Laughter turned to jeers and abuse. Homosexuality was anathema to most Victorians, and the fact that Wilde was a married man with children only served to heighten public disgust. He never forgot the scorn to which he was subjected as he stood there in the rain:

For a year after that was done to me I wept every day at the same hour and for the same space of time. That is not such a tragic thing as possibly it sounds to you. To those who are in prison, tears are part of every day's experience.

Women also underwent the humiliation of transfer in public. On 11 August 1893, an article in the *Sun* newspaper talked of the shock felt by people at the sight of four female convicts, handcuffed and chained together, being escorted by two female warders and a male warder. (PCOM 7/452)

Given all the misery of prisoners' lot, it is astonishing that there were so few mutinies or eruptions of mass violence in Victorian prisons. One of the more significant disturbances was at Chatham in 1863 when Major Arthur Griffiths was governor. Beginning as a protest against bad soup, it later escalated when the men were assembling on parade for labour. One man refused to obey and threw down his cap; others followed his example, and the whole yard was soon in uproar. Troops had to be called in to quell the riot. The ringleaders were flogged, and other prisoners forfeited remission and gratuities.

Looking back on it almost forty years later, Griffiths was proud of the way the disturbance had been suppressed:

Everything worked with clock-like precision; the worst that could be said was that it was too mechanical, the inmates were treated too much en masse, with no attempt at distinguishing between them. They were as one in the eyes of authority, a single entity, ground under the hard and fast rules of the prison system. The wheels went on, round and round, with ceaseless, methodic movement, and everyone must conform, and either fall out or be crushed; the happiest were those who allowed themselves to be carried along without protest or hesitation, adapting themselves automatically to the monotonous movement.

Arthur Griffiths, *Fifty Years of Public Service*, 1904

Religion

Prisoners who hoped to draw spiritual comfort from their religion were soon disappointed. The daily visit to chapel was regimented, one batch being marched in after another had just quit their seats. Only three denominations were recognized – Church of England, Roman Catholic and Jewish. Other faiths were effectively banned, and atheists were forced to attend services along with everyone else. The chapel was divided into tiers, each two foot higher than the one in front. Inmates sat in coffin-shaped stalls, watched over by warders in elevated positions.

While most Christian worship brought people together in a shared experience, the separation system tried to isolate each individual completely. In a long footnote, Mayhew and Binney explained why the plan failed:

> The chapel is a great place for communication among prisoners under separate confinement. Such communication is carried on either by the convict who occupies (say) stall No.10 leaving a letter in stall No.9 as he passes, or else by pushing a letter during divine service under the partition door of the stall; or, if the prisoner be very daring, by passing it over the stall. Sometimes those who are short men put their mouth to the stall-door and say what they wish while pretending to pray; or, if they be of the usual height, they speak to their next door neighbour while the singing is going on.
>
> *The Criminal Prisons of London*

The authors were referring to Pentonville, but their comments were relevant to any Victorian prison. Inmates found ingenious ways to communicate, such as tapping on the walls of a cell. If pipes ran from one cell to another, they were a much more efficient means of conversation. During meals, some men would scratch what they wished to say on their tin dinner-cans. In the presence of warders, all of them soon learned to speak without apparently moving their lips. While conducting a service, a prison chaplain did not realize that he was presiding over dozens of muted conversations or covert exchanges of letters.

Hymns were sung with fervour as prisoners seized their one legitimate opportunity to open their lungs. In *A Burglar's Life Story in Glasgow* (1897), David Fannan mourned the loss of lively hymns:

> We sang Sankey's hymns with such gusto as to attract the attention of
> the prison authorities ... Considering such joyous song inconsistent with
> the sombreness of prison life, they forbade the hymns and sent us back
> to the psalms and paraphrases with their plain puritanic tunes.

The more rousing a hymn, the greater the opportunity for illicit conversation. Under the cover of a barrage of sound, prisoners could also sing ribald ditties.

In older prisons like Newgate and the Marshalsea, chaplains did little more than recite daily services and attend executions. Those in the new convict prisons, like the Reverend Whitworth Russell at Millbank, worked much longer hours and had a far wider range of duties. There was a crusading impulse among Victorian chaplains, typified by the Reverend John Clay during his 36 years in the Lancashire county gaol at Preston. Rehabilitation was his aim: 'I consider the *reformation* of criminals a paramount object in their discipline' (Walter Lowe Clay, *The Prison Chaplain: A Memoir of Rev. John Clay*, 1861).

Clay was dedicated. Every morning at ten, he spoke to every prisoner who had requested to see him, and dealt with their problems or complaints. He gave lectures in chapel to different classes of criminals. He visited prisoners being punished, and said prayers in each of the three infirmaries. Clay also had to read every prisoner's letter that came in or went out of the prison, a chore that involved an annual 3,500 missives. He kept a detailed journal, supervised the prison schools, gave two sermons on Sundays and administered the sacrament to an average of a hundred communicants. Every second of spare time was taken up in visiting prisoners in their cells. He wrote that:

> These duties are not merely formal and routine, but demand much mental as well as bodily Exertion. My whole Time is devoted to my Calling. I cannot sleep a single Night out of the Institution without the Permission of the Committee and I am almost as much a prisoner as any of the Inmates of the Establishment.

Others might share his ideals, but few could match Clay's total commitment. In view of the dangers involved and the unpleasant nature of some duties, the post of chaplain was not an appealing or financially rewarding one. Prisons tended to get clergymen who were unable to secure better employment elsewhere. Disillusion among the inmates was bound to spread as a result. When he was in Wormwood Scrubs, David Fannan had an interview with the chaplain:

> I told him very honestly about my past life, made a clean breast of my crimes and asked what hope there was of God's forgiveness. Rising up from his seat with hands raised in horror, Holy Joe said – 'God will have nothing to do with such a character as you, you're past redemption.'
>
> *A Burglar's Life Story in Glasgow*

Hurt by the rebuff, Fannan hoped for a more positive response from the chaplain when he was transferred to Millbank, only to discover that the unhelpful 'Holy Joe' had also been moved there.

Oscar Wilde was equally scathing about the men of the cloth he encountered:

> The prison chaplains are entirely useless. They are, as a class, well-meaning but foolish, indeed silly, men. They are of no help to any prisoner. Once every six weeks or so, a key turns in the lock of one's door and the chaplain enters. One stands, of course, at attention. He asks whether one has been reading the Bible. One answers 'Yes' or 'No,' as the

case may be. He then quotes a few texts and goes out and locks the door. Sometimes he leaves a tract.

Selected Letters of Oscar Wilde

Chaplains were faced with an insurmountable problem in that they were identified as part of the repressive regime in which they were employed. Instead of offering succour, they simply went through a sterile routine in their grotesque chapels, the architecture of which was a travesty of Christian fellowship. Some showed kindness; others grew cynical; others again took refuge in meaningless quotations from the Bible. The convict prisons had not been designed with religion in mind, and its potentially beneficial effects were always minimized. The irony was that the authorities considered their use of religion in convict prison a glorious success, believing that they had evolved a system in which prisoners were bound to show moral improvement.

The glorious success was thrown into sharp relief by a comment made in 1848 by the former chaplain of Clerkenwell, who said that, out of the one hundred thousand prisoners who had passed under him, he knew of only two cases of true repentance towards God. Subsequently, he admitted, he found himself disappointed in both of them. In the big convict prisons, as in the small local ones, the curative effect of religion was more apparent than real. Souls were in desperate need of salvation, but the well-intentioned shepherds of the Victorian prison system were ill-equipped to save them.

Select committees, royal commissions, parliamentary debates, reports, reforms, militarism and muddled thinking were the bricks from which Pentonville, Brixton, Chatham, Dartmoor, Portland, Dover, Porstmouth, Parkhurst, Wormwood Scrubs and other prisons were built. Under the practical, energetic, earnest Victorians, the penal system was gradually centralized, but the high hopes for a Spartan regime of silence and separation were ill-founded. Instead of forcing inmates to repent, it either broke them or sowed implacable hatred in their hearts. Instead of being places for the rehabilitation of criminals, prisons were houses of sorrow, resentment and despair.

CHAPTER FIVE

No Place for a Woman

I visited Newgate in the beginning of the month of May, and went round, first, the female side of the prison ... and found it, as usual, in the most degraded and afflicting state; the women were then all mixed together, young and old; the young beginner with the old offender; the girl, for the first offence, with the hardened and drunken prostitute; the tried and the untried; the accused with the condemned; the transports [sentenced to transportation] with those under sentence of death; all were crowded together in one promiscuous assemblage; noisy, idle and profligate; clamorous at the grating, soliciting money and begging at the bars of the prison, with spoons attached to the ends of sticks. In little more than one fortnight, the whole scene was changed, through the humane and philanthropic exertion of Mrs Fry.

Henry Grey Bennett MP, 1817

The scene which confronted Henry Bennett in Newgate, later described in his correspondence, was truly demoralizing. Apart from the fact that women now had their own quarters, the prison had changed little over the centuries. The swirling criminal underground of Elizabethan London had kept Newgate well supplied with female prisoners. They included those charged with prostitution, keeping a disorderly house, drunkenness, giving false measure, counterfeiting, concealing the death of a bastard child, maiming animals, stealing property and committing murder. Debt was a common offence.

While held on remand, the innocent mixed with the guilty. If women had not been corrupted before they entered Newgate, they were by the time they left. Countless young women were seduced, tricked or forced into sacrificing their virginity. Promiscuity and its attendant diseases were the order of the day.

Those held in the Fleet might at least have the consolation of marriage, performed by a clergyman-prisoner on the grounds that the area was outside the jurisdiction of the bishop of London. Cheap, swift and valid, Fleet weddings were immensely popular at a time when conventional services of matrimony were heavily taxed. Almost 3,000 Fleet marriages took place in the four months ending February 1705. The practice was finally abolished by the Marriage Act of 1753.

Female criminals could be formidable. Moll Cutpurse was a prime example. Her crimes included those of the thief, bawd, fence, forger and highwaywoman. It was said that she was so spectacularly ugly that she would never make a living as a prostitute. Moll – alias Mary Frith, alias Mary Markham – therefore dedicated herself to gathering other illegal sources of income. Wearing men's attire and smoking a pipe, the drunken, bellicose Moll haunted theatres and public houses. Her exploits were so notorious that Thomas Middleton immortalized them in his play *The Roaring Girl* in 1604.

She was burned in the hand four times to indicate convictions, and was acquainted with almost all the gaols of the city. Even in middle age she worked hard at her trade: during the Civil War she waylaid General Fairfax of the Parliamentarians and shot him in the arm before robbing him and killing two of his servants' horses. Arrested and locked up in Newgate, she was later sentenced to death – but bribed her way out at enormous cost. She died in 1650.

The *Newgate Calendar* records the escapades of many female criminals, although none as colourful and rumbustious as Moll. Barbara Spencer, another woman of violent temper, was executed in 1721 for high treason as a counterfeiter. While held in Newgate, 'she behaved in the most indecent and turbulent manner; nor could she be convinced that she had been guilty of any crime on making a few shillings'. Penitent on the day of execution, she was much distracted by the mud and dirt thrown at her by the mob, which cheered as she was strangled with a rope then burnt to death.

Concentrating as it does on sensational cases usually ending at the gallows, the *Calendar* says little about women doomed to spend long periods in Newgate or other prisons awaiting trial or discharge from their debts. John Howard and many others drew attention to the squalid and inhumane conditions in which females were kept – but it was not until a new century dawned that an effective champion of women's rights appeared.

Elizabeth Fry

The name of Elizabeth Fry (see plate 10) is so closely identified with penal reform that it is easy to forget that, before she even crossed the threshold of a prison, she led a full life as a wife, mother of eight children and ardent Quaker. In February 1813, when she was 33 years of age, her priorities suddenly changed. She received a visit from Stephen Grellet, a French aristocrat turned American citizen and a Quaker minister with an interest in London's poor. Grellet was so unnerved by a visit to Newgate that he hurried to nearby Mildred's Court where Fry – Betsy to friends – resided, and was restored by hot tea and warm brandy. He and his companion, William Forster, another Quaker, recounted their terrible experience.

Seeing the male wards had been unsettling enough, but it was the female wards, where they witnessed violence, depravity and despair, that induced most compassion and disgust. Gaolers had tried to deter them by saying they would be putting themselves in danger, but the visitors insisted on inspecting the female quarters. There they saw women sleeping in three tiers: one row of bodies on the floor and the rest in two tiers of hammocks without any bedding. The stench of unwashed bodies and filthy clothing was overpowering. In an upper chamber reserved for the sick, the situation was even worse: women lay in the freezing cold on the bare stone floor. Covered in sores and coughing pitiably, they were surrounded by straw rank with urine, menstrual blood and afterbirth. Naked babies kept up a piercing lament.

Fry was profoundly moved. Sending out for some flannel cloth, she gathered a group of women Friends together and they spent hours sewing garments for the Newgate babies. Next morning, Fry and her friend Anna Buxton presented themselves at the prison and ignored the warnings of the governor, John Newman, about the risks of going amongst so many aggressive women. On entering the female wards, the visitors felt their flesh crawl as they moved through the masses of wild, howling, dark-eyed, unpredictable, malevolent creatures.

Their Quaker dress and their patent benevolence protected them; they provoked curiosity rather than attack. The two women went upstairs and were revolted by what they saw in the infirmary. Offering words of comfort to the mothers, they clothed the babies in the linen they had brought. When they returned the next day with more clothing and fresh straw, Anna Buxton said a few prayers, and Fry later wrote: 'I heard weeping and thought they appeared much tendered; a very solemn quiet was observed; it was a striking scene, the poor people on their knees around in their deplorable conditions' (Katharine Fry and Rachel Cresswell, *Memoirs of Elizabeth Fry with Extracts from Her Journals and Letters*, 1847).

It needed a third visit for all the babies to be properly clothed. Fry led the prayers and, in her serenely confident way, spoke to them of hope and love. In the space of three days, the visitors transformed the atmosphere inside the female quarters with a mixture of kindness, sympathy and practical help. It had taken courage to walk down the gloomy, vaulted corridors of Newgate and to inhale its foul air. After her third visit, Fry returned home, took off clothes impregnated with the stink of the prison and had a hot bath.

While her work had been appreciated by the women prisoners, it aroused reproach in her family. Her brothers and sisters could not understand why a woman of her age and background had taken up the torch of penal reform. Most upset was her brother, John, who had strongly opposed her involvement with the Society of Friends and her quest for a ministry. He found her activities highly embarrassing. In the event, domestic duties intervened. Fry was mistress of a large household with over a dozen servants; she was also preoccupied by the fragility of the family bank. To add to her problems, she learned in the autumn of 1813 that she was pregnant yet again.

Even with the best medical attention, childbirth was fraught with danger and physical pain. Having undergone ordeals during earlier deliveries, Fry took to strong drink in the hope of banishing the horrors. Her ninth child, Louisa, was born on 14 June 1814.

Prison reform

It was not until Christmas in 1816 that Fry returned to Newgate. In the interim, she had known great sorrow. The death of her brother, John, had been followed by that of five-year-old Betsy, her seventh child. Deeply shaken by the loss of the little girl, Fry was unable to keep up her regular visits to the sick and bereaved. In April 1816, after a long labour, she gave birth to a son. With nine children to look after once more, she had her hands full – yet she never lost sight of the urgent need for penal reform.

Her brothers, Joseph and Samuel, were now committed to the prison cause, as were her brothers-in-law, Fowell Buxton and Samuel Hoare. In their company she had already visited Norwich prison and the female quarters of Cold Bath Fields House of Correction. Fry had also been impressed when Buxton and Hoare had founded the Society for the Reformation of Prison Discipline; she approved wholeheartedly of its stated aim of improving prison conditions and encouraging rehabilitation among young offenders. It was with reform in mind that she went back to Newgate.

Once again she met with resistance, the turnkey refusing to let her into the female quarters at first. When she did finally gain entry and the massive door slammed shut behind her, she was in a totally different world from the one she usually inhabited. In the cold, dark prison with its smell of damp and decay, ragged women were begging at the grate, fighting over money, playing cards with a filthy pack or drinking. They greeted their visitor with jeers and obscenities. Seeing a young mother with a fair-haired girl, Fry went across to her and took the child in her arms. As a hush fell upon the yard, she asked a simple question – 'Is there not something we can do for these innocent children?' (*Memoirs of Elizabeth Fry*).

The effect was dramatic. Prostitutes, forgers, thieves and coiners listened to her with tears in their eyes as she talked about the need to prevent children from following their mothers into crime. Fry told them that she was a mother – she was still breast-feeding her son at the time – and how the anguish she felt at the death of her daughter had been eased by her faith in God. Relating the parable of the vineyard to the surging mass around her, she explained that sinners coming late to repentance were nevertheless welcomed into the fullness of salvation.

Nobody had spoken to the women like this before. They were accustomed to being pushed around by male turnkeys or leered at by male prisoners. Fry, in her snowy white clothes and her coal-scuttle Quaker hat, compelled attention with her dignity and her Christian certitude. The evangelist was roused in her. She had discovered her vocation. In February 1817 she made a first entry in her journal regarding her work at the prison.

> I have lately been much occupied in forming a school in Newgate for the children of the poor prisoners as well as the young criminals, which has brought much peace and satisfaction with it; but my mind has also been deeply affected in attending a poor woman who was executed this morning. I visited her twice; this event has brought me into much feeling by some distressingly nervous sensations in the night, so that this has been a time of deep humiliation to me, this witnessing of the effect of the consequences of sin. The poor creature murdered her baby; and how inexpressibly awful to have her life taken away.
>
> *Journals of Elizabeth Fry*, 24 March 1817

Setting up the school proved difficult. Governor Newman and the Reverend Cotton, the prison chaplain, listened politely to Fry's plans and agreed that they were laudable. They pointed out, however, that she had no experience of teaching the poor. Cotton, who had started a school for boys on the men's side in 1814, had been quickly disillusioned by its failure. Education, he feared, would never replace the idleness, drinking, swearing and gambling to which the women prisoners were addicted. Unwilling to upset the Prison Discipline Society by allowing Fry's experiment, Newman told her that they simply did not have a room available for use as a school.

They had reckoned without Fry's tenacity. She went back to the female quarters to consult the prisoners. On her return, she told the startled governor and chaplain that the women had agreed to set a cell aside and that they had chosen Mary Connor, a hitherto respectable young woman convicted of stealing a watch, as their teacher. Thus the first proper school in prison history was founded.

Fry's ambitions, however, extended well beyond the education of the

30 young female scholars who made up the class. In April 1817 she was instrumental in the creation of the Association for the Improvement in the Female Prisoners in Newgate, an organization pledged:

> to provide for the clothing, the instruction and the employment of women; to introduce them to a knowledge of the Holy Scriptures, and to forming in them, as much as possible, those habits of order, sobriety and industry which may render them docile and peaceable whilst in prison and respectable when they leave it.
>
> *Memoirs of Elizabeth Fry*

Exclusively female, the new society consisted of 11 Quakers and the wife of a clergyman in East Ham. The women agreed to take turns in visiting Newgate daily, to pay the salary of the resident matron, to provide funds for necessary materials and arrange for sales of work. To these declared aims, Fry added a personal one. On hearing of her plans for a workshop carrying out sewing and knitting in the prison, Buxton and Hoare asserted that the prisoners could never be taught a trade. Fry set out to prove them – and many other cynics – wrong.

Democracy rules

To the governor, the chaplain and Sheriff George Bridges, the workshop scheme sounded worthwhile but hopelessly unrealistic. In order to convince them, Fry arranged a meeting attended by 70 unkempt, unwashed and ragged women prisoners. Whereas the governor and his staff always controlled them by force, Fry sought to win their consent. With great patience, she explained the object and the clear benefits of the new scheme. Listening open-mouthed, the prisoners could not believe that they were being consulted about something that affected their welfare. Nothing could be done, they were told, until they agreed to the 12 rules drawn up by the Ladies' Association.

1. That a matron be appointed for the general superintendence of the women.

2. That the women be engaged in needlework, knitting or any other suitable employment.

3. That there be no begging, swearing, gaming, card-playing, quarrelling or immoral conversation. That all novels, plays, and other improper books, be excluded; and that all bad words be avoided; and any default in these particulars be reported to the matron.

4. That there be a yard-keeper, chosen from among the women: to inform them when their friends came; to see that they leave their work with the monitor; when they go to the grating, to see that they do not spend any time there, except with their friends. If any woman be found disobedient, in these respects, the yard-keeper to report the case to the matron.

5. That the women be divided into classes, of not more than twelve; and that a monitor be appointed to each class.

6. That monitors be chosen from the most orderly of the women that could read, to superintend the work and conduct of the others.

7. That the monitors not only overlook the women in their own class, but if they observe any others disobeying the rules, that they inform the monitor of the class to which such persons may belong, who is immediately to repeat this to the matron, and the deviations to be set down on a slate.

8. That any monitor breaking the rules be dismissed from her office, the most suitable in her class taking her place.

9. That the monitors be particularly careful to see that the women came with clean hands and face to their work, and that they be quiet during their employment.

10. That at the ringing of the bell, at nine o'clock in the morning, the women collect in the work-room to hear a portion of the Scripture read by one of the visitors, or the matron; and that the monitors afterwards conduct the classes from thence to their respective wards in an orderly manner.

11. That the women be again collected for reading at six o'clock in the evening, when the work should be given in charge to the matron by the monitors.

12. That the matron keep an exact account of the work done by the women, and of their conduct.

Memoirs of Elizabeth Fry

As the rules were read out by Fry, each one was voted on by a show of hands – and every prisoner in the room voted for all 12 rules. It was a democratic triumph, a phenomenon unknown before in the English penal system. Feral inmates were enthusiastically accepting the chance to live better and more productive lives. Only a fortnight after the new rules were adopted, a male visitor was taken to the women's side of Newgate; he recorded with astonishment that 'stillness and propriety reigned' (*Life of Elizabeth Fry* by Susanna Corder, 1853). When he entered the room, 16 female prisoners rose, curtsied respectfully and then, at a signal, resumed their seats and their employment.

It was not long before the lord mayor of London and several sheriffs came to witness the miracle. They were astounded by the sense of order and calm. As a result of the visit, the Corporation agreed to pay the matron a salary of a guinea a week, and donated £80 to the purchase of new dresses. The Corporation also dismissed the soldiers who overlooked the female yard, because their attentions made the women disorderly.

Elizabeth Fry and her colleagues had revolutionized Newgate. Hope, purpose and Christian values had ousted the aimlessness of former years; for the first time, prisoners earned self-respect. Inspired by her achievements, women in other parts of the country wondered if they could form their own Ladies' Association to help female prisoners. On Fry's recommendation, the 12 rules were later adapted and used in prisons all over Europe. Her success turned her from Quaker minister into zealous prison reformer. She set herself clear tasks – 'Read Howard, consult with clever and charitable men and endeavour to learn about the management of the best conducted prisons' (*Journals of Elizabeth Fry*). Her crusade had begun in earnest.

The 1818 inquiry
At the end of the Napoleonic Wars, crime increased in volume for the reasons already discussed; with well over 100,000 people in custody throughout the country, prisons were overflowing. Those released simply

swelled the ranks of the unemployed and criminal classes. In 1818 a House of Commons committee was set up to 'Report on Prisons in the City of London and Borough of Southwark'. One of those summoned to give evidence, in what was a tribute to her renown, was Elizabeth Fry. She talked about the poor diet, lack of prison dress and dirtiness of Newgate.

In her deposition, three main points were stressed. The first was that religious instruction was absolutely vital. Fry talked about the positive effects Christianity had had on women who knew nothing of its basic tenets. So popular had been her readings at Newgate that illiterate prisoners learned to read in order to be able to study the Scriptures for themselves. Although she was a Quaker, Fry assured them, her teaching was not sectarian.

The second necessity was to categorize prisoners according to their crimes and their previous criminal history. Once prisoners were assigned to a group, it should be kept distinct from the others. When convicts slept together, thirty in a room, disease and moral turpitude could easily spread. Given basins, soap and towels – and separated into smaller groups - prisoners could keep themselves clean and avoid the temptations that came with propinquity.

Fry's third recommendation related to employment that allowed the prisoners to earn money. It not only made profitable use of time, it trained prisoners for a more honest life on release. In practical terms, work produced saleable goods such as aprons, bags and rag dolls. During 10 months of her workshop's existence in Newgate, 80 prisoners had made 20,000 articles between them. Fry was proud to say that only three had gone astray. Not a single item had been stolen.

When the report, *Prisons of the Metropolis*, was published, it noted in a postscript that:

> the benevolent exertions of Mrs Fry and her friends in the female
> department of the Prisons, have indeed, by the establishment of a school,
> by providing work and encouraging industrious habits, produced the
> most gratifying change. But much must be ascribed to unremitting
> personal attention and influence.

The critics

Praise for Elizabeth Fry was not universal among parliamentarians. By her intervention in the case of Harriet Skelton, she irritated the Home Secretary, Lord Sidmouth. In March 1818 Skelton was sentenced to death for passing a forged banknote. Fry was distressed at the fate of one of her favourite prisoners, a quiet, well-behaved girl with an open countenance. A former maidservant to a solicitor, Skelton had been persuaded by her husband to commit the crime. Confident that she could secure a commutation of the death sentence, Fry appealed to the Home Secretary.

Sidmouth turned down her plea for a reprieve. He was fast losing patience with reformers, telling the House that they 'were removing the dread of punishment in the criminal classes' (House of Lords Debate on Prisons, 3 June 1818). Fry did not give up. Knowing that the Duke of Gloucester was sympathetic to the campaign against capital punishment, she persuaded him to visit Skelton in the condemned cell. After a harrowing hour with the young prisoner, Gloucester went to the Home Secretary to urge clemency. His appeal was rejected by Sidmouth, who resented Fry's methods.

Criticism of her came from other quarters. She was a woman in a world dominated by men: many people believed that it was inappropriate for a respectable matron to visit a dreadful prison, especially when she should have been caring for her family. Others felt that she was patronizing the unfortunate wretches in Newgate, foisting charity on them but making sure that they knew their place in society. Her sudden fame, some argued, had made her conceited.

Fry's sharpest critic was herself. On an occasion when Queen Charlotte was presiding over the examination of hundreds of poor children, Fry went to the Mansion House to view the event. The moment she appeared, attention was taken away from the Queen, the royal princesses, the lord mayor and the eight bishops present. Everyone was looking at the heroine of Newgate, saying her name in awe-struck tones. Even for a Quaker, such popularity was very intoxicating.

I believe that certainly it does much good to the cause, in spreading it amongst all ranks of society, a considerable interest in the subject; also a knowledge of Friends and their principles, but my own standing appears critical in many ways. In the first place, the extreme importance of my walking strictly, and circumspectly, amongst all men, in all things, and not bringing discredit upon the cause of truth and righteousness.

Journals of Elizabeth Fry

Fry had realized that a woman in the public eye would always be walking a tightrope. She sometimes faltered. Unused to political procedure and intrigue, she could be naive when dealing with parliament. Unaccustomed to national celebrity, she needed time to learn how to cope with it. Driven by inner convictions, she did not always recognize that her fervour made enemies as well as friends. She was a complex and fallible woman, and could be proud, selfish and ruthless.

Fry was conscious of her faults and prayed for forgiveness – but the work she had undertaken called for remorseless energy. When she committed herself to it with such blind fanaticism, those close to her were bound to suffer.

Crisis at Newgate

In the summer of 1818 trouble was brewing at Newgate, and when Fry visited the female wards, she felt a definite tension in the air. Turnkeys feared that a riot would occur when the women prisoners were due to be transported. If that were the case, Fry's reforms at the prison would lose some of their lustre.

Fry shuddered as she heard about the explosion of violence that had occurred on the eve of previous transfers to the convict ships. Those about to be transported went on the rampage, hurling furniture at turnkeys and prisoners, breaking windows, smashing pottery, lighting fires, ripping up clothing and drinking themselves into hysteria. Such a mob, Fry was warned, might even break into her beloved workshop for scissors and knitting needles to use as weapons. The prospect was frightening.

Confronting the problem directly, Fry spoke to relevant inmates. They were frankly terrified at what lay ahead. The notion of sailing to the other side of the world through all weathers in a leaky, stinking, overcrowded ship made them tremble with fear. Even more disturbing was the rumour that the vessels were nothing more than floating broth-els and that they would be treated as sex-slaves during the voyage and on arrival in the primitive colony. There was some truth in the rumour: a House of Commons committee had reported that: 'Women prisoners were received rather as prostitutes than as servants' (Anthony Babington, *The English Bastille*, 1971).

Something else alarmed the transports. While in Newgate, they had been treated with respect, allowed to work and given education. Once they left the prison, however, all the privileges of Fry's regime would be cruelly stripped away; they would be shackled together in open carts, helpless victims of the severity of the law. On their humiliating journey to the river, they would be mocked, taunted and jeered. Missiles would be thrown at them. If that was what they had to face, they would slake their anger on the prison itself in a parting act of revolt.

Armed with this information, Fry went straight to the governor and presented her case. She persuaded him that she could stifle the potential riot if he agreed that the women could travel to their ship in closed hackney-coaches. Newman gave his consent and in the event there was no disturbance. A sad but subdued procession of prisoners left Newgate in closed carriages, hidden from the eyes of the boisterous crowd stationed outside. Bringing up the rear of the convoy was Fry herself, a portly figure in her own carriage, carrying her Bible and a box of tracts as the vehicles rumbled on to Deptford.

Women from other prisons received less consideration. Chained together, and with hoops around their waists and legs, they were brought from custody in open carts or carriages. Some were bundled aboard a fishing smack to be taken to the *Maria*, lying at anchor in the river. Fry was appalled to learn that some women had had their infants torn from them, to be left behind. One of her colleagues vowed to appeal to Whitehall in the hope of reuniting mothers and children.

It was five weeks before the *Maria* finally sailed. During that time, Fry and the ladies worked hard to introduce order and comfort. They divided 128 convicts into groups of 12, based on their age and crime, urging each group to elect a monitor. They obtained scraps of material so that the women could stitch patchwork quilts on the voyage. Bibles, prayer books and religious tracts were issued to each monitor.

On the day of departure, the convicts were lined up on the quarter-deck in a blustery wind in front of Elizabeth Fry and the captain. She had achieved such eminence by now that sailors climbed in the rigging to hear her read from the Bible in her lilting voice. It was a moving occasion. Before Fry left the vessel, she knelt down and commended the *Maria* and its doleful cargo to God.

Fry's legacy

Elizabeth Fry's mission continued until her death in 1845, and she pursued it with unflagging zest, visiting prisons on the Continent as well as in England and taking a particular interest in the conditions for women convicts in the ships bound for Australia. In 1827 she published her *Observations on the Visiting, Superintendence and Government of Female Prisoners*. Having broken the social conventions herself, she urged other women to do so as well.

> During the last ten years much attention has been successfully bestowed by women on the female inmates in our *prisons*; and many a poor prisoner, under their fostering care, has become completely changed, – rescued from a condition of depravity and wretchedness, and restored to happiness, as a useful and respectable member of the community. Most desirable is it that such efforts should be pursued with patient perseverance wherever they have already been made, and that they should be gradually extended to all the prisons in the kingdom.
>
> But similar care is evidently required for our hospitals, our lunatic asylums, and our workhouses. It is quite obvious, that there are departments in all institutions which ought to be under the especial superintendence of females. Were ladies to make a practice of regularly visiting them, a most important check would be obtained on a variety of abuses which are far too apt to creep into the management of these establishments. Such a practice would be the means, not only of essentially contributing to the welfare of the afflicted sufferers, but of materially aiding those gentlemen, on whom devolves the government or care of the institutions.

Elizabeth Fry was a pioneer: at a time when women had no public role, she created one for herself. The power and influence that came with it were used to good effect. Evangelist, preacher and prison reformer, she changed the lives of thousands by her example and inspired people all over Europe, giving great impetus to the prison reformers who succeeded her. Fry not only studied the work of John Howard; in some ways this heroic woman actually surpassed him. Her legacy remains a rich one.

Government prisons

An Act of 1853 substituted penal servitude for transportation. At that time, there were 12 government prisons operating in England. Millbank, Pentonville, Wakefield and Leicester housed male convicts in solitary confinement. Chatham, Portsmouth and Portland held males who were employed in public works. Woking and Dartmoor took male invalid convicts. Brixton and Fulham had only female convicts, and Parkhurst received male juvenile offenders. All these institutions were under the control of the Home Office, which also had responsibility for the hulks.

Most female convicts were sent initially to Millbank, where they were employed for the first two months in coir-picking, stripping coconut fibre for use in mats and ropes. The next five months would be spent at bag making and coarse needlework. Once their aptitude had been assessed, they were selected as cooks, cleaners and laundry women. After 10 or 12 months, they were moved to Brixton, where they washed clothing for the staff, the male convicts of Pentonville and Millbank, and themselves. They were also employed at needlework for all the convict prisons.

In Fulham Refuge, a much smaller establishment, women were trained for domestic service and instructed in baking, cooking, laundry and housework. Some of the convicts became farm servants, and washing for other convict establishments was also undertaken there.

Brixton prison

Brixton prison began life as the Surrey house of correction. In 1819 local justices decided that they needed a new building for offenders, and Thomas Chawner, the county surveyor, was engaged to design it. What emerged in 1821 was a prison that could house 175 inmates in 140 single cells and 12 larger, three-bedded cells. It consisted of three-storeyed brick cell blocks with a chapel at the centre of them. At the heart of the structure was the octagonal governor's house, carefully sited so that the governor could oversee the prisoners working on the treadmills in the narrow, triangular yards within the polygonal cell blocks.

From the start, Brixton exceeded its capacity, and overcrowding was a perennial problem. Male convicts thought it one of the worst prisons in London because of its tiny cells, poor living conditions and harsh regime. It expanded to cope with increased numbers and, when it became a women's prison in 1853, additional accommodation was added so that between 700 and 800 female convicts could be locked up there. New arrivals were made to spend four months in solitary confinement and, when they later joined the general prison population, they were required to maintain silent association. It was not a system that Elizabeth Fry would have admired.

In their *Criminal Prisons of London*, Mayhew and Binny list the staff of Brixton in 1856. Emma Martin was the superintendent, and most of her officers and clerks were female. Under the five principal matrons were 32 assistant matrons, a small number to look after such a large intake. Women also filled the posts of cutter, work-mistress, school-mistresses (four), head nurse and cook. The Reverend J. H. Moran was the chaplain, and other men in the prison included the surgeon, the two superintendent's clerks, the foreman of works, the engineer, the gatekeeper, the baker, the watchman, the messenger, the carpenter and the plumber.

Mayhew and Binny noted the preponderance of women among the officers of the prison:

> the great body of officials there belong to the softer sex, so that the
> discipline and order maintained at that institution become the more
> interesting as being the work of those whom the world generally consid-
> ers to be ill-adapted to government. So much are we the creatures of
> prejudice, however, that it sounds almost ludicrous at first to hear Miss
> So-and-so spoken of as an experienced officer, or Mrs Such-a-one
> described as having been many years in the service, as well as to learn
> that it is some young lady's turn to be on duty that night, or else that
> another fair one is to act as the night-patrol ... those inclined to smile

at such matters should pay a visit to the Female Convict Prison at
Brixton, and see how admirably the ladies really manage such affairs.

Architecture

The authors saw little 'architectural or engineering skill' during their
inspection of Brixton, and felt that it compared unfavourably with
Pentonville. They did, however, praise the two new wings added to the
original crescent-shaped building:

These consist each of one long corridor, the character of which is
somewhat like the interior of a tall and narrow terminus to some railway
station; for the corridors here are neither so spacious nor yet so desolate-
looking as those at Pentonville, since at Brixton there are stoves and
tables arranged down the centre of the arcades, and the cells are as close
as those of the cabins in a ship, to which, indeed, the cells themselves,
ranged along the galleries, one after another, bear a considerable
resemblance.

In the older part of the prison, corridors were extremely long, narrow and
gloomy, with lime-coated walls. The doors of the cells were 'heavy cumbrous
affairs, with a large perforated circular plate in each, such as is seen on the
top of stoves, for admitting or shutting-off the heated air'. Each door was
fitted with a peephole and a 'huge ugly lock of the prison kind'.

Cells were small and contained a stool, a table, a deal box for keeping
clothes in or acting as a foot rest, a hammock to be slung from wall to
wall, rugs and blankets neatly folded up, a gas-jet and chimney. A barred
oblong window was set high up in the wall.

The whitewashed walls were intended to brighten up the cell, but
the unrelenting glare affected the eyes of some prisoners. Mayhew and
Binny were told that:

a gipsy woman was very violent during her incarceration, and it does
not require a great stretch of fancy to conceive the extreme mental and
physical agony that must have been inflicted on such a person, unaccustomed as she had been all her life even to the confinement of a house,
and whose eye had been looking upon the green fields ever since her

infancy; so that it is not difficult to understand how the four blank walls forever hemming in this wretched creature, must have seemed not only to have half-stifled her with their closeness, but almost to have maddened her with the intensity of their snow-like glare.

The gipsy woman was not alone in reacting strongly to being cooped up. The authors were told that the most difficult prisoners were those sentenced to transportation just before the Act that removed it as a sentence from the statute book. Wanting to be sent abroad, some of these convicts were enraged when they realized they would remain in England and eventually be discharged there. They became unruly, destroying their clothes, tearing up their bedding and smashing the windows. While they threatened violence against the officers, however, they rarely carried out the threat.

In his report for 1854, the medical officer made this comment about Brixton:

I may, perhaps, here be allowed to state that my experience of the past year has convinced me that female prisoners, *as a body*, do not bear imprisonment so well as male prisoners; they get anxious, restless, more irritable in temper, and are more readily excited, and they look forward to the future with much less hope of regaining their former position in life.

The Criminal Prisons of London

He added that male convicts had the advantage of being moved from prison to prison and of working outside in the open air. Female prisoners were stuck in the architectural monotony of Brixton, where cells, furniture, prison dress and everything else they set eyes on had a depressing sameness and where one day was an exact copy of the one that preceded it. A prison cell was no place for a woman.

Sweet women

As they crossed the gravelled courtyard at Brixton, Mayhew and Binney caught a first glimpse of the prisoners:

and so sweet and picturesque was their convict costume, that they had none of the repulsive and spectral appearance of the brown masked men at Pentonville, nor had they even the unpleasant, grey, pauper look of the male prisoners at Millbank.

For their part, the women did not think their dress either sweet or picturesque: it was a badge of shame. They were compelled to wear a loose, dark, claret-brown robe with a blue check apron and necker-chief. On their heads was a white muslin cap; on their arms was their prison number.

The chaplain compiled some interesting figures for the period November 1853 to December 1854. During that time, a total of 664 prisoners were admitted to Brixton. Just over 100 were illiterate and almost 200 read poorly. When he added the 53 who could read only a few syllables, he found that over half of the intake was 'imperfectly-educated'. Three hundred and fifteen women 'could read tolerably, but most … had learned in prison or revived what they had learned in youth'. Not one prisoner had received a moderate amount of education, confirming the chaplain's opinion that 'the beneficial effects of educa-tion are more apparent among females than men' (*Criminal Prisons of London*).

The Reverend Moran had taken the trouble to examine the history of each prisoner, and was able to divide them into distinct groups. The largest – some 453 in all – traced their ruin to drunkenness, bad company or a combination of the two. Ninety-seven had run away from home or from service. Eighty-four assigned various causes to their fall. Six had committed a crime on impulse. Eight claimed that they were in want, and the remaining 16 that they were innocent.

Meagre rations

The prison bread was made in a large, light building that adjoined the kitchen. While some prisoners did the baking, others were given the more menial task of fetching coal for the ovens. Work began early so that breakfast could be served promptly at seven-thirty. The ordinary prison breakfast comprised six ounces of bread and three-quarters of a pint of cocoa. Those who worked in the laundry, bakery and kitchen had eight ounces of bread and one pint of cocoa, small privileges that were coveted.

The prison allowance for dinner – the midday meal – was four ounces of cooked meat, a half pint of soup, half a pound of potatoes and six ounces of bread. Those who laboured in the kitchen and elsewhere were given five ounces of meat, one pint of soup, one pound of potatoes and six ounces of bread. Convalescents also had the latter rations, although mutton was served in place of beef.

Bread and gruel were the staple items on the supper menu, with amounts varying according to a prisoner's status. The convicts were divided into classes, each having its own dietary scale.

Meals were served to the prisoners in their cells, and this called for careful organization. A bell would ring, and matrons would enter the kitchen with prisoners who helped to load the food and drink on to large trucks which were wheeled along the landings. When everything was ready to be served, another bell rang and one of the wardresses would yell grace at the top of her voice: 'O Lord, bless this food to our use, and us to thy service, through Jesus Christ our Lord. Amen!' (*Criminal Prisons of London*).

After grace the cells were unlocked, and women would be handed their meagre meal from trays and baskets. When the food was served, another bell rang to signal silence. Any prisoner heard talking or making a noise was reported and punished. The distribution of knives was under close supervision: they were counted out and counted back in again. If one was missing, every cell was searched until it was found.

The airing yards

Prisoners were allowed to exercise for an hour between eight and nine in the morning; laundrywomen, whose work was laborious, only got half an hour. The airing yards with their plots of grass and flower-beds compared well with those of other institutions. Two hundred convicts at a time would pace around in couples, breaking the silence that was usually imposed by chatting away. Those on the inner ring of prome-nading prisoners were invalids, allowed to walk more slowly. The noise reminded Mayhew and Binny of the tumult of a marketplace.

All of the inmates were clean and tidy. Even though they wore identical uniforms, closer inspection revealed modifications. Some women adjusted their garments out of vanity. One carried coals at the bottom of her dress so that it would seem fuller. Another had taken the wire from around a dinner can and used it to stiffen her stays. A third – the visitors were reliably informed – had taken the ropes from her hammock and put them around the hem of her dress to body it out. A matron also confided that women had been known to scrape the white-wash off the walls of their cell to use as a cosmetic.

The punishment regime

Prisoners reported for misconduct had to appear before Emma Martin, the superintendent. Giving them the opportunity to speak in their own defence, she considered the circumstances of the offence before deciding on a punishment. Outbursts of violence were a regular feature of prison life. In a fit of temper, women would attack each other or vent their spleen on items in their cell.

During 1854 a total of 1,209 punishments were recorded. The figure is misleading as some convicts received the same punishment a number of times. Thirty-one convicts had to be handcuffed, and one put in a straitjacket. Two hundred and eighty-eight were confined to a refractory cell, roughly half of them on full rations while the others had only bread and water. A further 92 were placed on the bread and water diet. Two hundred and fifty-six were deprived of one meal or part of a meal. Thirty-four were confined to their cell, 70 were withdrawn from association and 428 were either reprimanded or admonished. Nineteen escaped punishment on special grounds.

The six refractory cells were small, dark and barely furnished. The window was covered with a screen allowing in restricted light through holes. It took time for the eyes to become accustomed to the gloom. Other cells were reserved for women who broke windows: a slanting iron screen was placed in front of the window to protect it. Loss of daylight was again part of the punishment.

The roll call of offenders suggests a large, turbulent prison population. In fact, the majority of prisoners obeyed the rules. In 1854 Brixton was especially proud of its record with regard to ticket-of-leave prisoners (those allowed out for a probationary period). Of the 200 women involved in the scheme, only four had been sent back to prison. For the rest of them, the fear of returning to Brixton in handcuffs was a strong deterrent.

Convict babies

Few aspects of the Victorian penal system could be described as even faintly touching, but Mayhew and Binny found one of them at Brixton. The convict nursery was a room in which mothers could play with their babies and enjoy an oasis of maternal pleasure. One of the matrons introduced Mayhew and Binny to the children – dressed in spotted blue frocks – as they played with rag dolls or were caressed by their mothers.

They met two-year-old Eliza, born in York gaol to a mother now serving a sentence of five years, and Jeannie, slightly older, born out of wedlock in Glasgow Prison. Little Sarah had been born in Brixton seven months earlier to a mother sentenced to four years' penal servitude. Since her imprisonment, the mother had not heard a word from her husband, a private in the Fusilier Guards.

All the children had been born inside the walls of a prison and had never known liberty. They were too young to understand the strangeness of their existence.

Like every other part of the prison, the nursery was controlled by strict regulations. The nursery breakfast consisted of a pint of milk for each child and tea for the mothers. As many as 30 children had been there at one time, but the Secretary of State had then forbidden Brixton to accept children born in other gaols. If a child was born before its mother came to Brixton, it was to be sent to the Union to be looked after by strangers. No child older than four years had ever been in the nursery.

The chaplain took a special interest in the nursery: he donated pictures for the walls, and his daughter presented the women with old frocks that could be adapted for wear by the children. He also encouraged his children to befriend those in the nursery, even taking one girl to Sunday school outside the prison so that she could see something of the world beyond the high perimeter walls.

The visiting authors drew an impassioned conclusion: 'There is, indeed, no place in which there is so much toleration, and true wisdom, if not goodness, to be learnt, as in the convict nursery at Brixton!'

Women's work

Yet even the mothers were never allowed to forget that they had been sentenced to hard labour. Time spent with their children was limited; they had to do their share of the prison drudgery.

The spacious wash-house was one of the busiest areas, filled with bare-armed women who stood on wooden gratings as they rubbed dirty flannels against a wooden grooved board, or turned the handles of the mangles set up at the centre of the room. A dense white mist of steam from the boiler enveloped them.

The drying-rooms were overhead, containing a giant clothes-horse over which towels and blankets were dried by blasts of hot air. The ironing-room was an equally unpleasant place in which to work, with damp clothes hissing, steam rising from them and the smell of burning flannel permeating the whole room. Gas stoves were used for heating the irons in summer because the open grates were far too hot. Laundrywomen worked hardest and endured the most uncomfortable conditions in the prison.

The bulk of the convicts were engaged in needlework, seated on stools outside their cells in serried ranks. They made a variety of garments for use in Brixton or other prisons, or for sale to outside contractors. None of the women endured the rigours of the male convicts involved in public works, but they were nevertheless taxed by a daily round that was conducted in silence, rigidly enforced and endlessly repetitive.

For most inmates, there were two consoling features of the prison experience. The first was attendance at chapel, a small, neat, simple yet handsome building with brown beams. Open pews on the ground floor and in the galleries at the rear allowed women to sit side by side without any partitions between them. Rising high above the congregation was the pulpit in which the chaplain conducted the services. Mayhew and Binney commented on the respect, gratitude and even affection shown by the prisoners towards him and his family: 'Indeed, we never met with a finer instance of Christian charity than we here found practised daily by this most righteous and unassuming family.'

The second consolation was the arrival of letters, a link with the outside world that was highly prized. Correspondence from family members or friends was distributed by the chaplain's clerk, and the illiterate would get someone else to read their letter for them. The urgent desire to maintain contact with loved ones was the spur that made many women learn to read and write while in Brixton. If a letter did not arrive on the day expected, women would be plunged into gloom. To know that someone loved, forgave and supported them made their sentence much easier to bear.

Florence Maybrick

Brixton set a pattern that was repeated elsewhere. But while most female convicts were uneducated women from the working classes, one more literate prisoner was able to create a record of her time inside, in her book *My Fifteen Lost Years* (1905).

Florence Maybrick was a Southern belle from Alabama, married to a successful Liverpool cotton-broker over twenty years older than her. In 1889 she was charged with poisoning him. Victorian public opinion was shocked by the revelation that she had had an affair, even though she had only sought comfort in the arms of another man when she discovered that her husband kept a mistress.

An all-male jury, influenced by a hostile judge, found her guilty, and Mr Justice Stephen, a sick man later committed to an asylum, pronounced the death sentence.

Because Maybrick had maintained her innocence, and because it was felt by some that she had not had a fair trial at the Liverpool assizes, there was a flood of letters, petitions and articles decrying the verdict. Leading Americans, including the President, put pressure on the Home Office. Sir Charles Russell, her defence counsel, wrote to the Home Secretary on 21 November 1895 that 'Florence Maybrick ought never to have been convicted and that her continued imprisonment is an injustice which ought promptly to be ended' (HO 144/1640/A50678).

Maybrick, meanwhile, was in Walton prison, and heard the sounds of the scaffold being erected. Three days before she was due to hang, the reprieve came. Her sentence was commuted to 15 years. A sensitive and hitherto respectable woman from the upper middle classes became one more number in the prison system.

The first nine months were spent in solitary confinement in Woking gaol on a diet of bread and gruel. Maybrick wore a brown dress marked with arrows, and had to make at least five men's shirts a week. Her medical examination had consisted simply of being weighed and measured. Her cell was so small and miserable that it drove her to instant despair: 'I sank to my knees, I felt suffocated. I sprang to my feet and beat wildly with my hands against the door, "For God's sake let me out! Let me out!"' (All quotations are from *My Fifteen Lost Years*.)

Maybrick's reaction was typical of women on their first day. Unable to sleep on the hard bed, she had insomnia every night that she was in prison. Her way of coping with her sentence was to compress her thoughts 'to the smallest compass of mental existence, and no sooner did worldly visions or memories intrude themselves, than I immediately shut them out as one draws a blind to exclude the light'. Maybrick relied on 'the opiate of acquiescence ... the keeping of my sensibilities dulled as near as possible to the level of the mere animal state which the Penal Code, whether intentionally or otherwise, inevitably brings about'.

In the winter, she recalled, the prisoners got up and ate their breakfast in the dark to save the expense of turning on the gas lighting. Female volunteers had been in the habit of assisting the chaplain by reading Scripture to individual prisoners. Maybrick recorded sadly that the services of the readers were also dispensed with on the grounds of cost.

When she was later transferred to Aylesbury prison, she worked in the kitchen:

My duties were as follows: To wash ten cans, each holding four quarts; to scrub one table, twenty feet in length; two dressers, twelve feet in length; to wash five dinner tins; to clean knives; to wash a sack of potatoes; to assist in serving the dinners, and to scrub a piece of floor twenty by ten feet ... the work was hard and rough.

All female prisoners complained of the abiding cold during the winter, but as an American from the Deep South Maybrick suffered particularly from the English climate. If there was rain or snow, she seldom had dry feet, and suffered catarrh, influenza, bronchitis and rheumatism at various times. She found wardresses in the prison hospital brusque and distant, with no tenderness to show her: 'Sympathy is not part of their official duty.' It was left to the sick to show care and affection to each other.

The prisoner pleaded for mercy on the grounds of ill health – but her claim that she had contracted tuberculosis and was spitting blood proved to be false. While in the hospital ward, she was observed introducing a knife into her vagina to draw blood that she then caught in a spittoon (HO 144/1639/A50678). She almost died when she severed an artery.

What outraged Maybrick was the way she was periodically searched:

> It was a bitter indignity. I was never allowed to forget that, being a
> prisoner, even my body was not my own. It was horrible to be touched by
> unfriendly hands, yet I was compelled to submit – to be undressed and
> searched. During the term of my imprisonment I was searched about ten
> thousand times.

Obstreperous prisoners could be handcuffed or even straitjacketed. Another method of restraint was hobbling, which bound arms and legs tight with leather straps. Standing against a wall in great discomfort, the prisoner had to be fed like a baby. Maybrick described the practice as barbarous.

Hope of early release was non-existent while Queen Victoria was alive because Her Majesty had approved of the original sentence (HO 144/1639/A5068). Six months after her death in January 1901, the Home Office reviewed the case. A memo to the Home Secretary stated that 'it would be possible to fix 15 years as the period at which she might be brought into licence. I think it would be well, if this decision is come to, to inform the American ambassador at the interview on Friday' (HO 144/1640/A50678).

Although some inmates railed against all authority, Maybrick recognized that the staff were working within strict guidelines – 'I served under three governors, each of whom was an intelligent and conspicuously humane man. They knew their prisoners and tried to understand them, but there is not much a governor can do of his own initiative.'

When Florence Maybrick neared release in January 1904, she was gripped by tension and troubled by disbelief – 'I felt as one in a dream. I could not realize that tomorrow, the glad tomorrow, would bring with it freedom and life.'

She felt that release was like being reborn. She had at last ceased to be a statistic and reclaimed her right to become a full human being once again, leaving behind her the experience of living in a 'mere animal state' in a Victorian prison.

CHAPTER SIX

Suffragettes and the New Century

I am fighting, fighting, fighting. I have four, five and six wardresses every day as well as the two doctors. I am fed by stomach-tube twice a day. They prise open my mouth with a steel gag, pressing it in where there is a gap in my teeth. I resist all the time ... The night before last I vomited the last meal and was ill all night, and was sick after both meals yesterday ... I am afraid they may be saying we don't resist. Yet my shoulders are bruised with struggling ... whilst they hold the tube into my throat. I used to feel I should go mad at first, and be pretty near to it, as I think they feared, but I have got over that, and my digestion is the thing that is most likely to suffer now.

Sylvia Pankhurst, 18 March 1913

During the closing decades of the Victorian era, the penal system became the focus of a number of inquiries or select committees, and there was a flurry of legislation. Two major additions were made to the statute book. The first, the Prison Act of 1877, did not come into effect until April of the following year. It brought local gaols under the control of central government in the person of Sir Edmund Du Cane, Surveyor-General of Prisons, who sought a better distribution of prisons in England and Wales. Wanting fewer and larger establishments, he drew up a list of closures: of the 113 prisons in existence, 45 were taken out of service. As a result of declining prisoner numbers, more gaols were closed over succeeding years.

The second and more far-reaching piece of legislation was the

Prison Act of 1898. This incorporated the recommendations of the Departmental Committee on Prisons (1895), otherwise known as the Gladstone Report because it was chaired by Herbert Gladstone, son of the former Liberal Prime Minister. The Committee had been formed in response to a series of articles in the *News Chronicle* newspaper that were highly critical of Du Cane's sterile, militaristic, punitive regime. Gladstone was charged with examining the administration of prisons and the treatment of prisoners. The Report recommended the improved classification of prisoners; the special treatment of certain categories of offenders, such as juveniles, habitual criminals and drunkards; the complete abolition of pointless, unproductive labour; and the introduction of associated work.

Until 1895 the declared purpose of imprisonment was to act solely as a deterrent. The Report advocated two main tasks: 'we start from the principle that prison treatment should have as its primary and concurrent objects deterrence, and reformation'. Confusion was thus introduced into the system. In his study of *The English Prison Officer since 1850*, J. E. Thomas points out that the prison service now had to cope with two mutually exclusive tasks. In a deterrent regime, the emphasis was on the control and punishment of the offender. In a reformative regime, by contrast, decisions would be made on the basis of the needs of an individual prisoner. The duty of the prison officer had suddenly become more complicated.

The man charged with implementing the Prison Act of 1898 was Evelyn Ruggles-Brise, who had succeeded Du Cane in 1895. He was a country gentleman and professional civil servant, educated at Eton and Oxford; an intelligent, conscientious man with a number of aristocratic contacts. In appearance, manner and style, he was a complete change from Du Cane, a career soldier who had ruled with an iron hand. Yet Ruggles-Brise was presiding over a system in which the military presence and ethos were still predominant. Seven of the eight governors of convict prisons were ex-servicemen. In local prisons, too, the majority of governors had been in the army or navy. Well over half of prison officers had been in the services.

Such men, used to maintaining discipline in a separation system, now had to adjust to Ruggles-Brise's priorities, later described in his book *The English Prison System* (1921) as 'retributory, deterrent and reformatory'. That meant learning new methods of control and developing a different relationship with prisoners. Ruggles-Brise turned out to be as autocratic as his predecessor, but his reign is notable for two cardinal reasons: he brought the despised separation system to an end and he established borstals as a means of taking young people away from the general prison population.

With its new overlord, new structure and new purposes, the penal system underwent radical changes as it came into the twentieth century. One of its first challenges was a new breed of offender – the suffragette.

The Women's Social and Political Union

At the start of the twentieth century, men who were happy to have a queen on the throne, and to forge a mighty empire in her name, were not prepared to yield one inch of their entrenched authority over the other sex. Victorian women were at the mercy of their fathers, husbands or employers. All the major decisions about their destiny were made by men. Towards the end of the nineteenth century, working-class women tried to find a voice by joining movements to improve their working conditions while those from the middle class joined more sophisticated organizations aimed at achieving female suffrage.

Formed in Manchester in October 1903, the Women's Social and Political Union (WSPU) was the most effective suffragist body because of its readiness to adopt militant tactics in pursuit of its objectives. Its founder was Emmeline Pankhurst (see plate 22), widow of a popular local leader of the Independent Labour Party. Mrs Pankhurst's three daughters – Christabel, Sylvia and Adela – were all involved to some degree in the new organization. The WSPU was given early encouragement and advice by Keir Hardie, leader of the Labour Party and, after the general election of 1900, one of its two members of parliament.

After two years of proselytizing and disseminating propaganda, the Union adopted a dramatic new policy in October 1905. Sir Edward Grey was the main speaker at a meeting held in Manchester Free Trade Hall in support of Winston Churchill, Liberal candidate in a parliamentary by-election. The meeting was attended by Christabel Pankhurst and Annie Kenney, a former Lancashire cotton-worker and the only working-class woman to join the senior hierarchy of the Union. When it was time for questions from the audience, the fearless Kenney stood up and asked: 'Will the Liberal government give women the vote?' (*Memoirs of a Militant*, 1924) The question was ignored, so Christabel stood up and repeated it.

The hall became increasingly restive. To calm things down, the Chief Constable went over to the two young women and said that Sir Edward would answer their question if they passed it up to him in writing. Although they did so, it evoked no response. Christabel and Kenney therefore climbed on their chairs and unfurled a home-made banner inscribed 'Votes for Women'. Evicted from the hall, they started a meeting outside and were arrested when they refused to be moved on by the police. Instead of paying a fine, they deliberately chose to go to prison: Kenney for three days and Christabel for seven.

At a stroke, the two women had garnered an immense amount of publicity for the WSPU and signalled a change of direction in its policy. The *Daily Mail* unwittingly helped by hurling the contemptuous name of 'Suffragettes' at them. It was gratefully accepted. When Christabel and Kenney were released from prison, they were welcomed by enthusiastic crowds.

During the 1906 general election, the suffragettes continued to harass Winston Churchill and were often thrown out of meetings. Churchill was duly elected as part of a Liberal landslide that did not bode well for their cause.

It was Christabel who insisted that the Union should move its headquarters to London so that it could be near the seat of government. Her mother protested that they had insufficient funds and that she had to continue her work as registrar in Manchester. She urged Christabel to complete her studies for a law degree, but her daughter was adamant. Annie Kenney was therefore sent off to London with WSPU funds (a grand total of two pounds) to join Sylvia Pankhurst, who was there on an art scholarship.

Mrs Pankhurst searched for someone to act as honorary treasurer to the WSPU. Keir Hardy recommended Emmeline Pethick-Lawrence, a woman who had done much charity work among the poor in the East End. From the moment the organization acquired its treasurer, the

19. Ann Smith, sentenced to two months' hard labour for stealing two shirts, from Wandsworth's photograph albums, 1873 (PCOM 2/291).

think the Governor, several times urged me to
break the hunger strike.

At about 5 p.m. the Senior Medical Officer returned
with, I think, 4 wardresses and the feeding
apparatus. The Doctor urged me to voluntarily
take food - I told him that was absolutely out of
the question. He did not examine my heart nor
feel my pulse; he did not ask to do so, nor did
I, directly or indirectly, say anything which
could possibly induce him to think that I would refuse to be examined. I offered no resistance to
being placed in position but lay down voluntarily
on the plank bed on the floor. I shut my mouth
and clenched my teeth. The Doctor offered me the
choice of a wooden or steel gag. He explained
elaborately as he did on every subsequent occasion,
that the steel gag would hurt and the wooden one
not, and he urged me not to drive him to use the
steel gag which however was the only one that
could overcome my resistance. After failing to
unlock my teeth with the wooden gag he used the
steel. He seemed, not unnaturally, annoyed at
my resistance. After being fed by the stomach
tube I was much overcome and I vomited. As the
Doctor left me he gave me a slap on the cheek, not
violently but apparently to express his contemptuous disapproval; he seemed to take for granted
that my distress was assumed. I said to him the
next day "Unless you consider it part of your
duty, would you please not strike me (or I may
have said slap me) when you have finished your
odious job."

He did not answer but never repeated the in-

20. (*left*) Report by Lady Constance Lytton, 18 January 1910, describing her forcible feeding at Walton Gaol when she was imprisoned as 'Jane Wharton'. The prison medical officer denied some of her allegations (HO 144/1054/187986).

21. (*right*) Letter from the Home Secretary to the Holloway governor urging that Mrs Pankhurst's condition be managed and monitored, 4 April 1913. Daily reports detailed the food offered to, and refused by, Mrs Pankhurst (PCOM 8/175).

22. (*far right*) Emmeline Pankhurst in 1908 (COPY 1/526).

23. (*lower right*) Interior of Holloway Prison. In 1912 suffragette Emily Davison threw herself from the landing onto the netting and then onto the metal stairs (PCOM 9/1330).

Prison Commission,
Home Office,
Whitehall, S.W.

No. _____

Confidential.

4th April 1913.

The Governor,

Holloway 1 Prison.

Please note that if Mrs Pankhurst starves herself, the Secretary of State wishes her to be kept constantly supplied with suitable and appetizing food. He wishes also, in case any question should arise, that an exact record should be kept (1) of the food supplied in her cell, and (2) of everything that is done in the way of inducing her to take food, and (3) in the way of medical treatment

H.

Secretary.

2

Noted and Deputy Medical Officer.
Informed.

RM Paton

4/4/13. Governor.

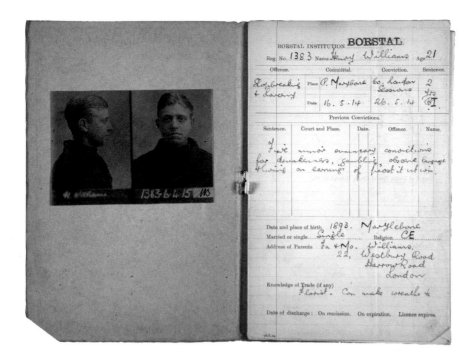

24. (*above*) Borstal record of Henry Williams, a former flower-seller sentenced for shopbreaking and larceny. Like other young men, he was given the choice of discharge into the army to serve in the First World War – and was killed in action at Amara in 1916 at the age of 23 (HO 247/71/86).

25. (*below*) Dartmoor conscientious objectors at work in April 1917.

Royal to the Works is desirable.

(2) I understand that a shelter shed is to be provided and it would be well that this should include seating accommodation for a midday meal (... tables) in bad weather, and a stove for heating Wat... ...tea. It would be of great assistance if ... ...ould provide this meal, a ded... ...arge for labour, if necessary. ...r ... to send out a meal of ...ese. Wh...her this would ... whether it should be ...uld only have water to ...rious side issue of the ...for the Committee to ..., it is the only difficult

... is one and a half miles

1.3.17

Mr. Whiskard,

I have visited Dartmoor and made arrangements for opening the Establishment as a Work Centre. The first batch of 150 men will arrive on Thursday the 8th instant. As these will come from Wakefield and Warwick and are used to the regime at those Centres their presence will enable a good start on established lines to be made as to the manner in which Dartmoor should be worked.

The hours of work in the neighbourhood are 9½ and these will be followed by Major Reade, the Manager.

The first 150 men will be required for domestic work, building repairs and for work on the prison farm and I anticipate that in about a fortnight quite 300 or 500 will be at the disposal of the Duchy of Cornwall authorities. I understand that number of men are ready for transfer.

The following matters require immediate consideration by the Committee.

Diet As the scale for 12 ozs. of Meat, Potatoes and Vegetables had been reduced to 9 ozs. at Warwick, and is, I understand to be so reduced at Wakefield, if this has not already been done, I advise Major Reade to commence with 9 ozs. as it would be easier to increase it afterwards than to reduce it. This is apart from any general reconsideration of the dietary.

This question has caused considerable commotion in the local public press, as will be seen from the enclosed newspaper cuttings.

Clothing In view of the inclement climate of Dartmoor, I consider that each man should have two pairs of boots and that a reserve stock of clothing should be kept for changing.

Cheap oilskins (8/- or 9/-) and Sou' Westers (about 1/-) should also be provided. The expense will be rather heavy at first, but economical in the long run being cheaper than the alternative of giving each man a second kit.

The Committee may consider it desirable to communicate with the Chief Constable of Devon on the question of the presence of such a large body of men in the village in the evenings and on Saturdays and Sundays. A certain amount of nervousness is felt by the villagers and Warders as to whether their children would be safe. There is only one policeman stationed in the village and he is not constantly there. As a help towards dealing with this question I arranged with Major Reade to set up a system of patrols chosen from the most reliable men who would help in keeping order.

I was unfortunate in not being able to consult the Duchy Authorities on the spot, although I visited the site of the intended operations. It would be well therefore that Mr. Peacock should be consulted on one or two points which arise

(1) An extension of the Telephone System Tor

Royal

26. Memo detailing the establishment of Dartmoor as Princeton Work Centre for conscientious objectors, 1 March 1917 (PCOM 7/12).

LEE'S TERRIBLE ORDEAL.

Man they Could Not Hang to Tell his Story in "Lloyd's News."

We give a photograph of John Lee, who has just been released from prison after serving a life sentence for the murder of Miss Keyse, at Babbacombe. Lee, who escaped the gallows because the drop failed three times to work, is writing an account of his experiences, the exclusive pub-

lication of which will begin in "Lloyd's Weekly News" next Sunday.

27. (*left*) Newspaper report announcing John Lee's decision to tell his story, from the *Chronicle*, 23 December 1907 (HO 144/1712/A60789).

28. (*below*) A note to the Home Secretary written while the authorities debated when to release John Lee from long-term detention after the failure to hang him (HO 144/1712/A60789).

5th October, 1906.

S. of S.

The case shows very strikingly how impossible it w⁴ be to substitute detention for life for the death penalty in this worst

Class of murders. Every one who knew the facts of Lee's crime was strongly of opinion that he sh⁴ never be released: and now the choice is between keeping him for 25 years or for 30!

29. (*left*) Request for execution equipment by Albert Pierrepoint, 29 September 1952 (PCOM 9/1772).

30. (*below*) Pierrepoint writing his memoirs in 1973.

31. (*above*) Civilian prisoners exercising in the yard at Wormwood Scrubs, Second World War (INF 2/43).

32. (*below*) Holloway prison hospital report on Ruth Ellis, 12–15 June 1955. It shows something of the monotony of prison life, as well the lack of emotional privacy – here Ruth is reported as being upset at having seen photographs of David Blakely's body (PCOM 9/2084).

when visited. Reading and writing for long periods. Taken diet fairly well.
Evening Report
Upset on return from solicitors visit had been crying. Said she had insisted on seeing the photographs of "David" They were worse than she imagined. States it is the first time she has cried since has been here. Taken supper. Soneryl gr iii given 8 p.

supreme power within it was shared between Mrs Pankhurst, Christabel, Mrs Pethick-Lawrence and her husband, Frederick. Their ability to work harmoniously together was the basis for their extraordinary success. Their policy was a bold one: women would take responsibility for their own advancement, targeting the government in the most militant and colourful publicity campaign ever seen.

Seeking imprisonment

The WSPU committed itself to a series of deputations to parliament, marches, demonstrations, meetings and heckling at by-elections. It courted publicity, and its numbers steadily rose. What set it apart from sister organizations was that its members were not only prepared to go to prison for their beliefs, they positively sought to do so.

Sylvia Pankhurst had no wish to become a paid employee of the Union. While she loved her mother and her sister, Christabel, she had private doubts about the way that they were leading the organization. Unlike them, she wanted to be an artist and not a political activist. At the same time, she wanted her art to serve the cause of social progress. Sylvia was soon at odds with the law. On 23 October 1906, a group of suffragettes demonstrated outside the House of Commons, then infiltrated the lobby to hold an illegal meeting there. Ten of them were arrested, including Sylvia's younger sister, Adela, and Annie Cobden Sanderson, daughter of Richard Cobden, former leader of the Anti-Corn Law League and a champion of British liberalism.

In court on the following day, the magistrate gave them a choice between promising to keep the peace or going to prison for two months. They were not allowed to plead their case. Sylvia was enraged that the women had been hustled off after a trial lasting less than half an hour. Storming into court, she told the magistrate that several women wishing to give evidence in defence of the prisoners had been denied access. Sylvia was dragged out and thrown into the street, where she tried to address the crowd. She was seized, charged with obstruction and abusive language and taken before the magistrate. As she refused to pay a fine, she was sentenced to a fortnight in Holloway.

Her first imprisonment left a deep impression on her, which she recorded in the sketches drawn inside Holloway prison and in her book

The Suffragette Movement: An Intimate Account of Persons and Ideas (1931).

There were three types of imprisonment at the time. The first division, for political prisoners, allowed inmates to receive unrestricted correspondence and visits; they could also practise their professions behind bars. In the second division, prisoners could only write and receive a letter monthly. In the third division, minimal correspondence would not even start until after two months. While the other suffragettes served their sentence in the second division, Sylvia was consigned to the third, and would therefore be completely cut off. She recalled the ride in a Black Maria.

> How long the journey seemed to Holloway, as the springless van rattled over the stones and constantly bumped us against the narrow wooden pens in which we sat. As it passed down the poor streets, the people cheered – they always cheer the prison van. It was evening when we arrived at our destination, and the darkness was closing in. As we passed in single file through the great gates, we found ourselves at the end of a long corridor with cubicles on either side. A woman officer in a holland dress, with a dark blue bonnet with hanging strings on her head, and with a bundle of keys and chains jangling at her waist, called out our names and the length of our sentences and locked us separately into one of the cubicles, which were about four feet square and quite dark. In the door of each cubicle was a little round glass spy-hole, which might be closed by a metal flap on the outside.
>
> *The Suffragette Movement*

Once they were all locked away, the wardress went from door to door to take particulars as to the profession, religion and so on of each prisoner. The suffragettes talked to each other over the top of the cubicles. When another van load of prisoners arrived, they were crammed into the same cubicles, sometimes as many as five in each:

> It was very cold and the stone floor made one's feet colder still, yet for a long time until I was so tired that I could no longer stand I was afraid to sit down because, in the darkness, one could not see whether, as one feared, everything might be covered in vermin.

This was the reaction of a sensitive young woman who had known the comforts and privileges of a middle-class upbringing. To be pitched into Holloway with prostitutes, thieves and drunks was a frightening experience for her. Ordered to undress and put on a short cotton chemise, Sylvia and the others had to surrender all of their valuables, duly registered so that they could be reclaimed on release. After being made to take a bath, they put on ill-fitting prison garb made of coarse calico and rough wool:

> A strange-looking pair of corsets were supplied to each of us ... The stockings were of harsh thick wool, and had been badly darned. They were black with red stripes going around the legs, and as they were very wide, and there were no garters or suspenders to keep them up, they were constantly slipping down and wrinkling around one's ankles.

Sylvia had just managed to scramble into a shapeless dress when they were ordered to put on shoes. Bundled together in a rack, none of the shoes seemed to be in pairs. They were heavy, clumsy and had leather laces that easily broke. She was issued with a cotton cap, fastened under the chin with strings and stamped in black with a broad arrow, and a blue and white check apron. The whole evening's intake was then led off to the cells:

> It seemed a sort of skeleton building we were taken through – the strangest place in which I had ever been. In every great oblong ward or block through which we passed, though there were many storeys, one could see right down to the basement and up to the lofty roof. The stone floors of the corridors lined the walls all the way round, jutting out at the junctions of the storeys like shelves some nine or ten feet apart, being protected on the outer edge by an iron wire trellis work four or five feet high, and having on the wall side rows and rows and rows of numbered doors studded with nails.

After climbing up stairs and walking along endless passages, they stopped outside an office for another roll call. Each prisoner was given sheets, a Bible and a number of other little books. They were then locked into individual cells. Sylvia's was small, whitewashed and with a bare stone floor. The window was near the ceiling in a heavy iron framework and barred on the outside. A flickering gas-jet cast a dim light. A small wooden shelf served as a table, and there was a stool beside it. Her utensils were made of black tin – a plate, a water can holding about three pints of water, a shallow washbasin and a small slop-pail with a lid. There were two small brushes for sweeping the floor, a little tin dustpan, and a piece of bath-brick wrapped in rags for cleaning the tins. Everything was placed in an order which, she later learned, was never to be changed. That was the rule.

Sleep on the plank bed was almost impossible. It was about two feet six inches in width and only a couple of inches from the floor. Sylvia found that:

> the bed is so hard, the blankets and sheets are scarcely wide enough to cover one, and the pillow, filled with a kind of herb, seems as if it were made of stone. The window is not made to open. The system of ventilation is extremely bad, and though one is terribly cold at night one always suffers terribly from want of air.

Sylvia was roused every morning by the tramp of feet and the ringing of bells. The light was then turned on. She had to wash in the tiny basin and dress quickly. When the door was unlocked, the wardress would bark a curt command: 'Empty your slops, twelve.' Back in her cell, she rolled her bed in the prescribed fashion; next came the cleaning of the tins. When the door opened again, there was a pail of water with which she had to scrub the stool, bed and table. All this was supposed to be done before breakfast, but it sometimes took longer.

Breakfast was served cell by cell. Sylvia's pint pot was filled with gruel, and six ounces of bread were thrust on to her plate. Once again the cell door clanged shut. After she had eaten, she began to sew: according to her work card, she had to produce 15 shirts a week. Chapel was at half-past eight. Forbidden to speak, Sylvia was marched there with the other prisoners and marched back when the service was over. Dinner was served at twelve o'clock – always six ounces of bread, with a pint of oatmeal porridge three days a week, six ounces of suet pudding twice a week, and on the other two days eight ounces of potatoes. Even in her student days, she had a more varied and appetizing diet than this.

The prisoners remained in their cells for the rest of the day, except on the three days when they were allowed out for exercise, which Sylvia looked forward to because it gave her a chance to see the sun. Dressed in drab capes, they walked single file in a circle, keeping three or four yards apart from other prisoners so that there could be no chance of communication. Back in their cells for the last meal of the day at five o'clock, they had more bread and gruel. Lights were then turned out, and number twelve had to endure another sleepless night.

The ordeal lasted for eight days. During that time, Keir Hardie, Lord Robert Cecil and others complained bitterly about the sentences meted out to the suffragettes. Many were scandalized that Richard Cobden's daughter was being treated by a Liberal government as a common criminal. Bowing to pressure, the government decided that the women should be given the status of first-class misdemeanants. Sylvia noted immediately that she was now entitled to exercise her profession. She was given pen, ink, pencils and drawing paper and, because she now had congenial work to do, the gaol 'lost the worst of its terrors'.

Other suffragettes were less fortunate, and protested that they were treated as common criminals. A petition from Alison Neilands (HO 144/1047) objected to the fact that she was given three months for pouring liquid into a ballot box. What she deemed as an act of political protest, entitling her to be put in the first division, was viewed by the magistrate as a case of electoral fraud. A file at the National Archives (HO 144/891) contains criticism of the harsh sentences meted out in 1908 by a magistrate named Hopkins, who routinely sent all suffragettes to the third division. Militant suffragettes had few friends on the Bench.

Sylvia Pankhurst's change to first-division status allowed her to record what she saw around her. Her prison sketches are simple, stark and realistic. They show convicts in differing stages of their daily routine, such as waiting in their cell for dinner, scrubbing the bed or sewing a shirt. What they reveal is the dreadful isolation and loneliness of prison. It operated, she said, 'as if it were still in the Middle Ages'. Her sketches go some way to supporting this claim.

Holloway prison

Holloway began life as the City house of correction. Opened in 1852, it was one of the 19 new radial prisons built in the earlier half of the Victorian era. It was designed by James Bunstone Bunting, the City Architect, and followed a standard pattern. Occupying a site of eight acres, the prison had four three-storeyed wings for adult male prisoners, each capable of holding 72 offenders; another three-storeyed wing held 56 juveniles; and a sixth wing of a similar type was set aside for 56 female prisoners (see plate 23). With its massive gatehouse, castellation and tall, central tower, the prison looked like a medieval fortress.

After 50 years as a mixed prison, Holloway became an exclusively female establishment in 1902. It grew very familiar to the suffragettes. In October 1908 Mrs Pankhurst, her daughter Christabel and Flora Drummond addressed a meeting in Trafalgar Square and thousands of handbills were distributed. All three women were later arrested on a charge of inciting to riot. Christabel spoke feelingly in court, condemning the proceedings as a Star Chamber as there was no trial by jury. But it was the dainty, dignified, politely defiant Emmeline Pankhurst who was most eloquent:

> Although the Government admitted that we are political offenders and therefore ought to be treated as political offenders are invariably treated, we shall be treated as pickpockets and drunkards; we shall be searched. I want you, if you can, as a man, to realise what it means to women like us. We are driven to do this, we are determined to go on with this agitation, because we feel in honour bound … it is our duty to make this world a better place for women than it is today.
>
> quoted in June Purvis, *Emmeline Pankhurst*, 2002

The magistrate showed no mercy. As they refused to be bound over to keep the peace, he sentenced Mrs Pankhurst and Flora Drummond to three months' imprisonment and Christabel to 10 weeks, all in the second division. As soon as they reached Holloway, Mrs Pankhurst demanded to see the governor and told him that suffragettes would no longer submit to being treated as ordinary law-breakers and therefore would refuse to be searched and to undress in the presence of wardresses.

She also claimed the right, as a political prisoner, to speak to her fellow political prisoners during exercise or whenever she came into contact with them.

The governor was prepared to compromise. While he agreed to waive the search and to allow the changing of clothes to be done in private, he pointed out that he had no power to meet her third demand. It would have to be referred to the Home Secretary, Herbert Gladstone, whose Report had led to the Prison Act of 1898. Mrs Pankhurst sent a petition to him, asking to serve her sentence in the first division, to have books and newspapers of her own selection, to be allowed to do literary work and needlework of her own choosing; to see her secretary and deal with correspondence relating to her public work; to associate to some extent with the other suffragettes in Holloway; and to wear her own clothing and provide her own food.

A severe migraine laid her low and she was moved to a hospital cell. She was still in pain when the governor brought the news that the Home Secretary had refused all of her demands. Mrs Pankhurst feared that Union activities would suffer while its two leading speakers – herself and Christabel – were incarcerated. As it happened, Flora Drummond was released early to rejoin the fight. She was in the early stages of pregnancy and had fainted in prison; on health grounds, she was let out of Holloway.

When her own health improved, Mrs Pankhurst flouted the silence rule by speaking to Christabel during exercise. Both of them were given three days' solitary confinement. When she told the governor that she would never submit to the silence rule again, Mrs Pankhurst was designated a 'dangerous criminal'. Kept once more in solitary confinement, she had no exercise or visits to chapel, and a wardress was stationed outside her cell to ensure that she spoke to nobody. She remained unrepentant.

Suffragettes who had served their sentences – articulate women with access to newspapers and magazines – knew exactly what Mrs Pankhurst and Christabel were suffering, and wanted to draw attention to Holloway's strict and inhumane regulations. The WSPU organized a huge demonstration led by a brass band. Sylvia Pankhurst, Flora Drummond and other released prisoners sat in wagonettes, some wearing home-made copies of the Holloway uniform. Reaching the prison, they circled it twice, cheering Mrs Pankhurst and Christabel. Thousands of people joined the procession and it became half a mile long.

When a second demonstration was held, the road to Holloway was blocked by a thousand policemen. In the face of unflattering headlines and ceaseless pressure, the Home Secretary eventually granted a concession: Mrs Pankhurst and her daughter were allowed to spend an hour of each day together. A vital breach had been made in the Holloway rules.

Opposition to the cause

This minor triumph was hailed by the suffragettes, but condemned by individuals and organizations implacably opposed to the notion of giving women the vote. People like Lord Cromer attacked the Union with unremitting anger and passion. The Women's National Anti-Suffrage League was founded in July 1908. One of its principal members was Mrs Humphrey Ward, the novelist and granddaughter of Thomas Arnold of Rugby. While she supported the movement for higher education for women, she opposed female suffrage on the grounds that women's influence was stronger in the home than in public life. Many middle-class women held that view.

The Men's League for Opposing Suffrage was formed in December 1908 and the National League for Opposing Women's Suffrage came into being two years later. All these organizations had links with the Edwardian establishment and the money to appeal to popular prejudice in their literature. They produced tracts, posters and postcards, vilifying the suffragettes and trying to marginalize them with satire or dismiss them with contempt.

Opposition was also shown in more direct ways. There were attempts to disrupt WSPU meetings or destroy their posters and banners. When Sylvia attended a meeting in Ipswich, she discovered that prominent Liberals had hired men to create a disturbance. The moment Sylvia rose to speak she was heckled, and fights broke out in the hall. Stink bombs were let off, making it impossible for her to continue for a while. Accustomed to being criticized by certain politicians, she found this kind of direct action much more difficult to handle. It showed the measure of resentment that the suffrage movement had stirred up.

Militancy

In the summer of 1909, the Union became even more militant. Marian Wallace Dunlop, a sculptor, entered the parliament building with a large stamp and tried to print in St Stephen's Hall an extract from the Bill of Rights of 1689. This stated that it was 'the right of subjects to petition the King' and that all prosecutions for so doing were illegal. She was removed from the building. When she repeated the offence, she was arrested and sentenced to a month's imprisonment.

Arriving at Holloway in a Black Maria, she refused to strip naked, don prison clothes or be searched. She demanded to be treated as a political prisoner and given the relevant privileges. When her demands were rejected, she became the first suffragette hunger striker, refusing to eat or drink anything at all. Dunlop had to be released 92 hours later in a state of collapse. Her stand had been injurious to her health but it had demonstrated her courage. Others followed her example. Fourteen women convicted of stone-throwing in July also went on hunger strike when their request to be treated as political prisoners was denied. The government was highly embarrassed by the stories they told on their release from Holloway.

In September 1909 the stakes were raised. Prime Minister Asquith was speaking at Bingley Hall in Birmingham. Women were refused admission, so a dozen suffragettes resolved to catch Asquith's attention. Climbing on to a roof nearby, two of them used axes to loosen slates, then hurled them at the Prime Minister's car as it drew up, breaking the windows and the lamp. The women shouted 'No surrender!' from the rooftop, and a hose had to be turned on them to force them down. Mary Leigh and Charlotte Marsh were sentenced to three months' and two months' hard labour, respectively, and taken off to Winson Green Prison. The other suffragettes, who had simply broken windows, received shorter sentences.

The *Daily News* urged Mrs Pankhurst to condemn her fellow-members for their outrageous conduct. While she had not authorized the attack, she was forced to endorse it and had to face much press criticism for doing so. A new development kept the story on the front pages. When the women in Winson Green went on hunger strike, they were forcibly fed. Suffragettes were horrified to learn that exhausted women were being held down so that a tube could be shoved down their throats or into their nostrils. It was a gross violation of their bodies as well as of their rights.

There was an immense public outcry. Newspapers were hit by a blizzard of protests. Questions were asked in the House of Commons by Keir Hardie and Philip Snowden, Labour MP for Blackburn. The Prime Minister was sent a memorial of protest signed by 116 doctors, many of them eminent in their field. Henry W. Nevinson and H. N. Brailsford, leader-writers for the *Daily News*, both resigned because of the editor's support for the government's action. 'We cannot denounce torture in Russia and support it in England', they argued. Resignation was a momentous decision for them and indicative of the strength of their feelings.

Winson Green, opened in 1849 as the Birmingham borough gaol, suddenly found itself at the eye of the storm. Opponents of women's suffrage felt that the prisoners were getting exactly what they deserved, but their fate aroused large-scale public sympathy and made people look more critically at a penal system in which such things could take place. That women should be subjected to a procedure so painful, dangerous and humiliating was felt to be quite unacceptable.

Lady Constance Lytton

Stone-throwing was a regular aspect of increased militancy. To further the cause, Lady Constance Lytton and Mrs Jane Brailsford damaged property in Newcastle, and were duly arrested. Sent to prison, Lady Constance went on hunger strike. When she was medically examined, it was found that she had a chronic valvular heart disease and was therefore unfit for forcible feeding. Released on health grounds in October 1909, she felt that she had been given preferential treatment because of her title.

Selina Martin was a working-class suffragette with no aristocratic connections. She went on hunger strike in Walton gaol, Liverpool. Just before Christmas 1909 she was forcibly fed even though it was against the law for remand prisoners to be treated in this way. Martin had been kept in chains at night and was frogmarched to the cell where she was to be fed. The action confirmed Lady Constance's belief that class was a factor in imprisonment. Accordingly, she dressed up as a working-class seamstress in January 1910 and joined a protest outside Walton gaol. When arrested, she gave her name as 'Jane Warton' and was imprisoned by the magistrate.

Because she was not recognized, no favours were granted to her. She went on hunger strike, but was given no medical examination. Under the guise of her assumed name, she was forcibly fed eight times before her true identity was discovered (see plate 20). The deterioration in her health was recorded by a medical officer (HO 144/1054/187986); when her sister came to get her out, Lady Constance's health had been broken and she became a permanent invalid. Newspaper accounts of her brutal treatment created a barrage of protest against the government. The scandal arising from the case helped to persuade Herbert Gladstone to leave the Home Office to become the Governor of South Africa.

Glad to see his departure, suffragettes were not pleased when the new Home Secretary turned out to be Winston Churchill, a man who had conceived a loathing of the women's movement when its members continually interrupted the Manchester by-election in which he stood as Liberal candidate. Gladstone had been consistently deaf to their demands. There was little realistic hope that Churchill's hearing would be any better.

Emmeline Pankhurst

The year 1910 had started badly for Mrs Pankhurst with the death of her beloved son, Harry. When the storm over the case of Lady Constance broke, she was still in mourning. It troubled her that a woman with a heart condition had been put through the rigours of forcible feeding, and she was also distressed by the cruel treatment in Walton Gaol of Selina Martin. She began to wonder if hunger strikes were an appropriate weapon to use. In January 1910 she discussed with Christabel and Mrs Pethick-Lawrence whether or not the Union should call a truce.

In spring her own mother died and her sorrow deepened. Critics said that she had neglected both her son and her mother in favour of her duties in the Union. In their eyes, the break-up of families was an inevitable consequence of giving women the vote. Even within the WSPU Mrs Pankhurst met with reproach from those who felt she was exerting too much power and taking too much credit for any advances they achieved.

All her efforts were now concentrated on organizing a peaceful demonstration to show the strength of support for their cause. Planned for late May, it was postponed as a mark of respect after the sudden death of King Edward VII. When it finally took place in June, 10,000 marchers turned up with 700 banners and 40 bands. Contingents came from overseas as well. The event was an unqualified success, and £5,000 were collected for their funds.

Support for the movement grew steadily, and pressure on the Liberal government mounted. A Conciliation Committee was formed in parliament, consisting of members from all parties, and it drafted a Bill that embodied a moderate degree of women's enfranchisement. When Asquith refused to make it a governmental measure, Mrs Pankhurst led a march to parliament on what became known as Black Friday. She and her distinguished companions managed to get to the Strangers' Entrance, but the many detachments of supporters who tried to join them were repulsed with unexpected brutality by the police.

Acting on the orders of Home Secretary Churchill, the police refrained from making arrests and instead beat, kicked and forced the women back. Some were knocked to the ground and others suffered what were, in effect, sexual assaults, as uniformed and plain-clothes officers lifted the women's skirts and thrust their knees between their thighs. When Dr Jessie Murray and Henry Brailsford published a report of the violence, the most frequent complaint from victims was 'variously described as twisting round, pinching, screwing, nipping or wringing the breast ... often done in the most public way so as to inflict the utmost public humiliation' (*Emmeline Pankhurst*). Disturbing details of the incident can be found in MEPO 3/203.

Over a hundred suffragettes were arrested after the six-hour struggle. On the following day Churchill sanctioned their release, declaring that no public advantage could be served by their prosecution. It was a gesture to cover his embarrassment and to appease his critics in the press. For their part, the suffragettes felt that their softer approach had failed – yet a return to militancy had obvious disadvantages, one of which was to alienate public support at a time when they were still hoping that the

Conciliation Bill might eventually become law. Nursing their bruises, they considered their options. The truce was renewed.

Schism and violence

Hostilities were resumed in the autumn of 1911. Mrs Pankhurst was in America, seeking financial support for the movement. Irate at the government's continued vacillation over the Second Conciliation Bill, she sent a cablegram to be read out at a meeting of the WSPU: 'I share our indignation at the Government's insult to women and am ready to renew the fight. Shall return with practical help from America.' (*Emmeline Pankhurst*). On the following day Christabel, Mrs Pethick-Lawrence and a deputation from nine women's suffrage societies met with the Prime Minister – and were once again fobbed off.

It was time for action. On 21 November, windows were smashed at the National Liberal Federation, the offices of the *Daily Mail* and the *Daily News*, in shops, hotels and a bakery. Militancy was sharpened in December when Emily Wilding Davis, a well-known freelance suffragette, was arrested for trying to set alight the contents of a postbox in Parliament Street. Her six-month sentence enraged the members of the WSPU and spurred them on. A weary but still charismatic Mrs Pankhurst returned in January 1912 to discuss strategy.

The *Daily Telegraph* reported what took place on 1 March:

> A band of women set out on such a window-breaking campaign in
> the principal streets of the West End as London has ever known. For
> a quarter of an hour or twenty minutes nothing was to be heard in
> the Strand, Cockspur Street, Downing Street, Whitehall, Piccadilly,
> Bow Street and Oxford Street but falling, shattered glass ... The attack
> began practically simultaneously. It was one of the busiest periods of
> the day. Suddenly women, who a moment before had appeared to be
> on a peaceful shopping expedition, produced from their bags or muffs,
> hammers, stones and sticks, and began an attack on the nearest windows.
> Information was immediately conveyed to the police and all reserve
> constables were hurried out.

Over a hundred arrests were made – including that of Mrs Pankhurst – and stiff prison sentences were imposed. The government took a strong-arm approach. Warrants were issued for the arrest of the leaders of the WSPU. Mr and Mrs Pethick-Lawrence and Mabel Tuke, Honorary Secretary, were arrested, but Christabel escaped to Paris and ran the Union from there. Mrs Pankhurst, already in Holloway, was now on remand and facing new charges.

The cycle of violence, arrest, imprisonment, hunger strikes and forcible feeding continued. As militancy reached new heights, there was great concern in some quarters of the WSPU and open schism threatened. Along with many others, the Pethick-Lawrences left the Union, but were soon replaced by new recruits. Mrs Pankhurst said that she took responsibility for the actions of her members, but she had no control over wilder spirits such as Emily Davison, who had a record of rebellion in prison, including an incident where she threw herself from a landing, feeling that 'a tragedy was wanted' (PCOM 8/174). On 4 June 1913, this intense young woman attended the Derby and hurled herself beneath the feet of the King's horse as it galloped around Tattenham Corner. Horse and jockey were brought down.

Witnessed by a huge number of spectators, the incident was caught on newsreel and shown in the cinemas. The whole country soon knew what had happened on Derby Day. As a result of her injuries, Davison died and was hailed as a suffragette martyr by her friends. Six thousand people attended her funeral. The shocking event had drawn attention to the seriousness of the women's movement. Those who had been indifferent to its activities were now forced to view it in a new light: a cause worth dying for commanded respect.

Even though she was confined to bed, Mrs Pankhurst had been determined to attend the funeral. As soon as she left the house, however, she was rearrested. She had been in and out of Holloway, a victim of the notorious Prisoners (Temporary Discharge for Ill-Health) Act. It was the government's way of dealing with troublesome suffragettes. Under this Cat and Mouse Act, as it became known, a prisoner in poor health as a result of hunger strike could be released into the community. As soon as she had recovered sufficiently, she could be clawed back into prison.

Mrs Pankhurst was frail and mentally exhausted, but her spirit was indomitable. She weathered her visits to Holloway even though they became increasingly stressful. The prison authorities tried to tempt her with 'various appetising foods', such as filleted plaice, roast chicken with bread sauce, thin bread and butter and freshly made tea - but she continued to hunger strike (PCOM 8/175; see also plate 21). Each time she was released, a crowd was at the gates to welcome her, and press photographs later showed how much she had weakened. Public sympathy for her was strong; even those who opposed women's suffrage felt that the treatment she suffered in Holloway was scandalous. Nobody liked what they heard about the harsh conditions inside the establishment, and there was a growing demand for penal reform.

It would be wrong to think that Holloway and other female prisons were staffed entirely by uncaring viragos who enjoyed inflicting punishment on their sisters. Some female officers showed compassion. In her book *Memoirs of a Militant* (1924), Annie Kenney spoke up for the staff:

> Their work is monotonous and their lives are spent with the undeveloped and disharmonised souls on life's ocean. They are on their feet all day, and their pay when I was in prison was poor ... Some of them were far too good to be wasted there, and yet such kind, gentle natures could be greatly utilised there if the women prisoners could be divided up into groups, each group representing the different stages of personality or development or education, and these groups organised and utilised according to their capacity.

Prison turned Kenney into a prison reformer. It brought out the rebel in the Canadian Mary Richardson, one of the most militant suffragettes, always inclined to go further than the others. When she was taken before the governor and a visiting magistrate, both men, she was furious that they relaxed in their chairs while the matron was made to stand. She spoke on impulse: 'It is a disgrace that the matron should have to stand while you sit round in your comfortable chairs – a disgrace!' (*Emmeline Pankhurst*).

In the course of two years she was arrested nine times and was forcibly fed when she went on hunger strike. She persuaded the bishop of London to support women's suffrage and presented a petition to King George V by jumping on the running board of his carriage. Richardson smashed windows at the Home Office and in Holloway, set fire to a country house and bombed a railway station. Notoriety was secured in 1914 when she went to the National Gallery with a meat cleaver and attacked the Rokeby 'Venus', the famous painting of a nude female reclining on a bed as she looked into a small mirror. The target had symbolic significance.

The outrage was only one of many committed by the suffragettes. Sylvia Pankhurst listed some of the other actions taken:

> The destruction wrought in the seven months of 1914 before the War excelled that of the previous year. Three Scotch castles were destroyed by fire on a single night. The Carnegie Library in Birmingham was burnt. The Rokeby Venus, falsely, as I consider, attributed to Velasquez, and purchased for the National Gallery at a cost of £45,000, was mutilated by Mary Richardson. Romney's Master Thornhill in the Birmingham Gallery was slashed by Bertha Ryland, daughter of an early Suffragist... Many large empty houses in all parts of the country were set on fire, including Redlynch House, Somerset, where the damage was estimated at £40,000. Railway stations, piers, sports pavilions, haystacks were set on fire. Attempts were made to blow up reservoirs. A bomb exploded in Westminster Abbey, and in the fashionable church of St George's, Hanover Square, where a famous stained-glass window from the Malines was damaged ... One hundred and forty-one acts of destruction were chronicled in the Press.
>
> *The Suffragette Movement*

Sylvia, who frequently hid to escape arrest, was the editor of the *Women's Dreadnought* published by the East London Federation of the Suffragettes. Its edition on Saturday 20 June 1914 carried the defiant headline: 'No Price Too Great To Pay For Freedom'. One of the articles on the front page referred to a debate on hunger strikes. The Home Secretary, Reginald McKenna, who had replaced Churchill in 1911, said there were four ways of dealing with militant suffragettes: they could be allowed to die of hunger in prison (the most popular suggestion); they could be deported; they could be treated as lunatics; or they could be given the franchise.

He dismissed the first option, not out of common humanity, but because he felt that 'for every woman who died there would be scores who come forward for the honour, as they would deem it, of the crown of martyrdom ... and when there were twenty, thirty, forty or more deaths in prison, you would have a violent reaction of public opinion'. McKenna described the whole issue as 'a phenomenon without precedent in our history'. The edition of the *Woman's Dreadnought* that reported his speech went to press while Sylvia was still in prison on hunger strike, being forcibly fed.

The debilitated Mrs Pankhurst had fled abroad to avoid rearrest and another ordeal in Holloway. From the safety of France, she and Christabel watched the terrorist strategy of the WSPU unfold. Arson and serious damage to property earned suffragettes long sentences but these did not frighten off determined activists. When Mrs Pankhurst felt they were on the eve of success, the First World War broke out. She told WSPU headquarters that all militancy must cease until the crisis was over. The Home Secretary was notified of the truce, and responded by saying that he would only release suffrage prisoners if they agreed not to commit any further crimes. A few days later, he bowed to pressure and reversed his decision, announcing that all suffrage prisoners would be released unconditionally. The militant campaign had come to a decisive end.

The vote

Throughout the war, Mrs Pankhurst and the other leaders worked hard to promote the WSPU as a patriotic and responsible organization whose members were not the unconscionable terrorists they were sometimes portrayed as. By committing themselves to the war effort, suffragettes showed that they were decent, civilized women who could be useful members of society. It was only because of the intransigence of the Liberal government that they had been driven to such extremes.

In 1918 their long struggle bore fruit. The Representation of the People's Act granted the vote to any woman who had occupied land or property for six months or was married to a man so qualified. Voting was restricted to women over the age of 30, while men could vote as soon as they were 21. (This anomaly was removed in 1928.) Women were at last part of the political process.

Their success had been won at immense cost. Many still bore the physical and psychological scars of being forcibly fed in prison – but in gaining the vote, they felt that their suffering had been worthwhile. It had taken the experiences of women from the leisured class to expose the horrors of imprisonment and to draw attention, not simply to their own treatment, but to that meted out to the common criminals, who had no voice of their own. The WSPU shone a light in some dark and disgusting places. When they later wrote their memoirs, leading suffragettes revealed the lasting impact that imprisonment had had on them and showed a sympathy for all women – whatever their crimes – still confined within a tough, dehumanizing and unforgiving prison system.

CHAPTER SEVEN

Prisoners of Two World Wars

Some died in prison; some went mad; some broke down in health completely and never really recovered; some suffered terribly from insomnia – it was almost unbearable for them.

Harold Bing, Great War conscientious objector[1]

When Germany invaded Belgium in August 1914, Britain honoured its treaty obligation and immediately declared war on Germany. There was euphoria in the streets; the general feeling was that it would all be over by Christmas and that an Allied victory was a foregone conclusion.

Of the powers involved in the conflict, Britain was the only one that had not introduced conscription. It did not seem necessary. In the Crimean War and, more recently, in the Boer War, armies of volunteer soldiers had been mobilized. Recruitment posters went up and there was a good response from young men in search of adventure and stirring tales to tell their children. It never occurred to them that the new war was the culmination of a fierce arms race and would run to appalling casualties.

Disillusionment set in very quickly after the battle of Mons on 23 August 1914. The British Expeditionary Force lost 1,600 men, killed, wounded or missing in action. England was jolted. It had not been involved in a major war since the battle of Waterloo in 1815, and had enjoyed almost a century of peace and progress. It was the wealthy and

1 Imperial War Museum Sound Archives 358/11

stable hub of a huge empire. To many people, Germany had never posed any threat because the British royal family was of German descent – but the Kaiser had already declared war on his cousin, the Tsar of Russia, and he extended no favours to his relatives in the house of Saxe-Coburg-Gotha.

After basking in insularity for so long, Britain was shaken by the call on 9 September 1914 for half a million army volunteers. As the war became world war, the sheer scale of the conflict was borne in upon the nation.

Opposition to the war

The war was opposed from the outset by pacifists, left-wing groups and various Christian organizations. Trade unionists objected to the notion of fighting their German comrades, arguing that they would be killing each other in the interests of their capitalist employers. The most active campaign was waged in the Glasgow shipyards, and agitators like Willie Gallacher and John Maclean served prison sentences for their part in organizing resistance. Union opposition slowly faded away when conscription was introduced and exempted many men in occupations vital to the war effort such as coal-mining, steel-working and rail transport.

Conscription was inevitable. The National Registration Act of 1915 had already implemented the listing of all men between the ages of 16 and 40. It was followed by the Derby Scheme of Attestation. This offered inducements to those willing to register as volunteers on call. One of the promises given was that no married man would be conscripted until the supply of single men had been exhausted. Another feature of the scheme was that men could seek the right of appeal for exemption from national service from specially created tribunals. They were led to believe that only by attestation could they earn the right of appeal, and some complied on that basis. Many, however, declined to do so.

Formed in 1915, the No-Conscription Fellowship (NCF) was to offer the strongest and most concerted opposition to the war. Its founder was Fenner Brockway, a brilliant journalist and a determined pacifist.

The NCF soon had 8,000 members, united in their resolve to 'refuse from conscientious motives to bear arms'. Clifford Allen became its chairman and Brockway was its honorary secretary. The NCF was extremely well organized, with branches all over the country. When the Military Service Act was passed in January 1916, making conscription a reality, there was a swift response from the Fellowship. A two-day meeting was held at Devonshire House, the Quaker headquarters in Bishopsgate, which was attended by some 2,000 young men of military age.

Beatrice Webb watched on the first day from the balcony of the circular hall. She was impressed by Clifford Allen: 'The Chairman was a monument of Christian patience and lucid speech – his spiritual countenance, fine gentle voice and quiet manner serving him well as the president of a gathering of would-be martyrs for the sacred cause of peace' (Beatrice Webb, *The Power to Alter Things: Diaries 1905–24*). Allen required all of his patience, because a large crowd of pro-conscription hecklers had gathered outside. They were joined by a group of sailors spoiling for a fight. Shouts and jeers could be heard clearly inside the hall.

Some of the sailors managed to force their way into the hall. Expecting resistance, they found themselves in the middle of an assembly of pale, polite, wide-eyed, harmless young men. After some good-natured mockery, the sailors agreed to withdraw. As the barracking was still in full flow outside, Allen decided that it would be safer not to incite the crowd with loud applause. As each speaker finished, therefore, the members waved handkerchiefs or pieces of paper to signal their approval.

Over 60 resolutions, mostly militant in tone, had been sent in by the various branches, so there was a great deal to debate. One thing that was firmly rejected was service in any non-combatant corps. Members would turn down all alternative work that might directly or indirectly serve the war effort. On the second day, Fenner Brockway read out the names of the 15 NCF members arrested as conscientious objectors. After each name, the delegates rose to their feet and waved white handkerchiefs or pieces of paper.

It was Brockway who read out their common pledge:

We, representing thousands of men who cannot participate in warfare and are subject to the Military Service Act are united in comradeship with those of our number who are already suffering for conscience's sake in prison or the hands of the military. We appreciate the spirit of sacrifice which activates those who are suffering on the battlefield, and in that spirit we renew our determination, whatever the penalties awaiting us, to undertake no service which for us is wrong.

Minutes of NCF meeting, 10 April 1916

It was a brave declaration, an absolute pacifist stance. These men were not merely resisting conscription, they were witnessing for peace. Arrests, beatings and ostracism had already begun, so they knew what might lie ahead. They had committed themselves, individually and as an organization, to breaking the law of the land, and would have to suffer the consequences.

Punishing the conchies

Conscientious objectors were a tiny minority almost universally reviled. When the nation was at war, it was unthinkable that anyone should actually defy the British Army. Long before the Military Service Act came into effect on 2 March 1916, conchies were bullied, baited and sometimes battered. They were looked down upon as cowards and traitors, too lily-livered to fight for the country of their birth and wholly lacking in patriotic feeling. Persecution took various forms. For some conchies it began with social exclusion.

Harry Stanton was the son of a Luton blacksmith:

One had a growing sense of isolation, that one was surrounded by people who thought in different terms, who spoke, as it were, a different language. It seemed useless to discuss the war with them; their standards of conduct were depreciated, though they would refuse to acknowledge it. Yet to me the very isolation gave me a strange sense of joy – perhaps an expression of my combatant instinct! The facile taunts and innuendoes of the 'man in the street' provided daily by the leader writers of the popular press, had the effect of stiffening my resolve.

Memoirs of Harry Stanton quoted in Felicity Goodall, *A Question of Conscience*

Military tribunals were hostile. They tried to make men feel guilty about defying a call to arms. They reminded them how many soldiers had already died trying to protect their country. The authorities could not understand a man who refused the opportunity to join up to exact revenge for these terrible losses.

Alfred Evans was an apprentice in a piano factory and came from a trade union background. Refusing to bear arms, he said he was willing to join the Royal Army Medical Corps on humanitarian grounds. The tribunal granted him an exemption certificate:

> I reported to the recruiting office in Ealing Broadway and saw a Lieutenant who asked for my exemption certificate and promptly tore it up. He then set an official document before me saying that I was to be put into the non-combatant corps and that I was to sign the paper and that I was told that I was not even to read it. I flatly refused to do this and he called the guard, two men and a corporal with fixed bayonets, and I was taken to Hounslow Barracks.
>
> Imperial War Museum Sound Archives 489/11

Harold Blake, a chemist from Northampton, refused to put on army uniform. He was seized, stripped and forcibly dressed by soldiers who abused him in foul language throughout. A heavy kitbag was strapped to his back and he was, literally, dragged 200 yards to the guardroom. When he fell to the ground, he was kicked hard several times. Blake was later court-martialled and sentenced to six months' hard labour.

George Frederick Dutch, a mild-mannered Quaker, also refused to put on army uniform:

> The Major was very unpleasant, hectoring. He said, 'Well all I can say is that in my opinion conscientious objecting is just another name for arrant cowardice.' He said, 'Take him away. Don't put a rag on him. He's got to dress himself.' And of course the NCO's did as they were told.
>
> IWM Sound Archives 356/10

Dutch was made to sit almost naked in a tent with his army uniform beside him. It was November and he was exposed to the biting cold because the sides of the tent were rolled up. Though he sat there for days, frozen to the core, he would not give in. In the end, a doctor had to intervene to save his life.

Horace Eaton was one of many conchies sent to Richmond Castle with the Non-Combatant Corps (NCC). He kept a diary of events at the camp:

> One young fellow who refused to put on khaki was stripped and left on the parade ground with only his shirt on, for a good while. Two NCC chaps took off their caps to him in a sign of admiration – and one said, 'Stick it, lad.' A captain overheard the remark and ordered his arrest under DORA [Defence of the Realm Act] and he was put in prison for fourteen days.
>
> *A Question of Conscience*

Eaton recalled many similar stories. Men were punched, kicked and made to carry heavy kitbags. Taunted by their guards, they spent their nights in cold, dark, bare cells. A man named Cooper was so badly treated that his health declined and he went insane. The case was even brought up in the House of Commons, and questions were asked about army brutality. Several other conchies were driven to insanity by the vicious bullying they encountered at such camps.

For conscientious objectors like Eaton, being in the NCC meant hard work. They built an aerodrome at one point:

> We had various duties to perform – sometimes assisting to build the stables and other times cleaning out various places in the town for soldiers' billets. One day part of our company was sent to a railway station to unload a van for another company of soldiers. They moved almost everything except some rifles and ammunition and these they refused to handle. Regular soldiers had to be called in to finish the work. We expected trouble – but heard nothing further, so probably the captain had smoothed over the affair.

Sent to gaol

In 1915 Mark Hayler was one of the first to join the No-Conscription Fellowship. Then in his mid-twenties, he was working as a teacher in a boy's reformatory school. When he appeared before a military tribunal on March 3 1916, he was forthright:

I have long been of the opinion that war is totally wrong. I have worked
and striven towards what I consider the highest brotherhood of man
and my conscience will not permit me to undertake any duty under the
Military and Naval authorities.

quotes from IWM Sound Archives 357/28 and

Mark Hayler's letters in IWM

The tribunal decided that he must enlist, and Hayler's appeal was
dismissed. When he was summoned by the army, he did not respond.
The policeman sent to arrest him was embarrassed because he knew
the family well. In court the next day, Hayler faced an unsympathetic
magistrate and was remanded to the cells to await a military escort from
Aldershot. He spent the first night in the army sitting in a chair in the
corner of the guardroom. An obstinate man with a Quaker belief in
pacifism, he refused point-blank to obey orders. So he was imprisoned
in Wandsworth, which, with Wormwood Scrubs, Pentonville, Lewes,
Winchester and Maidstone – emptied when convicted criminals were
released to join the army – became a military prison for conscientious
objectors. Colonel Brooke, the governor of Wandsworth, was irritated
to hear that Hayler had repeatedly asked to see him on arrival. After
keeping the prisoner waiting, he eventually agreed to meet him but
showed no interest in what Hayler had to say, simply issuing a stark
warning: 'I've got a lot of men like you down below. They're in irons.'
Hayler was duly marched back to his cell. As a military man, Colonel
Brooke relished the challenge of trying to break the wills of conchies.
His harsh treatment of them would in time earn him a fearsome reputation – but he failed to break Mark Hayler.

On his release, Hayler was given civilian clothes and a train pass to
Norwood Junction. A telegram awaited him at home. He was to report
to his regiment in Aldershot. Ignoring the summons, he was arrested
again and told that he was now a private soldier in the 12th battalion of
the Queen's Regiment. When he refused to obey orders at Aldershot, he
was kept in a tent so that he could not 'contaminate' other soldiers, and
guarded by two men. Hayler was bemused – 'For refusing to be a soldier,
I am told I may have to forfeit my life. I cannot understand it. I thought
the days of religious persecution were over.'

After weeks of being bullied, derided and kept on short rations, Hayler was court-martialled. His sentence – to serve 12 months' hard labour at Winchester prison – was read out before the whole battalion. When he and two other conscientious objectors arrived there, he could hear on the other side of the big wooden door the jingle of keys – 'keys of slavery, drudgery, confinement and a living tomb'. Given prison garb absurdly large for him, Hayler began a year of sustained misery. He drew comfort from his faith and from the fact that he had many conchies around him. His prison letters were read out by the Croydon branch of the No-Conscription Fellowship, where the families of conscientious objectors behind bars or awaiting tribunals would gather for mutual support.

Eric Dott, an ardent Christian from a comfortable middle-class home in Edinburgh, served 112 days' hard labour in Wormwood Scrubs. He found the warders severe; they had scant sympathy for those who refused to fight for their King and country. Notwithstanding this, prison life was surprisingly bearable:

> The labour wasn't hard, they called it hard labour but I was sewing mailbags most of the time …We were in solitary confinement and I was allowed out for I think an hour for exercise and back to your cell again, and the exercise was strictly supervised so that you couldn't speak to anyone else … During that first period of solitary confinement we got no letters but after that month was up I was allowed to write home to tell them I was fine. The first month, it was very boring, but being young and with a good memory of all the things I knew, I didn't find it too bad, but some of the men found it awfully hard that first month. And then after a month there was less strictness. They came round with a tray full of books from the library and you could pick your book, and have reading then of your own choosing to some extent, which was a great help. And I remember I got *Nicholas Nickleby* and read the whole of it with great attention and interest.
>
> Interview with Dr Eric Dott quoted in *A Question of Conscience*

Dott was young, fit, intelligent and resourceful. For those less blessed, the boredom and the loneliness of prison life were intolerable. The restricted diet was also a serious problem. Clifford Allen lost three stones in weight while in prison and never fully regained his health.

To a vegetarian like Harold Bing, some of the food was inedible. Bing was only 18 when he was called up. Refusing to put on an army uniform at Kingston Barracks, he was told that he was the scum of the earth and part of the deplorable 'white feather crew' (IWM Sound Archives 358/11). At his tribunal, he was informed that he was too young to have a conscience. Bing was to spend a total of three years in prison. When he began his first sentence, there were repercussions for his family, which was rejected by its church as well as by its own relations.

Prison could be merciless. When he was sent to Wandsworth, C. H. Norman, a left-wing pamphleteer, spent the first three weeks in a straitjacket much too small for him. He was on hunger strike and kept fainting because of the tight bindings. In the same prison, a man named Roberts went mad, howled abuse at the warders and piled his furniture against the door of his cell. By way of punishment, he was savagely beaten and later died.

Imaginative prisoners soon found ways to communicate with each other. They learned Morse code and tapped out messages on pipes. They invented a rudimentary sign language for use on exercise. They slipped each other scribbled notes. While in Maidstone prison, Clifford Allen played chess with a man five cells away, whispering moves to him when emptying slops, then marking them up on the walls. Games could last as long as a month, but they kept the mind occupied. The idea caught on and half the prison population once took part in a chess tournament.

Fenner Brockway

The *Tribunal* was the NCF's weekly paper, reporting on the fates of conscientious objectors nationwide. In order to stay in print, it had to play hide and seek with the police. Like all of its editors, Fenner Brockway served time: by 1919 he had spent 28 months in a succession of prisons, one of over 6,000 conchies who were incarcerated during the war.

Brockway's first sentence started in July 1916, when he was sent to Pentonville, which he later described as the dirtiest of the prisons he experienced. Shortly after arrival, he heard footsteps in the courtyard and looked out to see a prisoner staring up at the sky. This was Sir Roger Casement, who was hanged the next day.

Brockway was moved to Wormwood Scrubs, then to Walton Gaol, where he produced a prison newspaper on lavatory paper with news, cartoons and letters. He found the rule of silence irksome, and eventually rebelled against it. He was one of five men who told the governor that they would henceforth speak loudly and openly whenever they chose. All 60 other conscientious objectors followed their example and they had 10 wonderful days of vocal liberation, talking happily during exercise, holding evening concerts through the cell bars and listening to Welsh prisoners singing hymns.

Retaliation was vicious. The silence rule was imposed with force and the five ringleaders were moved. Brockway was sent to Lincoln Prison, with three months on bread and water and eight months in solitary confinement. Sinn Fein leaders were being held there under fairly relaxed conditions and they came to his aid:

> My mind was saved by the Sinn Feiners. One day I heard steps outside
> my cell. I got on my stool and saw through the slit one of the trustees.
> He posted a very small package in to me, containing a pencil stub and
> a scrap of paper, and a message. It came from (Eamon) de Valera and
> said: 'Tell us what you want and we'll get it for you.' I ordered daily
> newspapers.

IWM Sound Archives 476/4

Each day he went out in the yard for his solitary exercise, Brockway found copies of the *Manchester Guardian*, the *Labour Leader*, the *Economist*, the *Nation* or the *Observer* hidden for him in one of the drains. To a journalist, they were precious gifts.

Ordeal in France

A shameful episode took place in May 1916, when 50 conscientious objectors were sent in four separate batches to France. It was a desperate measure, born of the conviction that conchies were traitors who deserved to be shot, and that some exemplary death sentences would make others think twice about refusing to join the army.

Howard Marten was one of those subjected to psychological torture:

We were forever being threatened with the death sentence. Over and over again we'd be marched up and read the notice – some man being sentenced to death through disobedience at the front. Whether they were true cases or not I don't know. It was all done with the idea of intimidating us. The military authorities didn't know quite how to react. It was something quite outside their experience. And it became clear that we weren't people who could be bullied into it.

IWM Sound Archives 383/6

The bullying nevertheless continued. Harry Stanton served 28 days in a Field Punishment Unit in Harfleur. He and a few others were 'crucified', tied to a cross with their arms outstretched and their wrists and ankles tightly bound. It was painful for those of average height but agonizing for shorter men who had to stand on their toes to relieve their arms of the dead weight of their bodies. Stanton was indignant:

What did seem to me shameful was that any voluntary soldier, who was offering his life in what he believed was his country's service, was liable to such punishment for quite a trivial offence or at the instance of a prejudiced superior.

A Question of Conscience

At Harfleur they had been manacled to the poles of their tents. According to Alfred Evans, conditions were far worse when they were sent to Boulogne:

We were handcuffed with our hands behind our backs and seventeen of us were put into a dark underground cage about twelve foot square …
the cage was made of heavy timber mounting with inch thick planks and one inch spaces between the planks which allowed a little light from the opening of the passage to filter through.

IWM Sound Archives 489/11

Seventeen conchies shared one latrine bucket with no lid. Unable to lower or pull up their own trousers, they had to rely on others to do it for them. Food consisted of four hard biscuits and eight ounces

189

of corned beef a day with heavily chlorinated water. Evans went down with dysentery and was transferred to a Stationary Hospital. Others, meanwhile, were being tied to a wheel or a gun carriage in an attempt to bring them to heel. Those who were starved and housed in pits kept up their spirits by singing and by holding debates.

When the court martials took place on Monday 6 June, the first batch of conchies were told that their sentences would be announced in front of the whole camp at Henriville. Some three thousand soldiers stood in formation along three sides of the parade ground. Everything had been staged to achieve maximum impact. The sight of ranks of uniformed men made the conchies feel uneasy and vulnerable. The adjutant read aloud the first name, the man's regiment and details of the offence – 'Sentenced to death by being shot.'

All of the prisoners shuddered. After a deliberate pause, the adjutant added that the sentence had been commuted to 10 years' penal servitude. He went through the same procedure with the others. Thirty men in all were sentenced to be shot – as they were allowed to believe – then had the death penalty commuted. They were shipped back to England to begin their long sentences.

Their fate had not gone unnoticed. A scribbled note had been hurled from the window of a train by one of the prisoners en route to France. A railway worker took it to the offices of the No-Conscription Fellowship. Frantic attempts to rescue the men were made and parliamentarians like Philip Morrell and Philip Snowden demanded guarantees from ministers that the men were safe. Churchmen, peace campaigners and some of the more liberal newspapers took up their cause. Even some of those opposed to the conchies felt that they were being cruelly treated. The government and the army squirmed at the bad publicity they received: Prime Minister Asquith had to promise that such brutal treatment of objectors would never happen again.

Work of national importance

In the summer of 1916 a new strategy was adopted. A central tribunal was appointed by the War Office to review the cases of all imprisoned conchies. Those found to be genuine would be released from prison if they agreed to undertake 'work of national importance' under the control of the Brace Committee. Although people like Clifford Allen poured contempt on the scheme from his prison cell, many were tempted, believing that their professional skills could be used for the benefit of the country. More than 4,000 prisoners appeared before the tribunal.

Two hundred and fifty of them were dispatched to Dyce Work Camp near Aberdeen – but instead of using their skills as teachers, doctors, lawyers, clerks, tradesmen and so on, they had to work almost ten hours a day in granite quarries. They slept in tents discarded by the army. Weakened by malnutrition and lack of exercise in prison, they found the daily round exhausting. Persistent rain turned the quarries into mud baths; a man who caught influenza died a few days later. Ramsay Macdonald, who had often spoken up for conscientious objectors in the House of Commons, was shocked when he visited Dyce. The conditions there were intolerable – 'If you are going to punish these men,' he said, 'punish them honestly' (*Hansard*, 19 October 1916).

Few people agreed with him. Their sympathies were reserved for the 400,000 casualties of the battle of the Somme. Why care about a handful of conchies when there were heroes to mourn? In December 1916 Lloyd George became Prime Minister, and his War Cabinet took a tougher stance, drawing up a strict Code of Rules for conchies. As Dyce had now been abandoned, they housed them in Dartmoor prison, euphemistically renamed Princeton Work Centre (see plates 25 and 26).

Around 200 conchies worked inside the walls of the bleak gaol built by French prisoners during the Napoleonic Wars. The other 800 or so went off to a farm or a quarry, crushing corn or carting granite for 10 hours a day. Eric Dott summed up the experience:

> We were all put on what they called work of national importance, which was just a farce because they just found digging for us to do. We were supposed to be laying a pipe line or something and it was of no importance. We never got it done anyway, but as long as we were there and doing this job and didn't try to go away we'd considerable liberty at Dartmoor.
>
> *A Question of Conscience*

As well as Quakers, there were Anglicans, Roman Catholics, Plymouth Brethren, Christian Scientists, Baptists, Methodists, Salvation

Army members and representatives of other religious denominations among the prisoners at Dartmoor. Mark Hayler was disappointed by the response to them: 'The bishop of Exeter refused the conscientious objectors the use of the church in the prison. If we'd been murderers we'd have had a free hand and could have sung "God Save the King"' (IWM Sound Archives 357/28).

Escapes were attempted from time to time, and there were those who defied rules, stirred up trouble and fought with warders. Even in the bitter winter of 1916–17 some inmates found Dartmoor more hospitable than other prisons – but they experienced deep-seated hatred among local civilians: on outside working parties, they were jeered at, jostled and even assaulted. With British casualties soaring overseas, tempers rose back at home, and conchies were a target for those who wanted to vent their spleen.

Arrests, imprisonments, harsh treatment and 'work of national importance' continued apace. When peace finally came in 1918, Bertrand Russell hailed the conchies as victors, and Clifford Allen claimed that they had 'broken the power of the military'. It is not a claim that stands up to analysis. The NCF had failed to prevent the passing of the Conscription Act or, after a short while, its extension to married men. Its members had suffered terrible hardship. Nearly seventy had died as a result and over half as many had been driven mad. When they were finally released in 1919, conchies were in poor health and had great difficulty finding jobs: Government appointments were closed to them and most teaching posts were beyond the reach of a pacifist with a criminal record.

By the same token, the government and the army had also failed. No matter how hard they tried, they could not cajole, frighten, subdue or control conscientious objectors. They not only wasted a disproportionate amount of time, money and manpower on a futile exercise, they created damaging headlines for themselves at a moment when the country needed to be reassured about the conduct of the war. The battle against the conchies had been a form of warfare with minimal gains on either side.

Peace and war
Delight and relief at the cessation of war were translated into a common desire for peace. The League of Nations was created in 1919 to strive for

disarmament, collective security and the settlement of disputes through diplomacy. The No More War Movement was one of many peace organizations that flourished in Britain. Its leaders came from the rank and file of the No-Conscription Fellowship; when it was founded in 1921, its members swore that they would 'never take part in war, offensive or defensive, international or civil, whether by bearing arms or handling munitions, voluntarily subscribing to war loans or using my labour for setting others free for war service' (quoted in Caroline Moorhead, *Troublesome People*).

Others joined the War Resisters' International. Harold Bing was recruited as a roving ambassador for the organization because he had learned French and German in prison. Few other jobs were open to him; when he opened the *Times Education Supplement*, he saw the warning 'No conscientious objectors' in many advertisements.

The mood changed sharply in the 1930s as the actions of Mussolini, Franco and Hitler threatened European stability. When Spain was racked by civil war in 1937, pacifism was no longer so easily defined: thousands of British idealists flocked to fight for the Republicans. People like Kingsley Martin, editor of the *New Statesman*, and Victor Gollancz, the publisher, maintained that it was possible to support the war but remain a pacifist at home. Fenner Brockway actually went to Spain to see what was happening. Because of internal divisions, the No More War Movement dissolved itself, the majority of its members joining the Peace Pledge Union.

When Germany began to flex its muscles and expand its boundaries, all hope of international peace vanished. Having annexed Austria in 1938, Hitler completed his occupation of Czechoslovakia in March of the following year.

In the Great War, conscription had been introduced late and badly managed. The government did not repeat the mistake in the Second World War. The Military Training Bill had a smooth passage through parliament in 1939 while Britain was still at peace. To signal its resolve, the government brought in a scheme for six months' compulsory military training for all men between 20 and 22.

Resistance was immediate. Fenner Brockway became chairman of the Central Board of Conscientious Objectors, a federation of 15

societies able to disseminate information swiftly. It also advised members
on how to conduct themselves before tribunals. Some, like Edward
Blishen, were given exemption because they agreed to work on the land,
a pointless exercise according to Blishen's book *A Cackhanded War* (1972).
Others, like Ken Shaw, a religious objector, were drafted into the Non-
Combatant Corps and ended up working in labour camps.

Absolutists encountered tougher treatment. Kenneth Makin was a
young Christadelphian whose request for total exemption was denied
by a tribunal in March 1940. When he refused to join the regiment to
which he had been assigned, he was court-martialled and sentenced to
60 days in Glasgow prison. Stripped by soldiers, he was ordered to put
on his uniform – but each time he was forcibly dressed, he tore off the
clothing. He was kept in solitary confinement on bread and water, and
after nine days of shivering in a cold cell was taken to Dalkeith hospital
with suspected pneumonia.

The pattern of the Great War was repeated – disobedience, court
martial, imprisonment. Word soon spread about the differing merits of
certain prisons. Lewes was the most popular because of its more lenient
regime, followed by Dorchester and Maidstone. Treatment of conchies
in Wakefield was strict enough to prompt a token strike, but this had
none of the force of the prisoner revolts in the Great War.

Winson Green in Birmingham was rated as the worst prison. Hull,
too, was noted for ill-treatment of its inmates. Arthur McMillan, an
accountant and devout Methodist, arrived at the prison in 1941 to hear
that a conscientious objector had been hurled down the stairs by an irate
sergeant and had a broken neck:

> We passed in and were met by a sgt. who instantly ordered us to face
> a wall ... the language of the warders is the filthiest it is possible to
> imagine ... They call you all the dirtiest names imaginable and every-
> thing is said at the top of the voice in a hoarse yell. To a Christian it is
> simply revolting and extremely shocking ...
>
> Arthur McMillan's unpublished letters, quoted in *Troublesome People*

McMillan's two companions were not in uniform and had refused to
carry their kitbags. They were lifted up, thrown hard against the main

gate, then forcibly stripped of their civilian clothing and given a savage beating:

> They were held by the throats till they got red in the face and I got really
> alarmed … Then they were held up against the wall by one sergeant
> while the others took turns at punching them in the stomach and below
> the belt … My two friends were naked when we went up to the cells and
> for a long time in that first evening I could hear the hysterical screams
> and yells of them and the noise of slaps and punches on bare flesh …

Conchies who avoided the horrors of military prison suffered in other ways. Many lost their jobs. Teachers were especially vulnerable: citizens sometimes refused to pay their rates unless conscientious objectors were ousted from the classroom. Council buildings in Manchester were stoned because it was known that committed pacifists worked there. And national anger at the stance adopted by conchies always intensified when there was bad news from the front. In the wake of a military disaster for the Allies, there would be local witch-hunts involving abuse, assault and vandalism.

Women who objected

In the Great War, female pacifists had been relegated to a largely supportive role, because they did not have to justify a decision not to fight. They looked after their families while their husbands were imprisoned, or replaced absent officers in organizations like the NCF. But their efforts were significant: for example, Catherine Marshall kept the *Tribunal* in print, and was brave enough to harbour wanted men on several occasions. There were numerous other women wholly dedicated to the cause. At the same time, however, some wives were vexed or frankly bewildered at the position taken by their husbands, and enormous pressure was placed on a marriage during an extended period of imprisonment; some fractured beyond repair, while others carried lingering resentment.

In the Second World War, female conscientious objectors could end up in gaol. Churchill announced his intention in December 1941 to call up single women between the ages of 20 and 30. They had toiled so willingly in munition and other factories during the earlier war that he expected little resistance. The Prime Minister was astonished to find how many women had developed a conscience since then. Those registering as pacifists were directed to civilian work or employed in ENSA (Entertainments National Service Association). Over 400 of them were sent to prison for refusing to act as fire-watchers or take on other war work.

Iris Radford was an 18-year-old Jehovah's Witness in Wales. She refused an order to work as a receptionist at a hotel used by Bevin boys, able-bodied youths from England sent to work in the mines and factories. Radford spent a month in Cardiff prison:

> I lived a sort of sheltered life, and to mix with the types that were in there was pretty awful, that was the worst part of prison. Lots of prostitutes who had been carrying on with American soldiers, found on the camps. It was a shock. Some of them had VD, these things you got to know made you a bit frightened.
>
> *A Question of Conscience*

Radford was made to put on coarse calico underwear, a grey woollen dress and heavy black shoes. Her single cell had a bed, a pillow and a rough blanket. Early in the morning she had to empty her slop bucket:

> And then breakfast would be brought, which was porridge made with water and your sugar ration for the day was about a tablespoonful if that, and then the dinner was usually awful. I can remember particularly having salt bacon and beans all tasting very salty and horrible, but you were always glad to eat it. I lost a stone in weight when I was in prison.

As her case had been reported in the local newspapers, she had to withstand animosity and taunting. Her aunt, involved in the war effort, told Radford that she was ashamed of her for letting down the family name, but her parents did not criticize her:

> My mother said it was the proudest day of her life when I went to prison. All her life she was a very strong Witness and it pleased her

greatly to think that I made a stand like that. My father was a really
good man and he said you have to have the courage of your
convictions ...

Though they were spared the brutal punishment given to some male
conchies, women suffered loss of liberty and humiliation. Nora Page
was one of many who ended up in Holloway prison for refusing to
assist in war work. She was inspected by the doctor, then issued with a
linen dress, dirty white cotton vest and pants, black stockings (but no
suspenders) and a dark-blue cape. She found the prison routine onerous;
also that the wardresses were indifferent to the non-threatening conscientious objectors, concentrating instead on criminals imprisoned for
theft or soliciting.

Page was joined in Holloway by Sybil Morrison, full-time organizer
for the Peace Pledge Union, who had been charged with breach of the
peace when she addressed a peace rally in Hyde Park.

Another inmate was Dr Kathleen Lonsdale, the first woman Fellow
of the Royal Society and a mother of three young children. She spent
her fortieth birthday in prison.

It is difficult to see what, beyond revenge, was achieved by locking up
so many women with profound religious convictions or a sincere belief
in pacifism. Imprisonment neither tamed them nor filled them with any
desire to join the war effort on release.

Oswald Mosley

Conscientious objectors were just one group that found themselves
imprisoned during the war. In May 1940 the government imposed
Defence Regulation 18B, legislation entitling the Home Secretary to
imprison without trial anybody likely to 'endanger the safety of the
realm'. Full use was made of it: political agitators, suspected spies, anti-
war firebrands and undesirables of every kind were locked up so that
they could cause no more unrest. Among them were Oswald Mosley
and his second wife, the former Diana Mitford.

Mosley's career sheds light on the shifting patterns of the inter-war
years. Elected as a Conservative in 1918 at the age of 21, he became
disenchanted with the Tory government in 1921 because of its use of the

savage Black and Tans in Ireland. After a period as an Independent, he became a Labour MP in 1926.

An ambitious man and a brilliant orator, Mosley was an active member of the Fabian Society and was passionately committed to the cause of peace – but he soon became frustrated with the Ramsay MacDonald government when his ideas on tackling unemployment went unheeded, and he formed his own party in 1931. The New Party garnered support from MPs of all parties – but at the subsequent election Mosley and his supporters lost their seats.

An admirer of Mussolini, Mosley went to Italy to see how he had achieved his success. When he returned to England, he drew all the existing Fascist organizations into the British Union of Fascists (BUF), a party seeking to establish a dictator, 'acting for the benefit of the people'. BUF rallies attracted thousands of people, hecklers being brutally treated by thugs in black shirts. It became firmly aligned with the vicious anti-Semitism of the Nazis. In 1936 Mosley married Diana Mitford in the presence of Hitler and Goebbels.

Matters came to a head in October of that year when Mosley tried to lead 7,000 black-shirted Fascists through the East End, an area with a large Jewish population. Some 100,000 Londoners built barricades, and a running battle was fought in Cable Street. Lorries were overturned, cars set on fire, bricks thrown and glass scattered on the ground to prevent a charge from mounted police. A Jewish tailor and his son were thrown through a plate-glass window. Dozens of people were badly injured during the riot.

From that point on, Fascist marches were a constant concern for the government. It is a paradox that a man who preached the virtues of peace should provoke so much violence. Many blackshirts were imprisoned, but it was not until 1940 that the BUF was dissolved and its publications banned.

Mosley's prison career was softened in no small way by his contacts in high places. In a letter dated 4 November 1941 and addressed to 'Dear Cousin Winston', Mosley's brother-in-law appealed to the Prime Minister to allow Mosley, currently in Brixton Prison, to be moved to Holloway where his wife was being held (PREM 4/39/45).

Churchill had already taken a personal interest in the case. A letter from Lady Alexander Metcalf dated 17 December 1940 had complained that Mosley had not had a bath since May, was locked up in his cell for 16 hours a day and was refused paper to work on a literary project. A Prime Minister's Minute of 22 December 1940 asks for precise details of Mosley's confinement:

> Does a bath every week mean a hot bath and would it be very wrong to allow a bath every day? ... If correspondence is to be censored, as it must be, I do not see why it should be limited to two letters a week.
>
> PREM 4/39/45

Mosley eventually joined his wife in Holloway.

Female conscientious objectors at the prison were frustrated that Mosley and his wife were given privileges as political prisoners, living in more comfort and on a far better diet. After further lobbying from the couple's supporters, Winston Churchill gave permission for them to live in a small house in the prison grounds, with fellow prisoners as servants and a garden where they could grow their own vegetables and even sunbathe. Their lifestyle had little in common with that of the average inmate, and showed how far rules could be bent within a rigid system. The couple was released in 1943 on health grounds when Mosley developed phlebitis; thereafter they were under house arrest, a much more acceptable form of imprisonment.

Political prisoners

The troubles in Ireland proved another source of inmates for British prisons in this period. The Easter Rising in Dublin in 1916 lasted almost a week before it was suppressed by British troops. Patrick Pearse, James Connolly and five other leaders were sentenced to death and shot. Other Irish rebels were imprisoned on the British mainland.

Some of them were in Pentonville when Sir Roger Casement was hanged there. Knighted for his work in Africa, Casement was a highly respected former member of the Foreign Office. During the Great War he tried to persuade Germany to provide arms to the Irish to aid their fight for independence. He was convicted of treason. A smear campaign had already blackened his name: revelations in his diaries of homosexual encounters were passed around in secret, even though they had no bearing on the nature of his crime.

Irish political prisoners poured into British gaols during the inter-war years and beyond. One of the most colourful was Brendan Behan, who joined the IRA in 1939 at the age of 16 and went on an unauthorized solo mission to blow up a ship in Liverpool docks. He was arrested in possession of explosives and given a three-year sentence that began in Walton Gaol, then was transferred to Hollesley Bay Borstal in Suffolk. He later wrote about the experience in his autobiographical novel of 1958, *Borstal Boy*.

Behan returned to Ireland, but in 1942 he was sentenced to 14 years for the attempted murder of two detectives. He spent time at Mountjoy Prison and at the Curragh Military Camp before his release in 1946 under the amnesty. The following year he served a short sentence in Manchester for helping an IRA prisoner to escape. He read voraciously while behind bars and was inspired to write plays and short stories. Incarceration did not endear him to religion. 'The Bible was a consolation for a fellow in the old cell. The lovely thin paper with a bit of mattress stuffing in it, if you could get a match, was as good a smoke as I ever tasted' (*Borstal Boy*). His first stage success, *The Quare Fellow* (1954), depicted the vicissitudes of prison life as warders and inmates await the execution of the unnamed and unseen 'quare fellow'. Its original title was *The Twisting of Another Rope*.

The Hostage (1958), drawing once again on his experience of prison and the IRA – a young British conscript is held hostage by the IRA in a Dublin brothel – brought him even more fame, but it is *Borstal Boy* that gives a real insight into the nature and effects of incarceration.

* * *

During both world wars, then, Victorian prisons built specifically to hold convicted criminals became military establishments where conscientious objectors could be punished and political prisoners housed. During the inter-war years, prisons returned to their proper function, but space was quickly cleared in 1939 for a fresh batch of men unwilling to bear arms and women unable to compromise their pacifist principles by assisting the war effort.

In the Great War, almost 16,000 men registered as conscientious objectors. The number of conchies in the Second World War was well over 60,000, some 1,700 of them being women. They came up against a British army and penal system run by men in uniform, who inhabited a world of unquestioning obedience and neither understood nor respected conchies. Individuality and freedom of thought did not exist in the system: the authorities saw only men and women who deserved to be punished for their shameful lack of patriotism. Conchies were all one to them: enemies of the state with a number, a prison uniform and a single cell.

The most common accusation flung at conchies was that they were cowards, but it took bravery to withstand the physical and mental pain inflicted on them in prison (as well as the antipathy that greeted them outside). Given the severity of the treatment they received, the wonder is not that many conchies died, went mad or suffered chronic ill health as a result of imprisonment, but that the list of casualties was not substantially longer.

CHAPTER EIGHT

The Last Executions

Executions are intended to draw spectators. If they do not draw
spectators; they don't answer their purpose. The old method was
the most satisfactory to all parties; the public was gratified by a
procession; the criminal was supported by it. Why is all this to be
swept away?

James Boswell, *Life of Johnson*, 1791

As on any other subject, Samuel Johnson had a firm opinion on hanging.
When he left Lichfield in 1737 to try his luck in London, he soon became
acquainted with the strange mixture of solemn purpose and rollick-
ing entertainment found at a public execution. It was a circus for the
common people, a warning of the consequences of crime that became
a diversion rather than a deterrent. Eighteenth-century crowds did not
flock to Tyburn for moral instruction; they wanted drama, excitement
and violent action.

In 1783, the year before Johnson's death, the long procession to Tyburn
ceased when Newgate became the place of execution. A major part of
the ritual was swept away and the spectators were robbed of their fun.
Those in the condemned cells were now hanged outside the prison itself.
Instead of spreading out across the open space around Tyburn, onlookers were herded into a narrow street. The same riotous atmosphere
prevailed, but the more infamous criminals were denied what they saw

as their triumphal progress to the scaffold. With a shortened prologue to the execution, it was difficult to work up the same sustained hysteria. The mob, as Johnson noted, no longer derived full satisfaction from the event.

People also resented the decreasing number of executions, as juries found ways to acquit guilty offenders and judges sought excuses to pardon. Few of the capital statutes were regularly applied. In the last decade of the eighteenth century, less than a third of those condemned to die were actually hanged. By 1810 the figure was one in seven, and it was half that again by the 1830s. Transportation was still being used as a preferred alternative to execution, and abolitionists were steadily gaining ground. In 1832 there were 222 capital offences; five years later the number had been reduced to 16.

Samuel Romilly

There had always been people who thought capital punishment too barbarous and too readily employed, but they lacked a voice in the corridors of power. Samuel Romilly provided that voice. Born in the middle of the eighteenth century, Romilly was as a young man revolted by the whole apparatus of public execution, but it was not until 1806, when he was nearing 50, that he entered the House of Commons as a Whig member. Agitating for the repeal of the death penalty, he achieved a minor success in 1808 when he persuaded parliament to abolish an obsolete statute which made stealing 'privily' from a person a capital offence.

The national mood was not conducive to law reform. Memories of the French Revolution were fresh in everyone's mind, and the Napoleonic war was still being waged with ferocity. Nevertheless, Romilly carried on with missionary zeal. He and his supporters condemned the gallows because it was public and because it underlined the discretionary element of justice. They wanted neutrality and predictability in the justice system, contending that the authority of the judge to exercise discretion should be circumscribed. In their view, public executions were bad because they aroused the wrong emotions. Those who watched were simply hardened by the experience; it had no clear deterrent value. Prison would be a more humane and appropriate form of punishment.

In 1810 Romilly introduced his Shoplifting Bill, aimed at the aboli-tion of capital punishment for three minor property offences, including the theft of five shillings from a shop. Though he steered it carefully through the Commons, he saw his bill founder in the House of Lords. Charles Manners Sutton, Archbishop of Canterbury, and six other bishops voted against it. The pattern was repeated annually. Every time that Romilly tried to remove capital offences from the statute book, his proposals were rejected by the Lords.

One member of the upper house, however, did offer support. In his maiden speech in 1812, Lord Byron expressed his horror at the Framework Bill designed to impose the death sentence on those involved in the destruction of machinery:

> Is there not blood enough in your penal code, that more must be poured
> forth to ascend to Heaven and testify against you? ... Will you erect
> a gibbet in every field and hang up men like scarecrows? ... Are these
> the remedies for a starving and desperate populace? Will the famished
> wretch who has braved your bayonets, be appalled by your gibbets?
>
> *Cobbett's Parliamentary Debates*, 27 February 1812

After leading his campaign with fervour for years, Sir Samuel Romilly died before he could see it come to fruition, committing suicide shortly after the demise of his beloved wife in 1818. But he had planted the seeds from which reform could spring. The following year saw the appoint-ment of the Select Committee on Criminal Law as Related to Capital Punishment. In 1820 the death sentence was abolished for shoplifting, theft, sending threatening letters and destroying silk or cloth in a loom or frame. Capital punishment was abolished in 1825 for assaulting or obstructing a revenue officer.

When he became Home Secretary in 1828, Robert Peel began his revision of the criminal code. In 1829 he founded the Metropolitan Police Force. The same year witnessed the last execution for horse steal-ing and, two years later, the last execution for sheep and cattle stealing or maiming. In 1833 the last juvenile was hanged, and house-breaking no longer carried the death penalty. Gibbeting – hanging in chains upon a gallows – was ended in 1834. In the next three years, dozens of other crimes were redefined as outside the reach of the public executioner.

William Calcraft

From 1829 to 1874 William Calcraft was hangman of London and Middlesex, but he also officiated nationwide. At the time of his appointment, he was 28; his first assignment was to hang Esther Hibner at Newgate in April 1829. Having starved and flogged a young apprentice girl to death, Mrs Hibner was clearly a woman of violent character. She behaved so wildly when sentenced that she had to be straitjacketed. On the morning of her execution, she was carried to the gallows and hanged before a huge, excitable crowd. The long and controversial career of William Calcraft had begun.

In 1840 it fell to him to despatch François Courvoisier, one of the most celebrated killers of the day. The Swiss valet had murdered his master, Lord William Russell. In the crowd were Richard Monkton Milnes, an abolitionist MP, and the novelist William Makepeace Thackeray. What they saw had a profound impact on them. Calcraft was both brutal and incompetent. Using his customary short drop, he hanged Courvoisier with all the casual indifference of a butcher hanging a side of beef from a hook. Because the drop was not long enough to break his neck, the condemned man was slowly strangled to death, twitching uncontrollably and suffering agonies as the last breath was squeezed out of his lungs. Calcraft had given the crowd the gruesome spectacle for which they yearned and there were roars of approval.

Thackeray said that the event left on his mind 'an extraordinary feeling of terror and shame'. It was almost as if he had been 'abetting an act of frightful wickedness and violence performed by a set of men against one of their fellows'. His article 'Going to See a Man Hanged', appeared in *Fraser's Magazine*:

> Murder is such a monstrous crime (this is the great argument), – it is natural he should be killed … it is natural. That is the word, and fine philosophical opinion it is – philosophical and Christian. Kill a man, and you must be killed in return, that is the unavoidable sequitur. It is natural

and therefore it must be done. Blood demands blood. Does it? The system of compensation might be carried on ad infinitum – an eye for an eye, a tooth for a tooth, as by the old Mosaic law ... Where is the reason for this practice? ... revenge is not only evil, but useless.

Also in the crowd that day was Charles Dickens and he was at once appalled and fascinated – but unlike Thackeray, who averted his gaze at the moment when the trap opened, Dickens watched every second of the execution. In *Barnaby Rudge* (1841) the prolonged description of hanging – that 'obscene presence' – owed much to what he had observed outside Newgate.

In 1849 Dickens was outside Horsemonger Lane Gaol to witness the execution of Frederick and Marie Manning, condemned to death for the murder of Mrs Manning's lover. It was the first execution of a married couple for 150 years and aroused tremendous interest. Every effort was made to turn it into a major theatrical event. In spite of the protests from the prison chaplain, the Reverend John Rowe, a scaffold stadium was erected in the front gardens of neighbouring houses. On the eve of the execution a crowd of some 30,000 people gathered outside the prison in festive mood. Dickens paid two guineas on the following day for a vantage point on a roof.

Calcraft dressed for the occasion in his usual 'wide-awake hat' and shooting jacket. He claimed that 'I must keep my client in good spirits. Besides I am not a parson or an undertaker, and therefore decline to don funeral garments' (*The Life and Recollections of Calcraft the Hangman*, 1880). It was said of Calcraft that he would hang a man as he would hang a dog, and the same obtained for a woman. Husband and wife were executed with the same blundering cruelty. Dickens was so disturbed that he wrote an impassioned letter to *The Times*, which was published on 14 November 1847:

> When the two miserable creatures who had attracted all this ghastly sight about them were turned quivering in the air, there was no more emotion, no more pity, no more thought that two immortal souls had gone to judgement ... than if the name of Christ had never been heard

of in this world, and there was no belief among men but that they perished like the beasts.

While pleading for the abolition of capital punishment or, at the very least, that it take place within the walls of a prison, Dickens did not try to put the horrid memory from his mind. Marie Manning was to reappear in *Bleak House* as the murderous French maid, Hortense. Calcraft, meanwhile, went on hanging criminals in places as far apart as Perth, Taunton, Cardiff and Norwich. Paradoxically, in maintaining the tradition of a public executioner, he was also undermining it. While his performances on the scaffold might appease the blood-lust of the mob, they sickened many who watched them. When the Society for the Abolition of Capital Punishment was founded in 1846, replacing the Society for the Diffusion of Information on the Subject of Capital Punishments, its membership was not confined to liberal-minded MPs and sensitive novelists like Thackeray and Dickens. The call for total abolition came from a wider spectrum of society.

Though Calcraft liked to believe that he was a gentle and considerate hangman, he caused unnecessary pain to many of his victims by failing to break their necks when the trap opened. He often had to swing on their legs to despatch them. His most grotesque execution was that of the murderer William Bousfield, in March 1856. London's church bells were ringing merrily to celebrate the end of the Crimean War when the condemned man was brought out. Bousfield looked hideous: he had tried to commit suicide in his cell by flinging himself face down on a fire, but a warder pulled him away in time. His mouth and the lower part of his face were burned.

Calcraft was unusually nervous, having received death threats with regard to the execution. He wanted to get it over with as quickly as possible. As the prisoner was weak from excessive vomiting, he was carried to the scaffold in a chair – and was still seated when the trap opened. The chair fell through the gap, but Bousfield managed to get both feet back on the platform. When one of the warders pushed his feet away, the hooded figure with a rope around his neck swung his feet to the edge of the trap on the other side. It was a desperate bid to stay alive, and it set the crowd alight. Cries of encouragement were drowned out by the howls of abuse aimed at Bousfield. The mob felt cheated; they wanted to see him die.

Thinking his work was over when he released the trap, Calcraft had left the scaffold, and had to be called back immediately. The hangman wrestled with Bousfield, trying to push him through the trap, but – to everyone's horror – the prisoner contrived to swing away and keep his feet on the platform. He also struggled to raise his hands to the rope that was throttling him. Calcraft did not stand on ceremony. He and some warders forced Bousfield over the drop and held his legs down until he eventually expired.

Amazingly, after this shocking incident, no action was taken against Calcraft for his manifest ineptitude. At a meeting of the Court of Aldermen the following day, one of the sheriffs observed that 'no one was to blame, excepting that it may be said that the nervous agitation and alarm under which the executioner had acted led to a lamentable occurrence' (quoted in James Blond, *The Common Hangman*, 2001).

Calcraft bungled on into his seventies.

John Lee

Published memoirs of hangmen have always been popular among those of a ghoulish disposition, but they only tell the story from one point of view. John Lee was in a unique position to offer an insight into what it felt like to be a condemned man on the gallows. Three attempts were made to hang him at Exeter Gaol, and each failed. Lee served 22 years in prison and, on his release in December 1907, his version of events was published in instalments in *Lloyd's Weekly News* (see HO 144/1712/A60789; also plates 27 and 28), and subsequently in book form circa 1908 as *The Man They Could Not Hang*.

John Henry George Lee was the 19-year-old footman of an elderly spinster, Miss Emma Keyse, who lived in Babbacombe, Devon. On the morning of 15 November 1884, Miss Keyse was found in her dining room with her throat cut and her head battered. The room had been set alight. Lee – who had once served a prison sentence for theft – had been angered when his employer reduced his already paltry wage for a trivial

offence. Although the evidence against him was not entirely convinc-
ing, he was sentenced to death. The under-sheriff of Devon telegraphed
James Berry:

> … who I believed to be fully up to his work as an executioner to perform
> that office on Lee on Monday 23 February. On receiving his reply I
> immediately informed the Governor of the prison that the execution
> would take place on that day at 8a.m.
>
> HO 144/148

Berry's first experience as an executioner had been in March of the
previous year, when he had hanged two men in Edinburgh. Since then
he had added another 12 prisoners to his tally – including a woman, Kay
Howarth – so John Lee would bring the number to 15.

After travelling down from Bradford by train, Berry inspected the
scaffold erected in the prison coach house. He pulled the lever twice
and the trap doors opened on each occasion. What worried him was
the one-inch thickness of the trap doors, and he advised the governor to
replace them with three-inch doors that had stronger ironwork on them.
Berry also recommended that a spring be fixed to the wall to hold the
trap doors back so that they could not rebound.

On the Saturday before the execution the machinery was tested five
times with success, though no weight was used on the trap doors. It
rained heavily on Saturday and Sunday nights. The governor, Edwin
Cowtan, accompanied Berry to the coach house at a quarter past seven
in the morning on the Monday and watched the rope being fixed to the
beam. Everything seemed to be in order.

John Lee had been isolated in the condemned cell. He met no other
prisoners. Several clergymen tried to visit him – Lee thought with
the purpose of soliciting a confession – but he only saw the vicar of
Abbotskerwell, his own village.

On the morning of the execution, Lee was given tea and toast for
breakfast. The chaplain entered the cell and asked him to confess, but
Lee, who claimed to be quite calm, refused: 'I have nothing to confess.
I have finished with this world. I want to think about the things of the

next.' The prison bell began to ring his death knell: 'It was eight o'clock! For a moment I felt Death's cold fingers about my throat. But only for a moment. Now was the time to show how an innocent man could die.'

As the clock struck, the cell door opened and the governor entered with the chaplain and the hangman. Berry shook hands with Lee and remarked: 'Poor fellow. I must carry out my duty.' Lee saw that he was holding a large belt with straps, which was quickly buckled round the condemned man's waist. Lee's arms were strapped to it, and his wrists strapped together near the buckle.

The chief warder led the procession to the gallows, followed by the chaplain, Lee, a warder either side of him, a third warder, Berry, the governor and the Under-Sheriff:

> With slow paces we left the cell. We might have been following a coffin. The prison bell was tolling … In the corridor outside I saw several reporters. Even during this dreadful journey to the grave I held my head high. I walked with firm, unhesitating step. No man could say that I flinched. As we walked the chaplain read the burial service.

Lee noted that the prison van had been taken out of the coach house to make room for the scaffold. The officials stood back, and Berry took Lee to stand on the double-sided trap door in two halves, fixing a belt round his ankles.

While Berry was making the final preparations, the chaplain continued to read the burial service in a trembling voice:

> I felt the belt being pulled tight around my ankles. Next Berry put a big bag over my head. It was like a pillow-case except that it had elastic just where it fitted round the neck. I had I thought looked my last on the light of day. No qualms of soul tormented me. I was perfectly conscious of all that was passing.

Berry fixed the rope around his neck, pulling it so tight that it pinched Lee under the left ear. When the executioner asked him if he had anything to say, Lee answered firmly in the negative.

Berry then took hold of the lever: 'I held my breath and clenched my teeth. I heard the chaplain's voice. I heard the clang of the bell. I heard a wrench as of a bolt drawn and …' Nothing happened. The trap doors had failed to open. 'My heart beat! Was this death? Or was it only a dream? A nightmare? What was this stamping going on? Good heavens! I was still on the trap. It would not move! "This is terrible," I heard someone say.'

Blindfolded and pinioned, Lee stood there for over five minutes as the warders jumped on the doors to make them part:

> I was literally resting on my toes and every time the warders stamped the trap shook. Again and again the bolt was drawn, but it was quite evident that the mechanism would not work. Such an ordeal would be enough to kill most men, I suppose. But I remained perfectly quiet, and at last I was led off the trap.

Cap, rope and leg straps were removed so that Lee could be led out to a little storeroom nearby. Berry, meanwhile, got one of the warders to stand on the trap with his hands around the rope. When the lever was pulled, the doors opened. Lee could hear the dull thud as the experiment was repeated time and again. Berry was deeply upset when he came for Lee: 'Clasping his hands, he said: "My poor fellow, I don't know what I am doing!"' Some of the officials turned away, unable to watch such a disturbing scene again: the warders were white with shock and the chaplain was on the point of collapse.

Lee's legs were strapped, he was hooded and the rope was put around his neck for the second time. When the lever was pulled, however, the trap doors only moved two inches:

> The horrible stampings and hammerings were repeated, but all to no purpose. 'Take him off,' commanded someone, and I was made to step back two paces off. The rope was left round my neck, the cap over my head. I was stifling, choking for breath.

Anguished and bewildered, Lee waited for several minutes as someone tried to chip away the edge of the trap doors. It seemed as if they had swollen during the rain. For the third time, Lee was manoeuvred into position so that he could be hanged – but the trap doors only gave way instead of opening, despite the warders kicking at them. In the end, he had his leg straps removed and was led back to the storeroom, where his cap was taken off.

Lee did not realize that he had escaped death. The tearful chaplain explained to him that in English law he could not be put back on the scaffold again:

I did not know, and in any case I was too broken up for the moment to think. You must understand that each time the bolt was drawn I thought I was gone. The experience was made a thousand times worse owing to the fact that with the cap over my head I was practically in darkness. If I could have looked about me. If my hands or arms had been free, I would not have suffered so acutely. The darkness added to the horrible uncertainty of it all and made my agony almost unendurable.

The only consolation was that the grim enterprise had taken place in private; the last public hanging in England had been in 1868 when Michael Barrett had been executed for a Fenian bombing. There were no jeering hordes around Lee's scaffold. Like all those hanged, he had been due to be buried within the precincts of the prison. Lee was given a nasty jolt when they showed him the grave that had already been dug to receive his body.

To cover their embarrassment at the fiasco, the authorities commuted the death sentence to a long spell of penal servitude. Witnessed as it was by reporters, Lee's miraculous escape drew attention to the sheer horror of capital punishment, and more people began to call for abolition.

James Berry
There would be other humiliating accidents in Berry's career. Of the 130 people hanged by him, none caused him more anguish than Robert Goodale. On 30 November 1885 – the same year as the failed hanging of Lee – the prisoner had to be dragged to the gallows in Norwich Prison. By giving him too long a drop, Berry managed to decapitate him.

The editorial in the *Eastern Daily Express* on 1 December was scathing:

> we are persuaded that capital punishment is useless to prevent murders
> and that it is an offence to society. It shocks human nature. Every
> cultured sense revolts at the spectacle of a man legally done to death.
> We hope that never again shall we be called upon to record so awful and
> disgusting an occurrence as that which this day sullies our pages.

Berry, however, was no butcher like Calcraft: he preferred to meet his victims beforehand, offering comfort where he found true penitence. As a hangman, he had felt that there was a religious dimension to his work: he always prayed before an execution and sometimes tried to usurp the role of the prison chaplain.

Two executions at Hereford Gaol on 23 November 1885 showed the contrasting sides of Berry's character. John Hill and John Williams were sentenced to death for the murder of a young woman. When Berry visited Hill in his cell, he found the ex-soldier still glorying in his crime. Hill actually laughed in Berry's face, prompting the reply: 'Well, wait until morning when you stand on the edge of doom with a hempen rope around your neck. We'll see if you laugh then' (James Berry, *My Experiences as an Executioner*, 1692). It was an inexcusable taunt from a man who was there to offer reassurance.

John Williams, on the other hand, looked so dazed and pathetic in his cell that Berry took pity on the man. The hangman turned chaplain, talking softly to Williams and eliciting a list of his other crimes as well as details of the murder he and Hill had committed. Williams was in tears and Berry persuaded him to pray for forgiveness. Berry later recalled that he had left the cell with a feeling of exultation at having been used as an instrument of grace.

On his retirement, Berry became a Methodist preacher. No longer receiving an income as an executioner, he was a vocal opponent of capital punishment.

The Church

The Church of England played a leading role in the preservation of the death penalty. Judicial hanging required religious sanction to give it respectability. For century after century, prelates obligingly provided the intellectual and theological justification for public execution. One of the more articulate was Archdeacon William Paley, whose *Principles of Moral and Political Philosophy* (1785) supplied an authoritative justification for the criminal code.

Paley believed that the English system was well-nigh perfect, deterring crime by making many offences capital yet only exacting that penalty now and then:

> The charge of cruelty is answered by observing that these laws were never meant to be carried to indiscriminate execution … it is enough to vindicate the lenity of the laws, that some instances are found in each class of capital crimes, which require the restraint of capital punishment; and that this restraint could not be applied without subjecting the whole class to the same condemnation.

Paley was not troubled by the fact that innocent men might die on the scaffold:

> he who falls by mistaken sentence may be considered as falling for his country, whilst he suffers under the operation of those rules, by the general effect and tendency of which the welfare of the community is maintained and upheld.

In other words, anyone who was hanged – whether guilty or not – served the useful purpose of making others think twice before breaking the law.

There was almost unanimous support among churchmen for the view that capital punishment was a just and theologically sound practice. One of the few dissenters was the Reverend Bronlow Forde, ordinary at Newgate between 1799 and 1814. In a letter to Jeremy Bentham, he urged the total abolition of the death penalty for all crimes:

When the criminal is dead, both the crime and the punishment are forgotten. Let him live and labour and the public may benefit from his example whilst he himself is making some atonement for his crimes by his industry, and humbly endeavouring to make his peace with God. I have often wondered, with what small degree of devotion or right frame of mind certain persons have joined the second prayer in our Church service: 'Almighty God, who desires not the death of the sinner but rather that he may turn from his wickedness and live.' Strange it is that our religion is so mild and our laws so sanguinary.

Correspondence of Jeremy Bentham

Not only did the Church ratify hanging, it was represented at the event. Prison chaplains tried to prepare the minds of the condemned to meet their Maker and accompanied them to the scaffold itself. Until hanging was finally abolished, the death certificate had to be signed by the chaplain present at the execution. As we have seen, there were many opportunities for corrupt clergymen to make large profits by exploiting their position. The situation changed in the nineteenth century when convict prisons were built and when capital punishment was gradually limited to the crime of murder.

John Clay, chaplain of the Preston House of Correction between 1823 and 1858, relished his power. In *The Prison Chaplain: Memoirs of the Reverend John Clay* (1861) he sometimes sounds more like a psychiatrist than a clergyman:

A few months in a solitary cell renders a prisoner strangely impressible. The chaplain can then make the brawny navvy cry like a child; he can work on his feelings in any way he pleases. He can ... photograph his thoughts, wishes and opinions on his patient's mind, and fill his mouth with his own phrases and language.

Joseph Kingsmill, chaplain of Pentonville, adopted a different attitude. In *Chapters on Prison and Prisoners* (1854), he argued for the scriptural authorization of capital punishment and was contemptuous of those who showed more mercy to vicious killers than to their victims. He contended that abolitionists were wholly in error because 'death punishment for murder is perfectly consistent with the New Testament, necessary for the prevention of crime, and humane, in the largest sense, that is, as regards society at large'.

The duty of the chaplain was 'to assume, as a thing settled beyond all question, the guilt of the condemned and accordingly to direct the sinner to confess to God Almighty all his sins ... and next to acknowledge his crime'. Kingsmill believed that confession could be drawn out by a chaplain, while conversion was more problematical. He strongly opposed the administration of communion to the condemned as a vitiation of the principles of the Church of England: 'the admission of the foulest criminal to its participation on a few weeks of very doubtful repentance' he saw as 'nothing short of profanation and gross abuse of Divine Ordinance'.

Enjoying access to the condemned cell, a prison chaplain had an unrivalled power. Men and women facing death were at their most exposed. Chaplains had a unique opportunity to bring about a genuine reformation of character, and they did not wish to relinquish the influence they could bring to bear. For this reason, as well as for others, they condoned capital punishment and seized upon its incidental benefits.

In 1900 Dr Josiah Oldfield, chairman of the Society for the Abolition of Capital Punishment, wrote to all judges, bishops, Free Church leaders and prison chaplains, asking for their opinion on an experimental suspension of hanging. Many did not even bother to reply. Of those who did, not a single one favoured abolition. The two prison chaplains who responded advocated capital punishment as the best deterrent. At the turn of the century, therefore, hanging continued with the blessing of the Church.

The twentieth century

Edward King, Bishop of Lincoln, started to visit condemned men in 1887 at the request of the prison chaplain. In the time between sentence and execution, King felt that he was able to achieve marked spiritual progress. In some cases, prisoners were converted, confirmed and received Holy Communion before their deaths.

In the case of James Seaton, later bishop of Wakefield, a different type of conversion took place. In 1905 he was chaplain of Armley Gaol in Leeds. Taking up the appointment in the belief that the death penalty was contrary to Christian principles, his experience with condemned men led him to the opposite view. In a large number of cases, he found, convicted men acknowledged their guilt and accepted their death sentence.

The most notorious of the 10 people hanged in 1915 was George Joseph Smith, the Brides in the Bath killer. When he entered Maidstone Prison to await execution, Smith contemptuously handed back the standard issue Bible and Prayer Book to the chaplain, the Reverend Stott. After a while, however, he changed his mind, reading the Scriptures and asking to be confirmed. Archbishop Davidson sent his suffragan bishop of Maidstone to examine the prisoner and Smith was later confirmed. A sincere transformation seemed to have taken place though cynical warders described it as 'a religious dodge'. If his new-found faith helped Smith to acknowledge his guilt, it deserted him on the fatal day. He had to be dragged screaming to the scaffold.

Persistent voices continued to demand abolition of the death penalty. In 1908 there was an advance when the Children's Act prohibited capital punishment for those under 16. In 1920 the Penal Reform Committee of the Friends was formed, and the following year the Howard League for Penal Reform came into being when the Howard Association and the Penal Reform League amalgamated. These were small organizations, the majority of whose members were total abolitionists, and they launched active campaigns. In 1922 came another small success when the Infanticide Act abolished hanging for mothers who killed newborn children.

It was the execution of a woman that sparked off a full debate about capital punishment. In 1923 Edith Thompson was hanged because her lover, Frederick Bywaters, had killed her husband. Many felt that she was being punished for adultery as much as for murder. In spite of public petitions, Home Secretary William Bridgeman refused to grant a reprieve. Many princes of the Church defended the death penalty as compatible with Christianity. The most effective contribution to the debate came from Dr William Temple, Bishop of Manchester. At an abolitionist meeting held two weeks after Thompson was hanged in Holloway, a letter of Temple's that had appeared in the press was read out.

While believing that the state had the right to kill, he argued that the right should only be exercised in exceptional circumstances such as 'an outbreak of murder on such a scale as to create a general sense of insecurity of life'. For Temple the deterrent effect of capital punishment was outweighed by the glamour it held for unbalanced minds. The existence of capital punishment tended to undermine belief in the sanctity of life that the death penalty was there to safeguard. It also created 'a peculiarly vicious sort of sympathy with criminals'. On balance, he concluded, 'abolition would be found to result in fewer murders in the long run' (F. A. Iremonger, *William Temple, Archbishop of Canterbury: His Life and Letters*, 1948)

This view was not popular with his ecclesiastical colleagues, and Temple's letter provoked a snowstorm of correspondence advocating the retention of capital punishment. The debate raged on throughout the 1920s and Temple injected new life into it when, in January 1930, he preached the John Howard Sermon on 'the ethics of punishment'. In July of the same year, he was called before the House of Commons Select Committee on Capital Punishment. Temple was now archbishop of York, so his opinion carried even greater weight. He prepared a paper for the Committee, outlining his views, then justified them in person under questioning.

Temple believed that 'from the Christian point of view vengeance is entirely illegitimate'. The Sermon on the Mount was a denunciation of vengeance. The Old Testament laws of retaliation so often invoked by others – 'an eye for an eye' and so on – were a precise limitation of retaliation, not a licence. There should be a Christian emphasis on the reformation of the criminal:

The prospect of execution does not infallibly lead to penitence. A Christian society must seek the opportunity of evoking penitence through the remaining years of the criminal's life even if the state does not require the loss of liberty for the whole of his life. Christianity itself requires that punishment, as a repudiation of wrong, be inflicted; for the community can only exert a moral influence on the wrongdoer, if it manifestly repudiates his crime.

After collecting evidence from various sources, the Committee issued its report, recommending a five-year suspension of capital punishment. Abolitionists raised a cheer – but their relief was short-lived. A change of government meant that the recommendation never got anywhere near the statute book.

Modern hangmen

Hangmen in the twentieth century shared two crucial features. Most of them were northerners, and the profession had a dynastic element. James Billington, a barber from Bolton, was the chief hangman at the start of the century. His two sons, William and Jack, also learned the trade from him. Also on the list were William Warbrick and Robert Wade, both from Bolton, though they only officiated at a handful of executions. On one occasion, Warbrick contrived to fall through the trap while assisting James Billington.

John Ellis was a Rochdale mill-worker who turned to hanging. Among his victims were Dr Crippen, Frederick Seddon, George Joseph Smith, Sir Roger Casement and Edith Thompson. Ellis was succeeded by an Accrington-born engraver named William Willis, who often assisted Henry Pierrepoint, the former Bradford butcher. A fondness for drink handicapped Pierrepoint's career and he resigned his office in 1910. His younger brother, Thomas Pierrepoint, joined the official list of hangmen in 1906. William Conduit of Manchester made only brief appearances as an assistant but his fellow-Mancunian George Brown lasted much longer.

The most famous executioner, however, was Albert Pierrepoint (see plate 30), son of Henry and nephew of Thomas. Born in Bradford, he worked as a drayman for a wholesale grocer, but was anxious to enter the family business. When his Uncle Tom was away on duty, his aunt let him read the diary that her husband kept of his executions. Albert's first assignment was in Dublin on 29 December 1932, when he assisted his uncle in hanging Patrick MacDermott. He would go on to hang over 400 victims, many of whom were war criminals condemned at the Nuremberg Trials. When it became known that Albert had been handed such an important job, he became something of a hero in the press.

He fought shy of publicity throughout his life – then courted it with his autobiography, *Executioner: Pierrepoint* (1974). The book gives an accurate account of the process of an execution. It also lists the regulations that had to be obeyed. In the Memorandum of Conditions to which executioners were required to conform, the sixth rule was strictly enforced:

> He should avoid attracting public attention in going to or from the prison; he should clearly understand that his conduct and general behaviour must be respectable and discreet, not only at the place and time of execution, but before and subsequently; in particular he must not give to any person particulars on the subject of his duty for publication.

Prisons supplied the apparatus for executions (see plate 29); it was left to the hangmen to provide the necessary ropes and straps. Albert put these accessories to frequent and expert use. When he appeared before the Royal Commission on Capital Punishment in 1949, his deposition was straightforward:

> I have operated on behalf of the State, what I am convinced was the most humane and the most dignified method of meting out death to a delinquent – however justified or unjustified the allotment of death might be – and on behalf of humanity I trained other nations to adopt the British system of execution. It is a fact which is a source of no pride to me at all – it is simply history – that I carried out more executions of judicial sentences than any executioner in any British record or archive.
>
> *Executioner: Pierrepoint*

Notwithstanding his disclaimer, there is a clear note of pride here.

His autobiography gives a detailed account of the way that Albert replied to the searching questions of Sir Ernest Gowers, Chairman of the Commission. He weighed his words carefully before answering, and a wily streak emerges. Firmly committed to the operation of capital punishment, Albert did not foresee that he would make a significant contribution to its removal in the new decade.

Craig and Bentley

Christopher Craig and Derek Bentley tried to rob a Croydon warehouse on 2 November 1952. Thwarted by the arrival of the police, they could not escape from the rooftop where they were caught. Bentley was arrested and held by policemen. When Police Constable Sydney Miles approached Craig, Bentley is alleged to have shouted 'Let him have it!' – which of course can be interpreted in two ways. Craig shot the policeman dead, and projected himself and his accomplice on to the front pages of the national newspapers.

The callous shooting of a policeman was a mercifully rare event, and the case caused widespread public alarm. At the trial, however, it was not Craig whose life was at risk. Too young to hang at 16, he was given a long prison sentence. The 19-year-old Bentley, mentally subnormal, was sentenced to death – even though he had no gun and had been in police custody at the time of the shooting.

There was enormous public and parliamentary agitation for a reprieve, but it was denied by the dour Scottish Home Secretary, David Maxwell Fyfe. Large crowds formed at the gates of Wandsworth Prison on 28 January 1953, where Bentley was hanged by Albert Pierrepoint with the assistance of Harry Allen. Strenuous posthumous petitioning led eventually to a quashing of Bentley's conviction in 1998. It brought only token relief. His death had ignited the abolitionist debate and turned thousands against the notion of capital punishment. The public sense of guilt was stronger than its desire for revenge.

Christie and Evans

Timothy John Evans was executed at Pentonville on 9 March 1950 by Albert Pierrepoint and Syd Dernley. Evans had been found guilty of the murder of his wife, Beryl, and their one-year-old daughter. The chief prosecution witness was John Christie, who had the ground floor flat at Ten Rillington Place where the Evans family lived. Like Bentley, Evans was mentally subnormal and gave a poor account of himself in court. He claimed repeatedly that he was innocent, and accused Christie of the murders. The jury found him guilty and the judge donned the black cap.

In March 1953 John Christie moved out of Rillington Place and six bodies were later discovered, including that of his wife, Ethel. On his arrest, Christie confessed to the murders and to having sexual relations with five of his victims after their deaths. It was not long before the name of Beryl Evans was added to his tally, though, oddly enough, not that of her child. David Maxwell Fyfe had earlier said that it was impossible for an innocent man to be hanged – yet that was patently the fate of Timothy Evans. A hastily arranged inquiry under John Scott-Henderson QC concluded that the original verdict had been safe because Evans was also a psychopathic murderer, and that the two killers had operated independently at the same house in an identical way. Many dismissed this claim as nonsense.

Bentley and Evans were hanged for crimes they did not commit, shattering the myth that judges and juries did not make mistakes in murder trials. Abolitionists were in full cry. One of their leaders was Mrs Violet Van der Elst, a wealthy and eccentric woman who had started a series of street protests against hanging as far back as 1935. By engaging publicity agents, she acquired a sensational edge for her campaign. It never flagged. On the day of every execution, she would be outside the prison with her cohorts and banners. Pouring money freely into her crusade, she achieved the kind of success that more restrained abolitionists could never have achieved.

Ruth Ellis

Mrs Van der Elst and scores of other abolitionists were outside Holloway on 13 July 1955, when Ruth Ellis was hanged by Albert Pierrepoint and Royston Rickard.

Executions of women were uncommon. When Albert had hanged Louisa Merrifield at Strangeways Prison in 1953, she was only the sixth woman to have been executed in England since the death of Edith

Thompson in 1923. Merrifield's execution aroused protest, but it paled beside the uproar surrounding that of Ruth Ellis. One was convicted of poisoning a harmless old woman so that she could inherit her wealth, while the other had committed a crime of passion and moved in the glamorous world of motor racing. Merrifield was a dumpy, grim-faced, middle-aged woman, while Ellis was an attractive blonde who had worked as a model and club hostess.

In 1955 Ellis shot dead her former lover, the racing driver David Blakely, outside a public house in Hampstead. She made no denial of this. At her trial, mitigating circumstances were ignored. There had been provocation from Blakely when he discarded her. Ellis had been on a cocktail of drugs that affected her judgement. She had recently suffered a miscarriage. She had been driven to the murder scene by another lover who had provided her with the weapon. The jury heard none of this. They did not view her as a young mother driven to desperation. All that they saw in the dock was a flashy tart who had killed a man in a fit of rage.

Fifty thousand people signed a petition for mercy, presented by Canon Collins of St Paul's Cathedral. Donald Soper, the country's leading Methodist, wrote to the press appealing for a reprieve. Cassandra, the influential columnist in the *Daily Mirror*, asked the question on everyone's lips – Should Ruth Ellis Hang? He was convinced that she should not be executed. Nor should anyone else fall victim to this 'savagery untinged with victory'.

When Albert Pierrepoint left Holloway after the execution, he was besieged and jostled in a way that he had never known before. The crowd was vast and threatening. It was said that he regretted the execution and that it was largely responsible for his later resignation. His autobiography denies this. He claims to have felt that Ellis deserved to die and that her fetching appearance in court was responsible for all kinds of wrong publicity.

Mrs Van der Elst had led the chant outside Holloway: 'Evans – Bentley – Ellis'. The names would reverberate for years.

Abolition

After the execution of Ruth Ellis, the National Campaign for the Abolition of Capital Punishment (NCACP) was initiated to push for a change in the law. It soon had 20,000 members. It was chaired by Victor Gollancz, and its council members included Gerald Gardiner QC, Canon Collins, Christopher Hollis MP, Arthur Koestler and Reginald Paget QC. Sometimes uneasy bedfellows, they were nonetheless enthusiastic campaigners who gained wide and continuing publicity for the cause.

Momentum gathered, yet in November 1955 the government rejected all the recommendations of the Royal Commission on Capital Punishment. In 1957 the Homicide Act tried to create two categories of murder: one for which the penalty remained hanging and another for which the penalty was life imprisonment. The Act proved to be unworkable and without any noticeable deterrent effect. Between the passing of the Act and the introduction of the Abolition Bill in 1964 there was an average of three or four executions a year. Each one was an occasion for protest by abolitionists.

Ludovic Kennedy's *Ten Rillington Place* (1961), about the gross miscarriage of justice in the case of Timothy John Evans, was one of a number of books that called for abolition. Pamphlets and newspaper articles kept up the momentum. It was left to the Church of England to apply decisive pressure. When Archbishop Fisher was replaced in 1961 by Archbishop Ramsey, the Anglican community had a more liberal and humane primate. A new generation of younger and more critical bishops was making its appearance, supplanting diehard supporters of the retention of capital punishment. The mood within the Church was definitely changing.

Many prison chaplains spoke of the emotional strain of attending executions. They felt soiled and corroded by the process. Although they were present as priests speaking in God's name, they were troubled by guilt at condoning legal murder by their very presence. The ordeal was even worse for chaplains who had befriended a condemned man and given him spiritual comfort. The hanging of women had the most unsettling effect on those witnessing it, from the governor and the chaplain to the prison officers. Only a hangman like Albert Pierrepoint seemed impervious to such emotions.

When the Labour Party came to power in 1964, the issue was mentioned in the Queen's speech. Veteran Labour MP Sidney Silverman introduced a Private Member's Bill for abolition in December and time was allowed for debate. The public in general still favoured hanging by a margin of three to one, but abolitionists won the day in the Houses of Parliament. Much of their success must be attributed to the fact that Michael Ramsey, Archbishop of Canterbury, took charge of the Bill in the House of Lords. So often the nemesis of law reformers, the Church was now the champion of change. There was fierce opposition from people like Viscount Kilmuir – the former David Maxwell Fyfe – but the Bill eventually passed its second reading in the Lords.

The Murder (Abolition of the Death Penalty) Bill was sent up for Royal Assent on 8 November 1965 and became law. Fifteen men already sentenced to death were formally reprieved. The last people to be hanged in Britain were Peter Anthony Allen and Gwynne Owen Evans, two Preston-based dairy workers who battered and stabbed a man to death. Allen was executed in Liverpool on 13 August 1964 by Robert Stewart. On the same day Evans was executed in Manchester by Harry Allen. The long and sorry tale of judicial hanging had at last run out of rope.

Conclusion

Whilst we have prisons it matters little
which of us occupies the cells.

Bernard Shaw, *Man and Superman*, 1903

Imprisonment, then, was originally used as a means of detention for malefactors awaiting trial and sentence. As it was only a temporary home, the prison – castle, gaol, lock-up, shed – was not designed for the comfort of those incarcerated: it was a rough and ready place of transit. Prisoners had to pay for their accommodation and buy any additional privileges they desired. Wealth was decisive. The rich could live in relative ease while the poor decayed in communal cesspits. Gaol fever was a terror that affected all classes.

Prison involved loss – loss of family, loss of friends, loss of pride, loss of reputation, loss of earning power and loss of control. Most of all, it meant loss of liberty, and this has remained the basic ingredient of imprisonment until the present day. Those who broke the law were denied freedom of movement, isolated from society and kept behind bars. In medieval England and well beyond that period, they might also be put in irons and subjected to torture. During the eighteenth century, they would be locked in large common wards filled with the dregs of society. It was a brutalizing experience. Further losses could be incurred – loss of self-respect, of virginity, of faith.

In Victorian times, prisoners occupied a single cell in a silent system and were masked whenever they were allowed exercise. In the new convict prisons, isolation was total, often leading to great anguish and mental breakdown. Those without any insight into their own behaviour and its consequences were given long stretches in limbo to consider their crimes and repent. In theory, it must have seemed like a laudable Christian ideal. In practice, it either destroyed morale completely or filled a prisoner with such a burning resentment of the law that he would strike out in defiance of it on release.

Poverty and debt

The system treated poverty as a crime. Because they were seen as a threat to the stability of society, able-bodied vagabonds were whipped, branded, mutilated and even hanged on occasion. Gaols, workhouses and houses of correction had a never-ending stream of paupers coming through their gates. Those imprisoned for debt were put in the one place where they were unable to pay off their creditors. In 1776 John Howard discovered that debtors constituted 60 per cent of all inmates. By 1877 they accounted for only three per cent. The last debtors' prison – the Queen's Bench – was closed in 1862.

It took over 150 years to develop a rational approach to the problem of debt. In 1813 parliament set up a court to deal with insolvent debtors, thereby removing the need for regular legislative action. In 1844 the Insolvency Act abolished imprisonment for debts below £20 and permitted private individuals to go into bankruptcy, hitherto reserved for traders. In 1869 the Act for the Abolition of Imprisonment for Debt was passed – but it had a serious flaw: to default on a payment would not in itself result in imprisonment, but if a debtor had the means to pay yet neglected or refused to do so, he or she could be locked up for six weeks. Astonishingly, this provision lasted until the 1960s.

Prisoners' fates

Over the centuries, people reacted very differently to imprisonment. The moment he was locked up in the Tower of London, the only thing on Ranulf Flambard's mind was escape, and he had sufficient freedom of action to contrive it. Walter Raleigh, on the other hand, came to terms with his long incarceration in the Tower, using the time behind its high walls to fashion a new life for himself and his family, and producing his best-written work in the process. John Donne, who hunted with Raleigh for Spanish treasure ships off the Azores in 1597, was dogged by the disgrace of his brief time in custody for many years. The Fleet prison cast a very long shadow over his career.

John Bunyan made a virtue of a necessity, refusing the chance of release on a point of principle and creating, during his 12 years in Bedford gaol, enduring religious and literary texts. Edward Gibbon Wakefield was another who put his prison experience to good use. A gentleman by birth and a cousin of Elizabeth Fry, he was convicted of abducting a young woman and imprisoned in Newgate in 1826. The resulting *Facts Relating to the Punishment of Death in the Metropolis* (1831) was a powerful argument in favour of the abolition of capital punishment. Few people have described with such poignancy, compassion and pathos the sheer horror of awaiting an appointment with the hangman.

For a bird of paradise like Oscar Wilde, prison was an unrelieved ordeal. Stripped of his fine feathers, wrenched from his cultured, middle-class background, deprived of his work and derided for his homosexuality, Wilde was reduced to the same status as all the other prisoners. The humiliation was corrosive. While in prison, he was declared bankrupt and wrote a reproachful letter to his lover, Lord Alfred Douglas, published in part in 1905 as *De Profundis*. On his release in 1898, he went to France where he wrote *The Ballad of Reading Gaol*. Prison had destroyed Oscar Wilde, the *bon viveur* and literary sensation. It damaged his health, preyed on his mind and ate into his soul. He lived in obscurity in Paris until he died in 1900.

Ivor Novello was another creative artist whose sensibilities were outraged by a spell in prison – even though he only served four weeks. What made his disgrace more galling was the fact that a man who had written popular patriotic songs during the Great War was caught doing something as unpatriotic as misusing his petrol coupons during the Second World War. It was a bruising fall from grace for a man who had enjoyed admiration as well as a luxurious lifestyle. Although he continued to appear on stage after his release, Novello had been seriously diminished by his month as a convicted prisoner. He lived a blameless existence thereafter, dying in 1951.

Novello's predicament was not unusual – that of a basically honest and law-abiding person thrust into an establishment replete with career criminals. Serving a sentence alongside him was the young Frankie

Fraser, who had acquired his nickname of Mad Frankie by pretending insanity in order to avoid conscription in the Second World War. Fraser later became a feared enforcer for two notorious London gangs. He served a succession of prison sentences, including one of five years for leading a riot at Parkhurst in 1969. Incarceration simply hardened him and was a periodic interruption to a life of crime.

William Douglas-Home was another unlikely convict. Born into an aristocratic family, he was educated at Eton and Oxford. During the Second World War, he contested three parliamentary by-elections, standing as an independent candidate opposed to Churchill's war aim of unconditional surrender by Germany. He lost all three contests. In 1944, as an officer in the 141st Regiment, Royal Armoured Corps (The Buffs), he refused an order to attack Le Havre and was subsequently court-martialled and given a prison sentence.

Like the conscientious objectors, he was thrown into the unfamiliar company of murderers, thieves, arsonists and assorted criminals who adapted easily to the prison sub-culture. A peer of the realm was completely out of place. William Douglas-Home drew on his time as a convict to write his play *Now, Barabbas,* giving West End theatre-goers in 1947 a glimpse inside a typical English prison. While it may seem dated now, it was a clever ensemble piece that brought out the pain, confusion and camaraderie of life behind bars, together with its subtle homosexual undercurrent.

The 'screws'

Prison officers share the indignity of being locked up. As warders in medieval castles or gaols, they were able to make the most of their position by milking their charges of money in the most blatant and unscrupulous way. This was accepted as an occupational bonus rather than a crime. Only when John Howard realized that gaolers received no regular wage was this glaring anomaly tackled by the authorities – yet corruption continued, among chaplains as well as among warders.

The introduction of convict prisons in the nineteenth century brought a more ordered, centralized penal system into being. It was administered by prison officers on a fixed wage and with clear objectives. Its structure was paramilitary and it drew heavily on the army and navy for its manpower. Officers were there to enforce discipline and keep the prisoners to a strict daily routine.

When a reformative element was brought into play, officers were naturally perplexed. Trained to control offenders, they had neither the wish nor the skill to rehabilitate them, especially in conditions that robbed men of their self-confidence and weakened their ability to cope with life outside. Prison officers could not suddenly turn into social workers, psychiatrists and educationists. They were being asked to reconcile what many of them thought mutually contradictory tasks.

The point of prison?

Punishment or reform? Coercion or correction? Discipline or improvement? Arguments about the aim of the prison service have raged for countless years. Rule six of the Prison Rules for 1949 seemed clear: 'The purposes of training and treatment of convicted prisoners shall be to establish in them the will to lead a good and useful life, and to fit them to do so.' This directive was issued at a time when prison escapes or attempted escapes had soared to well over 1,000 a year, an indication of waning discipline. By 1964, at a time of crisis in the prison service, this earlier rule was altered slightly to become the first in the Prison Rules of that year. The second rule in 1964 advised that: 'Order and discipline shall be maintained with firmness, but with no more restriction than is required for safe custody and well-ordered community life.'

It is much easier to issue this guideline than to implement it. To prison staff, the emphasis on reform meant an erosion of discipline. While they found it increasingly difficult in the 1950s to control the behaviour of inmates towards them, they had no hope of controlling the conduct of prisoners towards each other. The justification for the free association of offenders was that it was natural, tended to be beneficial and was much preferred by inmates themselves. Victorians had dealt with the fear of contamination by keeping prisoners apart. By locking them up two or three to a cell and by allowing them freedom to mix with other inmates, the door was opened to all kinds of abuses – violence, intimidation, gambling, the exchange of contraband items and enforced or consensual sexual activity.

It is beyond the scope of this book to examine developments in the past 50 years or so. Suffice it to say that the perfect balance has yet to be struck between custodial and corrective aims. There have been several new scandals, new inquiries, new prisons, new initiatives and new types of crime to accommodate. Yet for all the money, effort and expertise that have gone into the penal system, the prison population continues to rise and the recidivist rate stays disturbingly high. Those who pose no threat to society at large are locked away at considerable expense to the taxpayer instead of being punished in alternative ways. Admittedly, for generations there have been those who have profited from the 'short, sharp shock' of a prison sentence. Set against those, however, are the untold multitudes that have been corrupted, alienated, brutalized, cowed or institutionalized by the penal system.

During his time as Home Secretary, Michael Howard MP gave it as his considered opinion that 'Prison works'. He forgot to tell us for whose benefit it does so. In the period covered by this book, it is difficult to find any beneficiaries. Those demanding retribution may have got some satisfaction, but those behind bars – prisoners and prison staff alike – would not have claimed that prison worked either as a deterrent or as an agent of reform. Where progressive ideas have been incorporated into the system, they have all too often been smothered by lack of resources and severe prison overcrowding. Being tough on criminals is a stance that will always win more votes than taking a liberal attitude towards male and female convicts.

After all these centuries, imprisonment is still evolving as a concept. Whether or not it is the most efficient, humane and productive way of dealing with offenders remains an open question.

A NOTE ON SOURCES

This book would have been impossible without the rich resources of the National Archives and the efficiency of its staff. I have also used the facilities of the British Library, the Imperial War Museum and many provincial libraries.

Prison records are complex, and are held by a variety of authorities including the National Archives, local record offices, individual prisons and the Prison Commission. The books *Tracing Your Ancestors in the National Archives*, *Using Criminal Records* and *Criminal Ancestors* (see Further Reading on p. 234) include useful introductions to the subject.

All document references in this book refer to National Archives' holdings. The following documents and document series are a good starting point for researchers. For fuller information search the catalogue at www.nationalarchives.gov.uk.

ADM 6 Service Records, Registers, Returns and Certificates, 1673–1960 [the hulks *Dolphin* and *Cumberland*]

CRIM 9 After Trial Calendars of Prisoners, 1855–1949

HO 6 Judges' and Recorders' Returns, 1816–40

HO 7/3 Bermuda – register of convicts on the ships *Antelope*, *Coromandel*, *Dromedary* and *Weymouth*, 1823–1828

HO 8 Convict Hulks, Convict Prisons and Criminal Lunatic Asylums: Quarterly Returns of Prisoners, 1824–1876

HO 9 Convict Prison Hulks: Registers and Letter Books, 1802–1849

HO 11 Convict Transportation Registers, 1787–1870

HO 17 Criminal Petitions, Series I, 1819–39

HO 18 Criminal Petitions, Series II, 1839–54

HO 23 Registers of Prisoners from national prisons lodged in County Prisons, 1847–1866 [includes material on the hulks]

HO 24 Prison Registers and Statistical Returns, 1838–1875 [includes material on the hulks]

A NOTE ON SOURCES

HO 26 Criminal Registers, Middlesex, 1791–1849
HO 27 Criminal Registers, England and Wales, 1805–1892
HO 47 Judges' Reports on Criminals, 1784–1829
HO 163 Criminal Cases Entry Books, 1899–1921 [executions]
HO188 Remissions and Pardons, 1887–1960

MEPO 6/1 Habitual Criminals Register, 1881–1882
MEPO 6/77–88 Habitual Drunkards: portraits and descriptions circulated to
  licensed persons and secretaries of clubs, 1903–1914

PCOM 2 Prisons Records, Series 1, 1770–1951 [includes prison registers for
  London and county prisons, and for the hulks, as well as prison books and
  journals]
PCOM 2/296–299 and 430–434 Habitual criminals registers, 1871–1875
  [Birmingham]
PCOM 2/300 Habitual criminals registers, 1875 [Cambridge]
PCOM 2/404 Alphabetical register of habitual criminals in England and Wales,
  1869–1876
PCOM 3 Male Licences, 1853–1887
PCOM 4 Female Licences, 1853–1887

PRIS 1 Fleet Prison: Commitment Books, 1686–1842
PRIS 2 Fleet Prison: Commitments Files, 1758–1842
PRIS 3 Fleet Prison: Discharges, 1775–1857
PRIS 4 King's (Queen's) Bench Prison and Queen's Prison: Commitment
  Books, 1719–1862
PRIS 5 King's Bench Prison: Abstract Books of Commitments, 1780–1815
PRIS 6 Queen's Prison: Commitments to Strong Room, 1847–1862
PRIS 7 King's Bench Prison and Queen's Prison: Discharges, 1776–1862
PRIS 8 King's (Queen's) Bench Prison and Queen's Prison: Execution Books,
  1758–1852
PRIS 9 Queen's Prison: Miscellaneous Books, 1842–1862
PRIS 10 King's (Queen's) Bench, Fleet, Marshalsea and Queen's Prisons:
  Miscellanea, 1697–1862
PRIS 11 Prison of the Marshalsea of the King's Household and Palace Court,
  and the Queen's Prison: Records, 1773–1861

Also contracts for the transportation of convicts in TS 18; hulks in T 38; Oscar
Wilde in DPP 1, HO 144, PCOM 9, TS 27; suffragettes in HO 45 and 144; conscientious objectors in ADM 1, CAB 1, CAB 21, CAB 37, CAB 41, CAB 65, CAB 75, KV 2,
MEPO 2, MEPO 3, PCOM 7 and PCOM 9; executions in MEPO 3 and PCOM 9; prison
burials 1834–1969 in HO 334.

233

FURTHER READING

Amanda Bevan, *Tracing Your Ancestors in the National Archives*, 7th edn (2006)

Allan Brodie, Jane Croom and James O. Davis, *English Prisons* (2002)

E. J. Burford, *In the Clink* (1977)

Richard Byrne, *Prisons and Punishments of London* (1989)

W. Hepworth Dixon, *The London Prisons* (1850)

Stewart P. Evans, *Executioner* (2004)

Susan Willis Fletcher, *12 Months in an English Prison* (1884)

Simon Fowler, *Workhouse* (2007)

Elizabeth Fry, *Observations on the Visiting, Superintendence and Government of Female Prisoners* (1828)

Felicity Goodall, *A Question of Conscience* (1997)

Jean Hatton, *Betsy* (2005)

David T. Hawkings, *Criminal Ancestors* (1992)

Denis Hayes, *Challenge of Conscience* (1949)

R. S. E. Hinde, *The British Penal System 1773–1950* (1951)

John Howard, *The State of Prisons in England and Wales* (1777)

W. Branch Johnson, *The Prison Hulks* (1970)

John Lee, *The Man They Could Not Hang* (c.1908)

Henry Mayhew and John Binny,

The Criminal Prisons of London and Scenes of Prison Life (1862)

Caroline Moorehead, *Troublesome People: Enemies of War 1916–86* (1987)

Norvall Morris and David J. Rothman (eds), *The Oxford History of the Prison* (1995)

Ruth Paley, *Using Criminal Records* (2001)

Emmeline Pankhurst, *My Own Story* (1914)

Richard Pankhurst, *Sylvia Pankhurst: Artist and Crusader* (1979)

Albert Pierrepoint, *Executioner: Pierrepoint* (1974)

Harry Potter, *Hanging in Judgement: Religion and the Death Penalty in England* (1993)

Philip Priestley, *Victorian Prison Lives* (1985)

Ralph B. Pugh, *Imprisonment in Medieval England* (1970)

June Purvis, *Emmeline Pankhurst: A Biography* (2002)

June Rose, *Elizabeth Fry* (1980)

Donald Rumbelow, *The Triple Tree* (1982)

J. A. Sharpe, *Crime in Early Modern England 1550–1750* (1984)

J. E. Thomas, *The English Prison Officer since 1850* (1972)

James Hardy Vaux, *Memoirs* (1819)

INDEX

Numbers in *italic* refer to plate numbers.

Act for the Abolition of Imprisonment for Debt (1869) 227
Act to Abolish Franchise Prisons (1852) 17
Allen, Clifford 12, 180, 181, 186-7, 191, 192
Allen, Harry 221, 225
Allen, John 58
Andrews, Edward 122-3
Anne of Lodburie 20
architecture, prison 69, 71, 102, 104, 109
Askew, Anne 11, 32-4
Assize of Clarendon 15-17
Association for the Improvement in the Female Prisoners in Newgate 136
Austin, Lieutenant 122, 123
Australia: transportation to 9, 72-3, 80, 98-100
Aylesbury prison 154

babies, convict 151-2
Balfour, Jabez 112-13, 117
Barrett, Michael 212
Barry, Charles 109
Baynard's Castle 25
Beaufort, Duke of 17
Beccaria, Cesare 66
Bedford gaol 67
Behan, Brendan 200
Bellamy, Anne 38
Bellerophon (prison hulk) *6*
benefit of clergy 14
Bennett, Henry Grey 130
Bentham, Jeremy 104
Bentley, Derek 12, 221, 222
Bermuda 97
Berry, James 12, 209, 210-11, 212-13
Bidwell, Austin 115-16, 118, 119

Bidwell, George 114, 115, 119, 120
Billington, James 219
Bing, Harold 179, 187, 193
Birmingham borough gaol 122-3
Blackburn, William 71-2, 73
Blake, Harold 183
Blakely, David *32*, 223
Blishen, Edward 194
Bodmin county gaol 70-1
Boleyn, Anne 30, 35
borstals 159
Bossy, Dr Peter 85, 86
Boswell, James 202
Botany Bay 72-3
Bousfield, William 207-8
Bow Street Runners 64
Brackenbury, Robert 29
branks 21
Bray, Dr Thomas 53-4
Bread Street Compter 47
British Union of Fascists (BUF) 198
Brixton prison 144-53; airing yards 149-50; consoling features 152-3; design and architecture 144-5, 146-7; history of female convicts 148; nursery 151-2; punishment regime 150-1; women officers 145-6; women's work 152
Broadmoor hospital 107
Brockway, Fenner 180, 181, 187-8, 193-4
Brooke, Christopher 44
Brooke, Colonel 185
Bunting, James Bunstone 166
Bunyan, John 48-9, 228
Buxton, Anna 132, 133, 136
Buxton, Fowell 134
Byron, Lord 204

Cade, Jack 23, 43
Calcraft, William 12, 205-8

Call, John 70-1
Campbell, Duncan 79, 80
Campion, Edmund 37
capital punishment *see* death penalty; executions
Capper, John Henry 84-6, 98
Capper, Robert 85, 86
Carnavon Committee (1863) 117
Casement, Sir Roger 187, 199-200, 219
Catherine of Aragon 30, 31, 32, 35
Cellier, Elizabeth 50
Censor (prison hulk) 78-9
Central Board of Conscientious Objectors 193-4
chain gangs 124
chaplains, prison 58, 110, 127-9, 215, 216, 224-5
Chatham Docks 115
Chatham prison 124, 125-6, 144
Chawner, Thomas 144
Chesterton, George Laval 109, 111, 113, 123
Children's Act (1908) 217
Christie, John 221-2
Church of England 214-16, 224
Churchill, Winston 159, 160, 171, 172, 195, 198-9
Clarence, Duke of 28
Clay, Reverend John 127-8, 215
Clerkenwell 129
Clink, the 10, 41-3
clothing, prison *6*, 107-8
Cnut, King 12, 20
Cobden, Richard 161, 165
Cobham, Eleanor (Duchess of Gloucester) 9
Cold Bath Fields prison *12*, 109, 111, 113-14, 134
Colquhoun, Patrick 84

Complaint of the Poor Commons of Kent 23
Connolly, James 199
conscientious objectors 25, 26, 12, 179-201; female 195-7; imprisonment of 12, 184-8, 194, 200; ordeal in France 188-90; treatment of 182-4, 194-5, 195; and 'work of national importance' 190-2
conscription 180, 181, 193
Courvoisier, François 205
Coventry 48
Craig, Christopher 221
cranks 11, 113-14
Cranmer, Archbishop 2, 30, 34
crime, increase in 77, 138
criminal registers 63
Crippen, Dr 219
Cubitt, William 113
Cunningham, Peter 106
Curthose, Robert 26, 27
Cutpurse, Moll 131

Dartmoor prison 25, 26, 114, 124, 144, 191-2
Davis, Emily Wilding 173
Davison, Emily 23, 174
de la Pole, William 30
death penalty: abolition of (1965) 225; campaign for abolition of 203-4, 217-18, 222, 224-5; see also executions
debtors 11, 17, 44, 50, 51, 52-3, 102, 227
Defence (prison hulk) 87, 88, 89-95, 100
Defence Regulation 18B 197
Defoe, Daniel 54; Moll Flanders 74; Robinson Crusoe 74
Dekker, Thomas 47
Derby Scheme of Attestation 180
design, prison 102-3, 104
Dickens, Charles 101-2, 206-7; Little Dorrit 11, 101-2
diet: Brixton 148-9; Holloway 164-5; prison hulks 91; Victorian prisons 116-18
Dingley, Robert 65
Discharged Prisoners Act (1774) 68
discipline: Victorian prisons 120-6
diseases: spread of in prisons 55

dissectionists 60
Dixon, W. Hepworth 81
doctors, prison 118, 119
Donne, John 44, 47, 227-8
Dorchester prison 194
Dott, Eric 186, 191
Douglas-Home, William 229
Drummond, Flora 166, 167
Du Cane, Sir Edmund 115, 157, 158
Dudley, Guildford 34, 35
Duncombe, Thomas Slingsby 85
Dunlop, Marian Wallace 169
Dupont, Captain Charles 82
Durham gaol 52
Dutch, George Frederick 183
Dyce Work Camp (Aberdeen) 191

Eaton, Horace 184
Edward I, King 27-8
Edward IV, King 28
Edward VI, King 34, 36
Edwards, John and Solomon 76
eighteenth-century prisons 11, 51-75; building of 71-2; conditions in 51, 52-3, 54, 68; in literature 73-5; reform proposals 65, 66-70; spread of diseases 55
Elizabeth I, Queen 36-7, 38, 43
Ellis, John 219
Ellis, Ruth 32, 12, 222-3, 224
Entertainments National Service Association (ENSA) 197
Evans, Alfred 183, 189-90
Evans, Elizabeth 45-6
Evans, Gwynne 225
Evans, Timothy John 12, 221-2, 224
executions 3, 12, 57-60, 61-2, 70, 202-25; abolishment for certain crimes 204-5, 217; abolition of death penalty (1965) 225; and Calcraft 205-8; campaign for abolishment of death penalty 203-4, 217-18, 222, 224-5; and Church of England 214-16; decrease in 203; eighteenth-century 57-60; hangmen in twentieth century 219-20; last people to be hanged 225; last public hanging 212; medieval

women 20-1; and Newgate Calendar 61; at Tower of London 30-5; of women 217-18, 222-3, 224-5

Fannan, David 127, 128
Fawkes, Guy 39
fees, prisoner 18, 46, 67, 68
female convicts 12, 125, 130-56; babies born in prison 151-2; at Brixton prison 145, 146-51; conditions 130-1, 132, 134; diet 148-9; Elizabeth Fry's reforms 132-44; and Florence Maybrick 12, 153-6; and government prisons 144; at Newgate 130-1, 132-3, 134; and prison hulks 80-1; punishment regime at Brixton 150-1; and religion 139; and transportation 9, 56, 57, 141-3; and work 152
Ferrers, Earl of 62
Fielding, Henry 63-4; Amelia 74; The History of Tom Jones, a Foundling 74
Fielding, John (the Blind Beak) 64
First World War: and conscientious objectors 179-92; introduction of conscription 180; and suffragettes 177
Fisher, John (Bishop of Rochester) 32
FitzStephen, William 41
Flambard, Ranulf 9, 26, 227-8
Fleet, the 10, 11, 46-7, 51, 52, 53, 68, 102, 131
flogging 11, 123-4
forced feeding: suffragettes 12, 169-70, 171
Forde, Reverend Bronlow 214-15
fossa 21
Fox, George 48
Foxe, John: Book of Martyrs 33, 36
franchise prisons 16-17
Fraser, 'Mad' Frankie 10, 228-9
Fry, Elizabeth 10, 12, 110, 132-44; and 1818 inquiry 139; criticism of 140-1; legacy of 143; reform at Newgate 134-7, 139; and transportation of female convicts 141-3
Fry, John 133, 134

Fulham Refuge 144
Fyfe, David Maxwell 221, 222, 225

Gallacher, Willie 180
Ganymede (prison hulk) 99
Gaol Act (1823) 103
gaol deliveries 16
Gardiner, Stephen 42-3
gibbeting 204-5
Gibson, Thomas 64
Gladstone Committee 114, 116, 158
Gladstone, Herbert 158, 167, 171
Goldsmith, Oliver 75
Gollancz, Victor 193, 224
Goodale, Robert 212-13
Goodcole, Henry 45-6
Gordon Riots 56
government prisons 144
Gowers, Sir Ernest 220
Graham, Aaron 85
Graham, Sir James 116
Great Fire of London 46, 47
Grellet, Stephen 132
Grey, Lady Jane 2, 34-5, 36
Grey, Sir Edward 159
Grey, Sir George 85
Griffiths, Major Arthur 125-6
Gruffydd ap Llewellyn 19
Guilding, Reverend J.M. 97
Gunpowder Pot (1605) 39, 40
Guy, Dr William 117

Hall, John 54-5
Hamilton, John 62
Handland, Dorothy 99
hanging *see* executions
hangmen 12; medieval 20-1; modern 219-21
Hanway, Jonas 65-6, 70
Harcourt, Henry 117, 124
hard labour 65, 87, 92-4, 112-16
Hardie, Kier 159, 160, 165, 170
Haylar, Mark 184-6, 192
Health of Prisons Act (1774) 68
Henry II, King 15
Henry III, King 16, 18, 27, 28
Henry VIII, King 30, 31, 32, 33, 35, 36, 42
Hibner, Esther 205
Hill, John 213
History of the Press Yard, The 54
Hoare, Samuel 134, 136
Holland: prisons in 68, 69-70

Holloway, Henry 123-4
Holloway prison 23, 161-4, 166-8, 174-5, 197
Holyoake, George Jacob 119-20
Homicide Act (1957) 224
Hooke, Robert 70
Hooper, John 47
Horsham gaol 66, 70, 71
hospital ship 95-6
Houghton, Simon 46
houses of correction 49, 65
Howard, Catherine 35, 36
Howard, John 4, 50, 66-70, 71, 72, 73, 132, 144, 227, 229; *The State of Prisons in England and Wales* 11, 68, 71, 83-4
Howard League for Penal Reform 217
Howard, Michael 231
hulks, prison 11, 57, 73, 76-100; and Capper 85; closure of 100; conditions aboard 78, 79-80, 81, 84, 86, 99; criticism of and public protest against 81, 83-4, 85; daily routine on board 90-1; death of prisoners 84, 93-4; diet 91; escape attempts and mutinies 83, 87-8; female convicts 80-1; first 78-80; hard labour undertaken by inmates 87, 92-4; and hospital ship 95-6; inquiry into treatment of convicts at Woolwich 85-6; prisoner records 88-9; and prisoners of war 81-3; religion and schooling 94-5; stationed in Bermuda 97-8; and transportation 98-100; warders' discipline 91-2
Hull prison 194
hunger strikes: and suffragettes 169, 170, 171, 176

Infanticide Act (1922) 217
Insolvency Act (1844) 227
irons 18, 19
Ivette of Bolsham 21

James I, King 39, 40
Jebb, Captain Joshua 107, 109-10
Jesuits 37
Jews 27
Johnson, Samuel 202
Jonson, Ben 44

Jordan of Bianney 17
Justitia (prison hulk) 72, 78-9, 80

keepers, prison 18, 45, 46, 69
Kennedy, Ludovic 224
Kenney, Annie 159-60, 175
Kidd, Captain 61
King, Edward (Bishop of Lincoln) 216
Kingsmill, Joseph 215-16

Lanfranc (Archbishop of Canterbury) 14
League of Nations 192-3
League for Penal Reform 72
Lee, John 27, 28, 12, 208-12
Leeds prison 120
Leigh, Mary 169
Lewes prison 120, 194
Lilburne, John 47
Limerick gaol 72
literature: eighteenth-century prisons in 73-5
lock-ups 16
London 22, 41-2, 103-4; prisons of 24-48
Loney, William 57
Lonsdale, Dr Kathleen 197
Lorrain, Reverend Paul 58-9
Lovett, William 110-11, 117
Luddite Riots 77
Lytton, Lady Constance 20, 170-1

Macdonald, Ramsay 191
McKenna, Reginald 176-7
Maclean, John 180
McMillan, Arthur 194-5
Maidstone prison 12, 187, 194
Makin, Kenneth 194
Manning, Frederick and Marie 206-7
Marsh, Charlotte 169
Marshall, Catherine 195
Marshalsea 10, 43-4, 51, 68, 101-2, 127
Marten, Howard 188-9
Martin, Emma 145, 150
Martin, Kingsley 193
Martin, Selina 170, 171
Mary I, Queen 34, 35-6, 42-3
Maybrick, Florence 12, 153-6
Mayhew, Henry and Binny, John: *The Criminal Prisons of London and Scenes of Prison Life* 11, 78, 87, 88, 89-95, 105, 106, 126-7, 145-7, 151-2
medical care: hulks 95-6;

Victorian prisons 118-20
medieval prisons 10, 12-23;
    conditions 17-19; escapes
    18-19; royal prisons 15-16;
    as symbols of hatred and
    burning down of 23; use of
    torture 19-20; and William
    the Conqueror 13-14
memoirs, prisoner 58
*Memoirs of the Right Villainous
    John Hall, The* 54-5
Men's League for Opposing
    Suffrage 168
Merrifield, Louisa 222-3
Metropolitan Police Force
    77, 204
Middleton, Thomas 131
Military Service Act (1916)
    181
Millbank 71, 104-6, 117, 118,
    127, 128, 144
Misson, Henri 58
Mitford, Diana 197, 198
Monastic Constitutions 14
Mons, Battle of (1914) 179
Montfichet Castle 25
Moran, Reverend J.H. 145,
    148
More, Thomas 29, 31-2
Moreau-Christophe, M.L.
    114
Morrell, Philip 190
Morrison, Sybil 197
Mosley, Oswald 197-9
Mountjoy prison (Dublin)
    107

National Campaign for
    the Abolition of Capital
    Punishment (NCACP) 224
National League for
    Opposing Women's Suffrage
    168
National Registration Act
    (1915) 180
neck-trap 13
Neilands, Alison 165
Nevill, Lord William 113;
    Penal Servitude 117, 118
Newgate *11, 13,* 10, 44-6,
    53-5, 68, 127; breaking out
    of infectious disease (1750)
    55; burning down of (1780)
    56; conditions 45, 50, 51;
    construction of windmill
    55; as den of inequity 53-4;
    establishment of workshop
    scheme 136-8, 139; execu-
    tions taken place outside
    202-3; female convicts

130-1, 132-3, 134, 141-3;
    Fry's campaign for reform at
    10, 134-8, 139; keepers 45;
    rebuilding of 45, 50, 55, 70
Newgate Calendar 61-2, 131-2
Newman, Governor John
    133, 135
No More War Movement 193
No-Conscription Fellowship
    (NCF) 180-1, 186, 187, 190,
    192, 193, 195
Non-Combatant Corps
    (NCC) 181, 183, 184, 194
Norman, C. H. 187
Norman Conquest 10, 13,
    14-15
Northumberland, Duke of
    (John Dudley) 34, 35
Novello, Ivor 9-10, 228
Nuremberg Trials 220

oakum picking 11, 112, 115
Oldfield, Dr Josiah 216
Orton, Arthur *see* Tichborne
    Claimant

Page, Nora 197
Paley, Archdeacon William
    214
Pankhurst, Adela 159, 161
Pankhurst, Christabel 159,
    160, 166, 167, 174
Pankhurst, Emmeline *21, 22,*
    159, 166, 169, 171-2, 173,
    174-5, 177
Pankhurst, Sylvia 157, 159,
    160, 161-3, 167, 168, 176
Papists Act (1778) 56
Parkhurst 144
Parr, Catherine 33
Payne, W. 112
Peace Pledge Union 193, 197
Pearse, Patrick 199
Peasants Revolt (1381) 23, 46
Peel, Robert 204
Penal Reform Committee of
    the Friends 217
Pentonville *9,* 106-9, 110, 111,
    120, 126-7, 144, 187
Peterloo Massacre (1819) 77
Pethick-Lawrence, Emmeline
    160, 161, 174
Philip, Captain Arthur 72-3
Pierrepoint, Albert *29, 30,* 12,
    219-21, 222, 223, 225
Pierrepoint, Henry 219
Pierrepoint, Thomas 219
pillory 13
Pitt, Moses 52, 53
political prisoners 199-200

Popham, Alexander 68
Portland prison 121-2, 144
Portsmouth prison 124, 144
poverty 227
Preston prison *15*
Prison Act (1877) 157; (1898)
    158
prison chapel 126 *see also*
    chaplains, prison
Prison Discipline Society 113
prison officers 229-30
Prisoners 'Temporary
    Discharge for Ill-Health'
    Act 174
Prisons Act (1835) 103
Prisons of the Metropolis 139
prostitution 53
Prynne, William 47
'public works' prisons 115-16,
    144
punishments 57, 103; early
    12-13; of female convicts
    at Brixton 150-1; medieval
    women 20-1; Victorian
    prisons 123-4

Radford, Iris 196-7
Raleigh, Sir Walter 40-1, 227
Ramsey, Michael (Archbishop
    of Canterbury) 224, 225
Reading gaol 118
religion: and female convicts
    139; and Millbank 105;
    and prison hulks 94-5; and
    Victorian prisons 126-9
Representation of the People's
    Act (1918) 177
Richard of Devizes 41-2
Richard III, King 28-9
Richardson, Mary 175-6
Richmond, Duke of 66, 70,
    103
Robinson, William 53
Romilly, Samuel 203-5
Rossa, Jeremiah O'Donovan
    108
Royal Commission on Capital
    Punishment (1949) 220
Royal Oak (prison hulk) 81
royal prisons 15-16
Ruggles-Brise, Evelyn 158-9
Russell, Bertrand 192

Salford gaol 118
Salter, F.M. 22
Sanderson, Annie Cobden
    161
scolds 21
'screws' 114, 229-230
scurvy 118

Seaton, James 217
Second World War 193-9
Seddon, Frederick 219
separation system 11, 103, 105, 109-11, 124, 159, 226, 230
Seven Years War (1756-63) 81
sewing 112-13, 115
Shaw, Ken 194
Shearwood, Thomas 45-6
Sheppard, Jack 102
shot drill 114
Sidmouth, Lord 140
silent system 103, 108, 109-11
Silverman, Sidney 225
Six Acts 77
Skelton, Harriet 140
Smith, George Joseph 217, 219
Smith, John 61-2
Smollett, Tobias 75
Snowden, Philip 170, 190
Society for the Abolition of Capital Punishment 207, 216
Society for the Promotion of Christian Knowledge 53
Society for the Reformation of Prison Discipline 134
Soper, Donald 223
Southwell, Robert 37-9
Souville, Tom 83
Spencer, Barbara 131
Spiers, James Edward 9
Stanton, Harry 182, 189
stocks 13
straitjackets 122-3
'strong and heavy punishment' 19-20
suffragettes 12, 157-78; and Black Friday 172; and First World War 177; forced feeding 12, 169-70, 171; and hunger strikes 169, 170, 171, 176; imprisonment of Pankhursts at Holloway 161-5, 166-8, 174-5; increase in militancy and violence 169-70, 173-6, 177; increase in support for 172; and Lady Constance Lytton 170-1; opposition to cause 168; wins vote 177-8; and WSPU 159-61, 167, 171, 173, 174, 177, 178
suicide attempts: Victorian prisons 120
Swansea prison 17
Swift, Jonathan 74
Sydney, Lord 72

Temple, Dr William 218-19
Thackeray, William Makepeace 205-6
Thomas, J. E. 158
Thompson, Edith 217, 219
Tichborne Claimant (Arthur Orton) 117, 118
Tolpudde Martyrs 99
Topcliffe, Richard 38
torture 11, 19; in medieval prisons 19-20; in Tower of London 32-3, 36, 38, 59
Tower of London 1, 10-11, 19, 24-41, 227; changes to 27-8; construction of 13, 24; design and location 25; executions 30-5, 40; princes of 28-9; torture at 32-3, 36, 38, 39; treatment of Jews 27
transportation 56-7, 72, 203; end of 71; and female convicts 9, 56, 59, 141-3; to Australia 9, 72-3, 80, 98-100
Transportation Act (1784) 72
treadmill 15, 11, 113, 114
Treason Act (1535) 32
Trenfield, Dennis 89
Tribunal 187, 195
Tun 20
Tyburn 3, 11, 60, 202
Tyler, Wat 43

Unité (hospital ship) 95

vagrancy 49
Van der Elst, Violet 222, 223
Vaux, James Hardy 84, 99
Vengeance (prison hulk) 83
Victorian prisons 11, 101-29, 157, 226-7; architecture 109; building of 104-8; diet 116-18; discipline 120-6; disturbances in 125-6; and hard labour 112-16; illnesses and diseases 117; medical care 118-20; punishment 123-4; and religion 126-9; routine on arrival of prisoners 107-8; rules and regulations 108, 120-1; silent and separation system 11, 103, 105, 109-11, 124, 159, 226, 230; suicide attempts 120
Vryheid (ship) 81-2

Waad, Sir William 39
Wade, Mary 9, 73
Wakefield, Edward Gibbon 98, 228

Wakefield prison 49-50, 109, 144, 194
Walsingham, Sir Thomas 37
Walton gaol 20, 170, 171
Wandsworth prison 16, 19, 120, 185, 187
War Resisters' International 193
Warbrick, Robert 219
Ward, Mrs Humphrey 168
Ward, Ned 51
warders 124
Warrior (prison hulk) 5, 7, 87, 88, 95
Webb, Beatrice 181
West Indian fever 97
Wild, Jonathan 61, 63-4
Wilde, Oscar 11, 118, 119, 124-5, 128-9, 228
William the Conqueror 12, 13-14, 24, 25-6, 26
William Rufus (II), King 26
Williams, John 213
Williams, William 104
Willis, William 219
Winchester prison 18, 186
Winson Green prison 7, 169-70
witches 21
Wither, George 44
Woking gaol 144, 154
Woman's Dreadnought 176, 177
women: conscientous objectors 195-6; early punishment of 13; executions of 217-18, 222-3, 224-5; gaining of vote 177-8; medieval punishment of 20-1; prisoners see female convicts
Women's National Anti-Suffrage League 168
Women's Social and Political Union (WSPU) 159-61, 167, 171, 173, 174, 177, 178
Wormwood Scrubs 14, 17, 18, 31, 120, 186
Wyatt, Sir Thomas 47

York prison 18

AUTHOR'S ACKNOWLEDGEMENTS

Warmest thanks are due to my wife, Judith, who read every draft; to Sheila Knight, my perceptive editor, who kept a close eye on the text throughout; to the ever-helpful staff at the National Archives; and to all the prisoners, prison staff, prison visitors and probation officers I've met over the years and with whom I've discussed the inherent faults of the system. Finally, I'd like to thank my good friends, Nobby and Anne Bennett, who didn't realise that our casual chats about Canterbury Prison, and others in which they both worked as officers, helped to fuel my enthusiasm for this project.

TEXT AND PICTURE ACKNOWLEDGEMENTS

Many primary and secondary sources have been consulted in the writing of this book. The following works have proved particularly valuable for the light they shed on individuals' prison experiences: Felicity Goodall, *A Question of Conscience* (1997); John Lee, *The Man They Could Not Hang* (c.1908); Caroline Moorehead, *Troublesome People* (1987); Florence Maybrick, *My Fifteen Lost Years* (1905); Sylvia Pankhurst, *The Suffragette Movement* (1931); Albert Pierrepoint, *Executioner* (1974); June Purvis, *Emmeline Pankhurst* (2002).

Every care has been taken to trace copyright holders. However, we will be happy to rectify any omissions in future editions.

The author and publishers are grateful to the Imperial War Museum, London, for permission to reproduce the words of conscientious objectors from its Sound Archives.

Pictures except nos 4, 10, 25 and 30 can be seen at The National Archives, and are © Crown copyright unless another source is given here.

1 William York 5, 7, 11, 13 *Illustrated London News* 4, 25 TopFoto.co.uk 10 The Print Collector/HIP/TopFoto 15 Arthur James Winter 14, 17, 18 Charles Peck Fletcher 22 Bernard Kruger 27 *Chronicle* 30 Ian Tyas/ Getty Images.